The Psychophysiology of Consciousness

The Psychophysiology of Consciousness

EUGENE N. SOKOLOV

DEPARTMENT OF PSYCHOPHYSIOLOGY
MOSCOW STATE UNIVERSITY

TRANSLATED AND EDITED BY

ALEXANDER M. CHERNORIZOV
KIRILL A. CHERNORIZOV
DOUGLAS M. BOWDEN

OXFORD
UNIVERSITY PRESS

OXFORD
UNIVERSITY PRESS

Oxford University Press is a department of the University of Oxford.
It furthers the University's objective of excellence in research, scholarship,
and education by publishing worldwide.

Oxford New York
Auckland Cape Town Dar es Salaam Hong Kong Karachi
Kuala Lumpur Madrid Melbourne Mexico City Nairobi
New Delhi Shanghai Taipei Toronto

With offices in
Argentina Austria Brazil Chile Czech Republic France Greece
Guatemala Hungary Italy Japan Poland Portugal Singapore
South Korea Switzerland Thailand Turkey Ukraine Vietnam

Published in the United States of America by
Oxford University Press
198 Madison Avenue, New York, NY 10016

Library of Congress Cataloging-in-Publication Data
Sokolov, E. N. (Eugene Nikolaevich), 1920–2008
[Ocherki po psykhofiziologii soznanie. Russian]
The psychophysiology of consciousness / by Eugene N. Sokolov; translated and edited by Alexander M. Chernorizov, Kirill A. Chernorizov, Douglas M. Bowden.
pages cm
Includes bibliographical references and index.
ISBN 978–0–19–993435–5
1. Consciousness. 2. Neuropsychology. I. Title.
BF311.S64665 2013
153—dc23 2012034685

The *Psychophysiology of Consciousness* was originally published in Russian under the title *"Ocherki po Psykhofiziologii Soznanie" (Notes on the Psychophysiology of Consciousness).* This translation is published by arrangement with Moscow State University.

9 8 7 6 5 4 3 2 1
Printed in the United States of America
on acid-free paper

CONTENTS

E. N. SOKOLOV (1920–2008)

Eugene N. Sokolov will be remembered as one of the great neuroscientists of the late twentieth century (Chernorizov et al. 2008; Spinks et al. 2008). Working at the intersection of psychology, neurophysiology, and mathematics, he was among the first true cognitive neuroscientists.

In the 1950s Sokolov introduced the orienting reflex as a physiological window onto mental models of external reality. In the 1960s he introduced the concept of neurophysiological measures and cognitive distance as corresponding attributes of physical and mental reality. During the next fifty years he demonstrated the power of multidimensional vector mathematics to represent relations between the brain's neural model and the mind's mental model of reality.

In the course of his lifetime as an experimental and theoretical scientist, Sokolov published twelve books and more than 400 articles on the brain–mind relationship. Thousands of citations of his work are now found in the international academic literature. This, his last major work, summarizes the contributions of a lifetime and integrates them with major themes that are shaping twenty-first-century research on the relationship between the brain and the conscious mind.

Evgenii Nikolaevich Sokolov was born in 1920 to a family of civil servants in Nizhnyi Novgorod, a historic city on the Volga River about 400 km northeast of Moscow. As a young man he received schooling and a year of naval engineering study at an industrial technology institute in his home city. Through private tutoring he acquired language skills, which, when his education was interrupted by World War II, enabled him to serve four years as a translator with an army intelligence unit on the German–Russian front.

After the war he resumed his education in Moscow, first in a foreign language institute and later as a graduate student in the Psychology Institute of the prestigious Academy of Sciences of the USSR. There he made a puzzling observation with regard to Pavlov's "*chto eto*?," "what's that?," or "orienting" response to novel stimuli. He focused on the fact that after an unexpected stimulus is repeated a few times, the orienting response disappears. This observation marked the beginning of Sokolov's persistent interest in habituation of the orienting response as a sign that the brain incorporates predictable stimulus events into a dynamic neural model of external reality.

In 1950, after obtaining the Russian equivalent of a Ph.D. in experimental psychology, Sokolov was appointed to the faculty of the Department of Psychology of Moscow State University. He advanced rapidly to full professorship and, in 1971–72, established the university's Department of Psychophysiology, which he was to chair for more than 30 years. He pursued an exceedingly productive career of interdisciplinary research and teaching that ended only with his death at the age of 87, May 14, 2008.

Western science was introduced to Sokolov in 1954 when an 11-person team of Soviet psychologists, reported by the *New York Times* as "traveling outside their own country for the first time," attended the 14th International Congress of Psychology in Montreal. The event attracted both academic and media attention, because Soviet and Western scientists had had virtually no communication since the 1920s. The *Times* featured the symposium at which Sokolov presented his paper on a topic that would be characterized today as "behavioral neuroscience and perception." Those attending the Congress grasped immediately the significance of the work, and Sokolov became known internationally as an outstanding member of the young, postwar generation of Soviet psychologists.

International interest in Sokolov's work was fueled by the 1963 publication in English of his book *Perception and the Conditioned Reflex*, as well as by later translations into Spanish and Japanese. Reviews by esteemed Western psychologists appeared in major international journals, including *Brain,* the *Journal of Experimental Psychology,* and the *Journal of Electroencephalography and Clinical Neurophysiology.*

In 1969 Sokolov was invited to give ten lectures at the Universities of Cambridge and Oxford. In 1974 he was a visiting professor at MIT. His work attracted attention for several reasons. First, it illustrated the importance of physiological responses as indicators of covert effects of external stimuli on neural functions, a major emerging interest of experimental psychologists. Second, the theory integrated the concept of a neuronal model with the concept of a cognitive model of external reality in a way that generated hypotheses testable by neurophysiological and psychophysiological methods, which powerfully supplemented the techniques of classical psychophysics.

During the 1960s Sokolov turned to single unit recording, electroencephalography (EEG), evoked potentials, and electroretinography to elucidate the neuronal mechanisms that link perception, memory, and motor responses. He and colleagues worked with a variety of animal species, including the snail, fish, frog, rabbit, and macaque. The 1970s marked a gradual return of his scientific effort to a focus on perceptual mechanisms in the human. This gave rise to numerous experiments conducted by his collaborators and students. They applied a variety of methodologies: neurophysiological, behavioral, psychophysical, statistical, and mathematical.

Studies of central visual networks by Sokolov and colleagues revealed a mathematical commonality among the mechanisms that mediate the perception of specific features of visual stimuli, such as color, brightness, line orientation, and motion, and that apply to both simpler organisms and to man. Such investigations led eventually to a general vector model for the encoding and recording of information that links perceptual and memory processes to adaptive motor mechanisms. The theoretical model, built of elements with neuron-like functions, became the basis for the conceptualization of artificial sensory "organs" in robots. This effort resulted in a number of publications, including the book *Neurointellect: From Neuron to Neurocomputer*, co-authored with H. Vaitkevicius (1989).

Extensive multidimensional scaling studies of color and brightness discrimination and psychophysical studies of color discrimination in humans, complemented by basic electrophysiological evidence from studies of color receptors in the snail and retinal unit activity in fish and frog, led to Sokolov's *spherical model of color vision*. The first English-language presentation of the spherical model was given at the International Congress of Psychology in Leipzig in 1980.

In the 1990s Sokolov extended the spherical model, which was based on the perception of basic attributes of visual stimuli, to a more general model that encompassed other perceptual-cognitive functions, specifically the perception of emotional facial expressions and executive control mechanisms. By integrating evidence from human psychophysics, neurophysiology, and mathematical modeling he developed a unified model to characterize quantitatively the complex relations between objective and subjective aspects of reality.

Over the years Sokolov received many international honors for his work. Interestingly, in the context of this English version of his final work, the first formal recognition of scientific distinction occurred in the United States. In 1975 he was elected to the U.S. National Academy of Sciences and, in 1976, to the American Academy of Arts and Sciences. In 1984 he was elected to the Finnish Academy of Sciences and Letters and received the Pavlov Gold Medal Award from the Academy of Sciences of the USSR. In 1988 he became the first Russian scientist to receive the Award for Distinguished Contributions from the Society of Psychophysiological Research. And in 1998 he was recognized by the International Organization of Psychophysiology as one of the five most acclaimed neuroscientists of the twentieth century; he received the Century

Award for "major discoveries and invaluable contributions [that] served as a source of inspiration and encouragement for others and helped shape the present and future course of psychophysiology and related neurosciences."

Throughout his career Sokolov was fascinated by that most mysterious of neuroscientific problems, the mechanism of consciousness. For many years he conducted for the Department of Psychophysiology at Moscow State University a series of lectures entitled "The Psychophysiology of Consciousness." He updated the lectures for each presentation. Much of the material covered in those lectures is found in this volume.

D. M. Bowden
G. Paramei
A. M. Chernorizov

PREFACE

The mechanisms that give rise to the subjective phenomena of perception, conceptualization, and semantics are the fundamental objects of psychophysiological research. Traditionally, psychophysiological experiments were based on recordings of autonomic responses and changes in electrical activity of the brain. The work reported here extends the methodology of psychophysiology to neuronal mechanisms of mental phenomena. The electrical activity of the brain is considered to reflect neuronal cell activity and autonomic responses are regarded as results of activity in neuronal networks.

Studies of the neuronal mechanisms of mental phenomena have led to separation of neurons into two categories: neurons indirectly connected with consciousness and *consciousness neurons*, which are directly associated with this psychic function. Activation of a specific consciousness neuron is associated with a corresponding subjective experience. In accord with the hypothesis expressed by Penrose (2005), it is proposed that the specificity of the subjective process associated with activation of particular consciousness neurons is determined by the generation of coherent photons in cytoskeletal microtubules of those neurons. The origin of complex subjective images lies in hierarchically organized networks of consciousness neurons. Temporary loss of consciousness, as in fainting or concussion, occurs when consciousness neurons are disabled, while neurons, whose function is necessary for life but which are not directly associated with consciousness, continue to function.

The separation of neurons into two categories has led further to the concept of *distributed consciousness,* according to which consciousness neurons form a multidimensional subjective space that is spherical in structure. This means that subjective phenomena can be represented on multidimensional spherical maps formed by sets of consciousness neurons. The concept of distributed consciousness is supported by the occurrence of focal lacunae in maps of consciousness.

The spherical structure of consciousness reflects a universality of the spherical model of cognitive processes. This universality is confirmed by the fact that the spherical *perceptual space* in a given domain coincides with the spherical *semantic space* of terminology representing the percepts of the domain. Perceptual and semantic differences correlate quantitatively with the amplitudes of evoked potentials when the stimuli they represent change from one to another. The amplitudes of evoked potentials in turn are determined by the magnitude of spike trains in phasic neurons that "measure" the differences between stimuli. A striking example of the coincidence between different indices of subjective spaces is seen in the correspondence of the color hypersphere as determined by psychophysical experiments to the color hypersphere derived from the amplitudes of evoked potentials in response to replacement of one color stimulus by another. The sphericity of color space has been repeatedly confirmed by recording the responses of visual system neurons to interstimulus differences.

Further experiments have shown that the semantic space defined by estimated differences between the names of colors also exhibits a spherical structure that coincides with the space defined by difference estimates for the colors themselves, the perceptual color space. Moreover, it has been found that the amplitudes of evoked potentials in response to replacement of the name of one color by that of another provide evidence for the sphericity of the semantic structure of color concepts. Universality of the spherical structure of color vision across species other than humans has been confirmed in behavioral and psychophysiological experiments in animals ranging from monkeys, rabbits, and frogs to fish. Extension of the spherical model to other domains of cognitive function was demonstrated in psychophysical experiments showing that verbal estimates of differences in images of facially expressed emotion and of differences in the names of emotions correspond identically to the distances between points on surfaces in spherical space.

Thus, the recurring appeal of the spherical model of cognitive processes is a consequence of the fact that the model has emerged as a universal representation of a variety of cognitive processes in both humans and animals.

I want to express my deep gratitude to colleagues in the Department of Psychophysiology and the Department of Higher Nervous Activity of Moscow State University for their collaboration in the experimental research and their productive discussion of the ideas to be found in this book. Special thanks go to editor M. I. Cherkasskaya for her enthusiasm and valuable counsel.

E. N. Sokolov
Doctor of Biological Sciences and Professor
Moscow State University

Introduction

We refer to the strategy of the current work as the *human neuronal model of psychophysiological research*, a search for the neuronal mechanisms of subjective phenomena. The ultimate goal is the integration of psychophysiological data with corresponding neurophysiological data into a unified mathematical model composed of neuronal elements. With external stimuli as inputs, such a model should output the responses obtained by psychophysiological methods. Simultaneously, neuronal elements of the model should reproduce the responses of real neurons. We have found that a spherical model of cognitive processes fully meets these criteria (Fomin et al. 1979).

Elements of the spherical model include a set of receptors that connect to predetector neurons. The predetectors form an ensemble that connects to an ensemble of detector neurons, which are selectively tuned to specific combinations of output from predetectors that encode the stimuli at their input. In the model, stimulation of the predetectors is represented by equal-length vectors of excitation. Thus, stimuli at the input project onto a spherical surface in multidimensional space. The dimensionality of the space is determined by the number of predetectors in the ensemble. Differences between stimuli correspond to the distances between points that represent the stimuli on a sphere.

The spherical model has been confirmed repeatedly at both the psychophysiological and neurophysiological levels in relation to color vision. Multidimensional scaling of matrices compiled from subjective estimates of color differences has shown that different colors are distributed on the surface of a sphere in four-dimensional Euclidean space. The subjective differences between colors coincide closely with the geometric, chord distances between colors on the surface of the sphere (Izmailov and Sokolov 1991; Leonov and Sokolov 2008). When the color of a stimulus changes suddenly, subjects show a negative peak in the evoked potential (EP) with a latency of 87 msec (N87). The amplitude of the EP at N87 correlates closely with the subjective difference between the colors. Multidimensional scaling of matrices compiled from N87 amplitudes reveals a four-dimensional spherical color space that is identical to the space obtained from the subjective evaluation of color differences (Izmailov and Sokolov 2004; Leonov and Sokolov 2008).

The model also applies to color memory. Multidimensional scaling of a matrix of subjective evaluations of differences between color names results in a four-dimensional *semantic color space* that corresponds to the perceptual color space. Sudden substitution of the name of one color for that of another on a monitor evokes a *semantic negative potential* with a peak latency of 180 msec (N180). The amplitudes of semantic N180s correlate closely with the subjective differences between the names of the same colors (Sokolov 2003). The close correspondence of these findings suggests that the direct perception of color and the perception of the learned names of the colors are both coded by excitation vectors of equal length. The differences between perceived colors and between the names of the colors are equal to the absolute value of distances between the corresponding vectors.

The neuronal mechanisms of color discrimination have been investigated by recording the spike activity of neurons in the visual cortex of rabbits using the same sudden change of color paradigm. It has been found that cortical neurons generate bursts of spikes within an interval of 40 to 90 msec after the change of stimulus that correlate closely with amplitude of the EP to the same change. Multidimensional scaling of the matrix of spike discharges generated in response to color changes revealed a four-dimensional color space that coincided with the rabbit's color space derived from the matrix of EP amplitudes (Polyansky et al. 2005). The similarity between the magnitude of spike discharges in visual cortical neurons and the size of EP amplitudes from the same areas suggests that a common neuronal "computation" evaluates the absolute value of vector differences as a measure of color differences (Sokolov 2003).

Thus, systematic research on color vision has demonstrated the ability of the spherical model to integrate psychophysiological and neurophysiological data related to perceptual processes. This opens new perspectives for explaining other mental processes, including consciousness.

Although the existence of consciousness is perceived subjectively by every human, it is very difficult to give a strict definition of the term. Consciousness, which originates somewhere in brain structures, is a purely personal property that is inaccessible to the external observer. Only indirectly can one convey the content of consciousness—for example, by spoken or written communications, or drawings and paintings. The difficulty posed by indirect reproduction of the content of consciousness is illustrated by the experience of an artist who sketches portraits of individuals based on verbal descriptions of facial features, whether of a close friend or of a face seen but once. Although the process is continuously checked and controlled by the person who committed the face to memory, the portrait is never identical to the image stored there.

Consciousness involves activities that are expressed in creative work, in plans of future actions, and in the formulation of scientific concepts, the generation of engineering designs, and the production of artworks. Creativity itself constitutes the nucleus of consciousness (Pribram 1991). Consciousness reaches its highest levels in creative self-consciousness, which is directed toward the spiritual enhancement of personality.

According to Schrödinger (2000), the emergence and development of consciousness is associated with a biological transformation. Although individually acquired skills are not transmitted genetically, some habits are inherited over generations. Schrödinger explains this process in terms of Darwinian evolutionary theory. Mutation results in organic change at the genetic level, which leads to changes in individual behavior that determine the further selection of individuals. This process is illustrated by the development of birds' ability to fly. Acquisition of the ability to fly allows them to build nests in trees, which in turn determines selection for nestlings advanced in that ability, which is further determined by random mutation. Over many generations improved flying ability appears at the genetic level.

Thus, consciousness can be defined as the flow of individual subjective experience: sequential changes of images, thoughts, intentions, and feelings. The question of the mechanisms of consciousness, however, remains open. Discussing the physical principle that generates consciousness, Schrödinger poses a fundamental question: What material processes are directly associated with consciousness? Avoiding the attribution of consciousness to inanimate matter, Schrödinger further states that not every neural process, not even every cerebral process, is associated with consciousness. Only those modifications or "differentials" that distinguish a new event from the preceding one penetrate into the conscious sphere.

Here follows the question: What determines the specificity of *consciousness neurons*? There are two possible answers: (1) the specificity of consciousness neurons lies in their intercellular mechanisms or (2) the specificity of consciousness neurons is a network effect that results from interactions among neurons.

Crick and Koch (2002) have also considered the hypothesis that only a specific set of neurons in the central nervous system is associated with consciousness. The majority of neurons involved in decision making are not associated with consciousness. Only the result of the process is represented in the form of an explicit image in specific consciousness neurons. Destruction or functional disruption of these neurons leads to inability to perceive certain specific categories of objects.

Based on the hypothesis that a limited number of consciousness neurons form object representations, Crick and Koch consider two possibilities:

1. Consciousness is in principle global.
2. Conscious perception of a specific category of objects is connected with a small group of neurons, by their estimate only 100 to 1,000 such neurons.

They compare a neuron's specialization to the expression of selected genes in specific cell types. They argue that "neurons of visual consciousness" are not located in primary visual cortex, area V1, but are distributed at a higher level. In discussing the question of neurons that perceive direction of movement, area V5, they point out that electrical microstimulation of neurons in V5, under conditions requiring a choice of direction of motion, determines the direction chosen. The authors propose further that visual consciousness is associated with neurons of the frontal cortex. In support of this view they cite functional magnetic resonance imaging (fMRI) data obtained on a patient with "blind sight," whose prefrontal areas 46 and 47 were activated only when he watched moving objects.

Removal of a monkey's frontal cortex leads to total blindness (Nicholls et al. 2001). Such an observation suggests that consciousness neurons located in these specific structures receive information from gnostic neurons (i.e., neurons responsive to specific categories of object) in dorsal and ventral areas of association cortex, which in turn receive projections from neurons in the primary areas of visual cortex. The latter are not themselves consciousness neurons.

In 1995, a special symposium was devoted to discussion of *Shadows of the Mind*, a monograph by R. Penrose (1994). S. A. Klein (1995) presented a review titled "Is quantum mechanics relevant to understanding consciousness?" Klein's main objection to the quantum mechanical interpretation of consciousness proposed by Penrose was that up to this point no neurophysiological process has required going beyond classical physics for an explanation, and that the problem of consciousness should be solved within the framework of classical physics. According to Klein, quantum mechanical hypotheses belong to the realm of metaphysics where questions are posed in a form not susceptible to scientific testing.

In responding to critical remarks regarding quantum mechanisms of information processing, Penrose referred to work of Jibu and colleagues (1994), which considered laserlike quantum processes in microtubules of the neuronal cytoskeleton. Such processes result from interaction between the electrical dipoles of water molecules in microtubules and quantum electromagnetic radiation. Microtubules function as a nonlinear optical coherent mechanism. Two phenomena were considered, superradiance and supertransparency. Superradiance is a quantum mechanical effect of water molecules ordered according to their energy level and specific time of coherent transition, which is much shorter than thermal fluctuation. Self-induced supertransparency is a consequence of short radiation, which escapes the decoherent influence of thermal fluctuations. It was proposed that the microtubular network converts the nerve cell into an "optical computer" and that optical computations in cytoskeletal structures are likely to be the substrate of consciousness.

In his response to critics, Penrose touched on the issue of individual neurons as substrates of consciousness. First he emphasized the differences between the cytoskeletal structure of neurons and other cells, concluding that only nerve cells are connected with consciousness. Developing this approach further, one could propose that only consciousness neurons possess a cytoskeleton in which the generation of coherent photons is possible.

Based on the above, one can entertain a hypothesis whereby consciousness, the flow of subjective states, is a form of activity of specific consciousness neurons. From this hypothesis follow a number of experimentally testable consequences:

1. A stimulus that causes a subjective phenomenon should lead to the activation of a specific consciousness neuron.
2. Electrical stimulation of an individual consciousness neuron should cause a subjective phenomenon specific to that neuron.
3. Destruction or functional disabling of an individual consciousness neuron should result in the disappearance of a subjective phenomenon specific to that neuron.

Modern microelectrode recordings of neural activity and the microstimulation of single neurons in clinical settings open the door to objective studies of consciousness, including testing the predictions that flow from the consciousness neuron hypothesis. Important progress in this direction has been made by a group headed by Professor E. Holmgren (Marinkovic et al. 2000). One study involved the use of 105 electrical stimulation sites in the search for a focus of epileptogenic activity in the prefrontal and temporal cortex of a patient. The following results were obtained:

1. Presentation of photographs depicting different emotional expressions provoked a depolarizing shift in event-related potentials (ERPs) in only one of all electrodes implanted in the prefrontal cortex of the right hemisphere.
2. Electrical stimulation through the electrode that responded to emotional expressions elicited visual hallucinations, such as “phantom” faces.
3. Extirpation of the epileptogenic zone of prefrontal cortex near the site of stimulation that led to phantom faces caused long-term selective loss of the perception of emotional expressions. No recovery of the perception of fear expressions was found even after three years of systematic observation.

Although the activity of individual neurons was not recorded in this work, the intention of the investigators was to study consciousness. The recording of neural activity and the electrical microstimulation of neurons in relation to consciousness represent genuine methodological progress.

The hypothesis of specific neurons of consciousness includes two further predictions, which may also be subject to experimental testing:

1. What is the difference between a consciousness neuron and a neuron not related to consciousness? The fact that the genome of an organism is identical in all its cells suggests that neurons of consciousness are characterized by the expression of a specific combination of genes. Hence, consciousness neurons should differ from neurons not associated with consciousness by the expression of RNA fragments and proteins that determine their specific properties.
2. The evolutionary process involves evolution of the genome, which along with mutations involves duplication of genes. Increased complexity of the genome opens the way to increased complexity of proteins. The evolution of consciousness is the evolution and improvement of neurons of consciousness based on evolution of the genome.

Let us return to the monograph by Schrödinger (2000), who suggested that the nervous system of *Homo sapiens* is still undergoing phylogenetic development. Hence, neurons of consciousness at different levels of evolutionary development should differ in DNA structure and consequently in genes expressed.

The hypothesis that consciousness neurons exist makes research on consciousness at cellular and molecular levels a suitable topic of neuroscience. At the same time, consciousness is an element of the subjective world, so the integrated study of consciousness belongs to the interdisciplinary field of psychophysiology.

The present work examines the concept of *distributed consciousness*. It is proposed that qualitatively different sensations arise within specific neurons of consciousness, which in turn form neural fields, or *neural maps*. A change from one sensation to another is determined by a shift in the focus of excitation on a neural map. This leads to replacement of activity in one consciousness neuron by excitation of another one. The mapping principle extends across perceptual and semantic patterns.

The question arises as to where neurons of consciousness are located: Are they distributed across brain structures or concentrated in a single center? The visual cortex is considered to be responsible for the perception of visual signals. However, preservation of the visual cortical area with total removal of other cortical areas in animals has shown that behavioral reactions to visual stimuli are lost: the animals behave as if blind even though neurons in visual cortex continue to respond to visual stimuli. In the work mentioned above, Marinkovic and colleagues have shown that in humans, visual patterns occur during focal electrical stimulation of the prefrontal cortex. An fMRI study carried out under the direction of L. Weiskrantz showed that the conscious perception of a visual stimulus involves activation of prestriate and dorsolateral prefrontal cortex, Brodmann area 46 (Nichols et al. 2001; Sahraie et al. 1997). During unconscious perception, or *blind sight*, the superior colliculi of the midbrain, together with the medial and orbital prefrontal cortex, are activated. According to Weiskrantz, the fact that conscious perception is linked with the activation of dorsolateral prefrontal cortex, while in unconscious perception such activation is absent, shows the importance of this area in conscious processes. The fact that prestriate cortex is activated during both conscious and unconscious processes means that this region is not directly linked with consciousness, even though it is important for processing visual information. This means that the dorsolateral prefrontal cortex, which receives information from both the ventral and dorsal visual streams, is responsible for consciousness. The transition from conscious to unconscious perception is associated with a shift in activation from dorsolateral prefrontal cortex to medial and orbital areas of the frontal lobe. This can be interpreted as evidence that neurons of visual consciousness are located in the dorsolateral area of prefrontal cortex. Primary visual cortex (area V1), which provides information to neurons of consciousness in the prefrontal cortex, is not itself directly associated with consciousness.

Consciousness neurons and the neurons that serve them constitute specialized cells that represent different modalities. The neurons that are not associated with consciousness form neural ensembles. When a stimulus acts on the system, a particular combination of excitations occurs in those ensembles. The combination of excitations can be represented by an excitation vector that is of constant length for all stimuli acting on the ensemble. The excitation vectors of constant length form a sphere in multidimensional space. The dimensionality of the sphere is determined by the number of primary neuronal predetectors in the ensemble. The excitation vector induced in the ensemble enters via parallel channels to a set of neuronal detectors. Each detector possesses a specific combination of synaptic contacts, which can in turn be represented by a vector of synaptic weights. The synaptic weights vectors are of equal length for all detectors, so the detectors form a spherical surface in the model. Each detector multiplies the incoming excitations by the weights of the synaptic contacts and sums the products. Formally this operation is a scalar multiplication of the excitation vector by the vector representing the weights of the synaptic connections. Because these vectors are equal in length, maximal excitation occurs in the detector whose synaptic weights vector coincides with the incoming excitation vector. Thus, a focus of excitation appears on the spherical surface formed by the detectors, which is associated with a subjective sensation specific to the detector. This is a general overview of the spherical model of cognitive processes, which unites sensation as an element of consciousness with its neural mechanism.

Consciousness neurons are influenced by signals from the brainstem reticular formation and the reticular formation of the thalamus. The first regulates global consciousness; shutting it down inactivates the consciousness neurons and leads to unconsciousness. The second represents a "searchlight of consciousness" that highlights a specific "module of consciousness," making it the object of attention. Moving the searchlight from one module to another allows the shift of attention from one object to another (Crick and Koch 2002).

PART ONE

The Spherical Model of Cognitive Processing

1

Vector Encoding in Perception

1.1. THE DETECTOR NEURON

Based on the results of psychophysical studies of human perception and recordings of individual neuronal activity in the brains of animals, the following model has been formulated. External stimuli are represented on a hypersphere in multidimensional Euclidean space (Fomin et al. 1979). Perceived stimuli are represented by vectors of equal length. Each point on the hypersphere corresponds to a specific stimulus and can be represented by either Cartesian or spherical (angular and radial) coordinates. In the case of the color space, which is four-dimensional, the relations between the Cartesian and spherical coordinates are defined by the equation set:

$$X_1 = R \sin\alpha \sin\beta \cos\phi;$$
$$X_2 = R \sin\alpha \sin\beta \sin\phi;$$
$$X_3 = R \sin\alpha \cos\beta;$$
$$X_4 = R \cos\alpha;$$

where α, β, ϕ represent three angles of a hypersphere;
R represents the radius of the hypersphere; and
X_1, X_2, X_3, X_4 represent the Cartesian coordinates of points on the surface of the hypersphere (Leonov and Sokolov 2005, 2008).

$$R = \sqrt{X_1^2 + X_2^2 + X_3^2 + X_4^2}$$

We use a four-dimensional space to illustrate multidimensional perceptual differences (Fig. 1.1) because a four-dimensional hyperspheric model has emerged in the analysis of experimental data obtained on the perception of visual features as different as colors and emotional faces (Izmailov and Sokolov

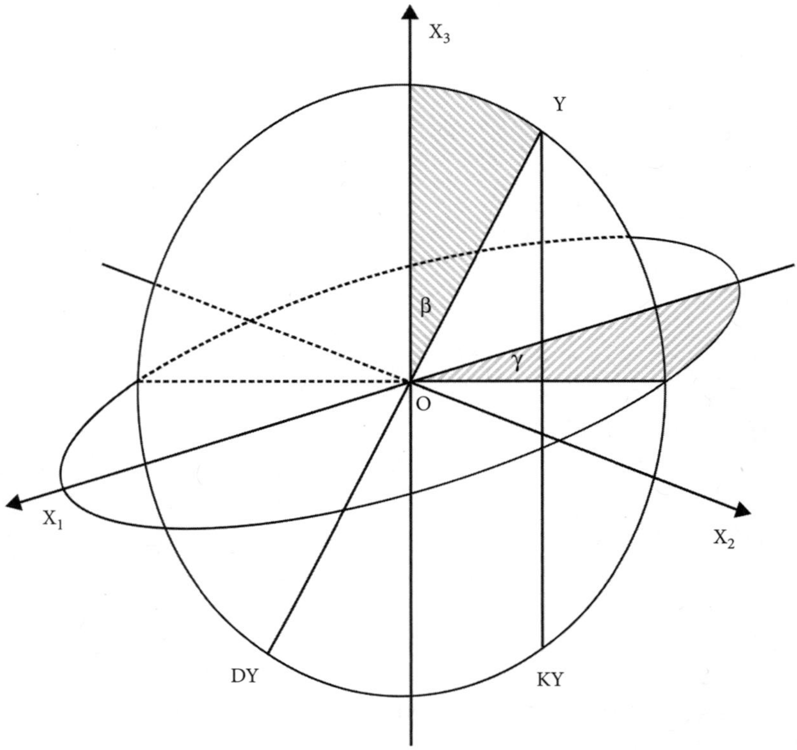

Figure 1.1 Chromaticity sphere. Y, reference color; KY, contrast color; DY, complementary contrast color; O, origin; β, saturation; γ, hue; X_1, X_2, X_3 as defined in text; X_4 (not shown) is held constant for three-dimensional representation. (Modified from Leonov and Sokolov 2008; with permission, copyright Wiley Periodicals.)

1991, 2004). In this model, Cartesian coordinates correspond to the excitation levels of predetector neurons and spherical coordinates correspond to the psychological characteristics of the stimuli. Thus, the spherical model of cognitive processes, which integrates physiological and psychological aspects of perception, is a true psychophysiological construct.

The hypersphere represents the set of stimulus detector neurons. Initiation of a specific sensation or perception is associated with localized excitation of one of the detectors that together form a spherical neural map (Fig. 1.2). Thus, individual sensations correspond to the excitation of specific neurons. As stimuli change, the focus of excitation moves over the detector map from one neuron to another.

The proposed model further implies that sensations arise during the local activation of detector neurons. The latter must be activated selectively. This is achieved by a specific synaptic mechanism. Each detector has on its dendrites

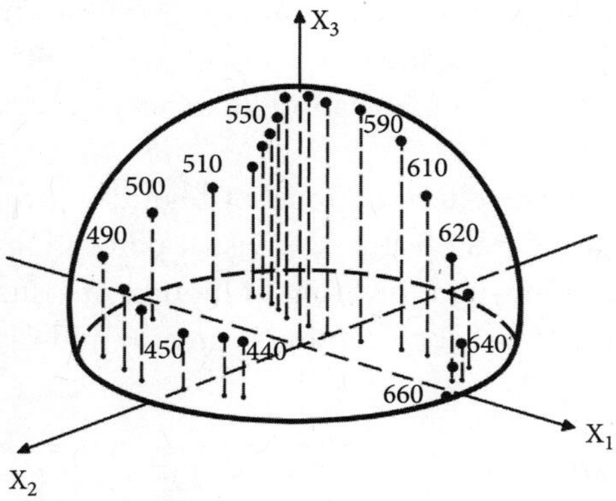

Figure 1.2 Spherical model of subjective color space. Points on the surface represent sensations evoked by monochromatic colored light stimuli; numbers represent the spectral wavelengths (nm) of stimuli that evoke the corresponding sensations. X_1, X_2, X_3 represent predetector response functions corresponding respectively to red–green, blue–yellow, and projection of bright–dark characteristics of the stimuli. The third axis (X_3) represents a projection of the achromatic plane (Z_3, Z_4) of the four-dimensional space (Z_1, Z_2, Z_3, Z_4) for colors of different brightness onto the three-dimensional space for equibright colors. (Modified from Paramei and Chernorizov 1991, with permission.)

a set of synapses of varied efficiency. Through these contacts detectors receive a combination of excitatory inputs from predetector neurons. The predetectors constitute an ensemble of neurons that generate a specific combination of excitations in response to each external stimulus. These excitations are addressed to all of the detector neurons that make up the detector map. Maximal excitation, however, is transmitted to the single detector whose combination of synaptic connections coincides with the combination of excitatory inputs from the predetectors. The selective excitation of one of the detectors in the detector map determines the sensation that emerges. Thus, the vector code represents not only the conversion of external signals but also the weight vectors of the synaptic contacts, the efficiencies of the detectors' synaptic connections.

This allows us to represent the responses of detectors as scalar products of the excitation vectors of predetectors and vectors representing the synaptic connections of detectors. The selectivity of detector responses is a mechanism for specifying one particular feature of the stimulus, its *specification*. Specification refers to the isolation of one of the properties of an object; it is not the same as *identification*, which refers to the comparison of a set of features with traces in long-term memory.

Apart from specification of the stimulus on a detector map, vector encoding includes a further cognitive operation, namely *computation* of the difference between stimuli. This difference can be represented as the chord distance between the intersections of the corresponding vectors with the spherical surface (e.g., the distances Y–DY and Y–KY in Fig. 1.1). In other words, the difference between stimuli equates to the absolute difference between corresponding vectors of excitation.

The universality of the spherical model of cognitive processes has been confirmed in studies of different features of visual perception such as color, light intensity, line orientation, and direction of motion of visual objects, as well as more complex forms of visual perception (Izmailov and Chernorizov 2005).

1.2. THE NEURONAL STRUCTURE OF COLOR SPACE

A spherical surface is the surface of a sphere every point of which lies at the same distance from the center. In contrast to the normal three-dimensional sphere, a spherical surface located in multidimensional space is called a *hypersphere*. To define the position of a point on a hypersphere requires *n* coordinates. When three coordinates are sufficient to position a point on the surface, the hypersphere reduces to a normal sphere. In the case of two coordinates, the hypersphere becomes a circle.

As stated above, and based on research of perceptual processes and recording of single neuronal responses in animals, the following hypothesis was formulated: Subjective perceptions of stimuli are represented on the surface of a hypersphere as individual loci that correspond to loci of activation of specific detector neurons (Fomin et al. 1979). In other words, different perceptions correspond to the excitation of different cortical neurons. The subjective perception and the specific detector neuron responsible for the perception occupy the same area on the surface of the hypersphere. The set of detector neurons lying on the hypersphere constitutes a *detector map*, particular points of which correspond to specific perceptions.

The subjective differences between perceptions represented on the hypersphere are measured as the chord distances between points representing the perceptions on a spherically curved surface. Perceptual differences are equal to the distances between the respective detector neurons. The hypothesis that subjective perceptions and the neuronal detector activity determining them lie on a spherical surface in multidimensional space has been tested extensively in psychophysical and neurophysiological studies of color vision.

The psychophysical method of testing the spherical hypothesis was as follows (Izmailov and Sokolov 1991). Two color stimuli were presented sequentially to an observer on a computer screen. The observer was required to rate the degree of color difference by a score on a 10-point scale from 0, in the case of complete identity, to 9, in the case of maximal difference.

By presenting different combinations of colors, a matrix of pairwise differences was created (Fig. 1.3). The matrix was analyzed by multidimensional scaling to determine the dimensionality of the color space. It was found that all of the color stimuli were distributed on a hypersphere in four-dimensional Euclidean space in such a way that all colors were represented by vectors of the same length. The coordinates of the color stimuli obtained from the multidimensional analysis enabled one to calculate the distances between the ends of vectors representing the colors and made it possible to compare those distances with the color differences obtained in psychophysical experiments.

It was found that the initial color differences correlated positively to a large degree with the distances calculated on the basis of the color coordinates obtained by multidimensional scaling. Thus, two main statements of the original hypotheses were confirmed:

1. The entire set of colors is represented by points on the surface of a hypersphere in four-dimensional space.
2. Differences between colors are measured in terms of the geometric, chord distances between the colors on the hypersphere.

The bridge between psychophysiological and neurophysiological studies of color vision in the human was the recording of evoked potentials (EPs) from the scalp as one color was substituted for another on the monitor screen. The change in color produced an EP with a negative peak of 87 msec latency (N87).

Subjective Estimation of Color Differences

Wavelength (nm)	440	450	460	466	520	525	554	570	575	600	613	625	635	650	675	white
425	1.2															
440	2.1	1.4														
450	2.4	1.9	0.5													
460	2.8	2.4	1.6	1.0												
466	6.5	6.1	5.8	5.8	5.6											
520	6.5	6.2	6.2	6.1	5.8	0.8										
525	6.8	6.4	6.2	6.1	6.2	2.7	2.5									
554	7.5	7.3	7.0	6.8	6.9	5.3	5.0	3.9								
570	7.4	7.4	7.3	7.4	7.2	6.0	5.5	4.1	1.5							
575	7.5	7.6	7.6	7.7	7.7	6.8	6.3	5.2	3.3	2.6						
600	7.4	7.6	7.7	8.1	7.9	7.3	7.3	6.8	4.6	4.2	2.9					
613	7.1	7.2	7.3	7.4	7.7	7.9	7.9	7.2	5.1	4.8	4.1	1.2				
625	6.8	6.9	7.0	7.3	7.5	8.4	8.3	7.7	6.2	6.1	4.8	2.7	1.7			
635	6.6	6.8	7.0	7.1	7.3	8.4	8.4	7.7	6.3	6.2	5.0	2.9	2.0	0.4		
650	6.5	6.8	7.0	7.1	7.4	8.4	8.4	7.8	6.7	6.5	5.3	3.2	2.4	1.0	0.7	
675	6.0	5.9	5.7	5.4	5.8	5.9	5.7	4.0	3.0	5.2	4.5	5.3	6.0	6.3	6.4	6.6

Wavelength (nm)

Figure 1.3 Mean subjective difference between colors of equal brightness; scale 0 to 9. Each pair of colors was presented 10 times in random order to three subjects. (Modified from Izmailov and Sokolov 1991, with permission.)

The peak amplitude of N87 increased with increasing perceived difference between the colors. When the colors were perceived as identical, the N87 component was absent. Thus, the amplitude of the N87 component reflects the subjective estimate of color difference.

The correlation coefficient between N87 amplitudes and observers' verbal scores of color differences showed a strong positive relationship. This provided an opportunity for neurophysiological study of the human color space based on measurement of N87 amplitudes in response to color changes. Analysis of the matrix of N87 amplitudes by the multidimensional scaling technique, again, revealed four orthogonal factors representing a hypersphere in four-dimensional space. This hypersphere coincided with the color hypersphere obtained by analysis of the matrix of subjective assessments of color differences. The N87 amplitudes correlated closely and positively with the distances between colors on the hypersphere, which had been calculated from color coordinates found in multivariate analysis of the matrix of the N87 amplitudes. The coincidence of the N87 amplitudes with the distances between the ends of vectors representing color stimuli meant that the N87 amplitude corresponds to the absolute values of the vector differences (Izmailov and Sokolov 2004).

The results of these studies suggested that the four factors that define the color hypersphere correspond to four types of monotonic neuron found in the lateral geniculate body (LGB) of primates: "red–green," "blue–yellow," "brightness," and "darkness" neurons (Fig. 1.4). These neurons are quite appropriately

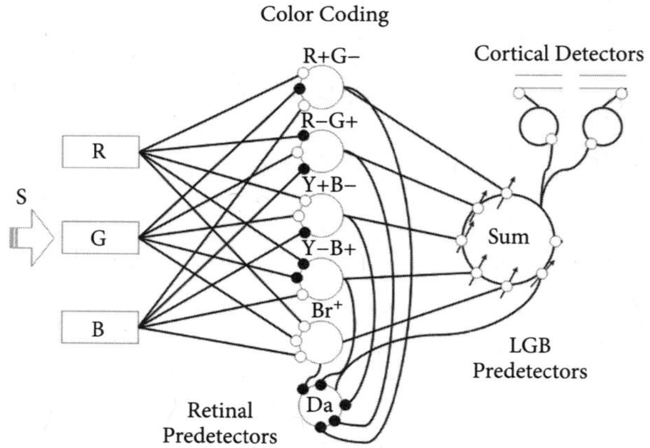

Figure 1.4 Anatomic circuit for neural coding of color. S: colored stimulus; R, G, B: retinal receptors most sensitive to wavelengths in red, green, and blue ranges respectively; R+G-, R-G+, Y+B-, Y-B+: four chromatic predetectors for coding red vs. green and yellow vs. blue effects; BR+, Da: two achromatic predetectors for Brightness and Darkness effects. Lateral geniculate body (LGB) predetectors are neurons that integrate inputs from retinal predetectors for output to Cortical Detectors of subjective colors.

referred to as *predetectors* because they constitute the inputs to color-selective detectors in the visual cortex. We propose that the selectivity of the responses of color detectors located in visual cortex is achieved because each detector has a specific set of synaptic contacts of varied efficiency, which is represented by their weighting factor in the model. The detectors receive excitatory inputs from the color predetectors located in the LGB. Combinations of synaptic weights of the color detectors form synaptic weights vectors. The synaptic weights vectors for all color detectors are considered to be of equal length. A color detector multiplies the presynaptic excitation by the weight for each synapse and sums the products. This operation constitutes a calculation of the scalar product of the excitation vector by the synaptic weights vector. The excitation vectors of the color predetectors have been shown experimentally to be equal in length. The lengths of the synaptic weights vectors, as proposed, are also identical, so their scalar product depends only on the angle between the vectors. The product, which determines the color selectivity of the color detector, is maximal when the directions of the excitation vector and the synaptic weights vector coincide.

The psychophysical study of color vision in humans led to the formulation of three hypotheses:

1. The selectivity of color detector responses is determined by differences in the orientations of synaptic weights vectors of equal length.
2. The magnitude of the color detector response equals the scalar product of its synaptic weights vector and the input excitation vector of color predetectors.
3. The magnitude of color difference is represented by the absolute value of differences between the excitation vectors of the colors presented in sequence.

These statements were verified neurophysiologically by extracellular recordings of neuronal activity in the visual cortex of rabbits (Polyanskiy et al. 2005). The same paradigm of instantaneous color change was used. A preliminary study of EPs recorded from rabbit visual cortex in response to the replacement of one color by another revealed a negative peak with latency of 84 msec (N84) (Polyanskiy et al. 2000). The similarity of this peak to the N87 component of the human EP suggested that the amplitude of N84 corresponds to the perceived color difference in the rabbit.

A matrix of N84 amplitudes was constructed from EPs recorded in response to color changes. The matrix of values was submitted to factor analysis to determine the dimensionality of the color space, which was found to be a hypersphere in four-dimensional Euclidean space. The coordinates of color stimuli on the hypersphere were used to calculate the distances between the ends of vectors representing the colors. The distances between colors on the hypersphere were found to be highly and positively correlated with the N84 amplitudes observed in response to color changes. It was concluded that the mechanisms of computing color differences in human and rabbit are very similar. The color space of the rabbit, however, differed from the human color space by a blank area in the portion of the hypersphere representing shades of red. This was consistent with the fact that the rabbit lacks photoreceptors responsive to the long-wave portion of the visible spectrum.

In a subsequent study using the paradigm of instantaneous color substitution, recording of the N84 EP peak was replaced by extracellular recordings of spike activity in individual neurons in the visual cortex of rabbits (Polyanskiy et al. 2005). Direct recording from cortical color detectors produced new results: the spike activity of the neurons in response to color changes consisted of an early 40- to 90-msec burst that coincided with the negative, N84 component of the EP. The number of spikes in this early discharge correlated positively with the amplitude of the N84 peak. These results suggested that the amplitude of N84 is determined by the early spike train.

The relationship between N84 amplitude and the number of spikes in the early discharge is consistent with the glial theory of origin of the negative peak in EPs. According to that theory, spike activity leads to a loss of neuronal potassium that depolarizes astrocytic glial cells, which occupy the space between neurons. This gives rise to a negative peak in the EP from the area. An increase in the frequency of spikes leads to greater passage of potassium, resulting in greater N84 amplitude.

A matrix was created for each neuron in this study. Each cell of the matrix contained the number of early discharge spikes in response to a specific color change. When the matrices were analyzed by factor analysis, it was found that each gave the same result, a hypersphere in four-dimensional space. This indicated that all color detectors in visual cortex receive the same *difference discharge* early in the processing of color information. The early spike train in visual cortex was followed by an inhibitory pause, which was followed in turn by a late spike discharge. The duration of the inhibitory pause depended on the number of spikes in the early discharge. The denser the burst of spikes, the more distinct was the inhibitory pause. This suggested that the inhibitory pause was based on lateral inhibition between color detectors activated in the early difference discharge (Polyanskiy et al. 2005). The early discharge originates in a population of phasic retinal neurons that measure the difference between excitation vectors that encode the changing stimuli.

The study on which the matrix of early spike trains was based included trials in which the second color was identical to the first. Such a sequence can be considered as the substitution of a stimulus for itself. In those trials the initial discharge and the inhibitory pause were absent, but tonic spike activity was observed. The spike frequency was different in different neurons. This was consistent with the concept that each color detector in visual cortex is selectively tuned for a certain color and responds to it for the full duration of the stimulus. As indicated earlier, the color selectivity of a detector is defined by its synaptic weights vector.

To test this concept, data reflecting each neuron's response to replacement of the stimulus by itself were collected in a common matrix for all of the neurons studied. It was hypothesized that such a matrix would contain information about individual response functions of color detectors, which in turn are determined by their synaptic weights vectors. It was expected that multidimensional analysis of the summary matrix of tonic responses of the color detectors would allow one to identify the basis for such activity and to construct a corresponding geometric space.

Multidimensional analysis of such a matrix showed that the synaptic weights vectors of the color detectors formed a four-dimensional space that was spherical in structure. Thus, the synaptic weights vectors of color detectors were of equal length. Scalar products of the synaptic weights vectors and excitation vectors of the predetectors computed on the basis of the early spike trains coincided closely with the tonic responses of the respective color detectors. This means that each color detector possesses a specific set of synaptic contact weights. Their tonic response to color stimuli can be represented as the scalar product of the vectors of excitatory input from the color predetectors and the vector of synaptic weights of the detector (Polyanskiy et al. 2005). The constant length of those vectors means that each detector responds with maximum tonic activity when the input excitation vector of the predetectors has the same direction as the detector's synaptic weights vector. Thus, the color space of predetectors and the space of the synaptic weights of color detectors coincide to form isomorphic hyperspheres in four-dimensional space. A color stimulus produces an excitation vector in color predetectors that acts on the entire population of color detectors. Maximal response to the unique pattern of input occurs solely in the detector whose synaptic weights vector coincides in direction with that of the excitation vector.

An important result of this research was the discovery of a population of brightness detectors in rabbit visual cortex. In contrast to color detectors, achromatic detectors of light intensity were found to be represented by a two-dimensional space, which was determined by two predetectors: *brightness predetectors* and *darkness predetectors*. The early spike discharge of intensity detectors to the replacement of one achromatic stimulus by another was represented by a semicircle in two-dimensional space (Fig. 1.5). The upper vertical semiaxis of the

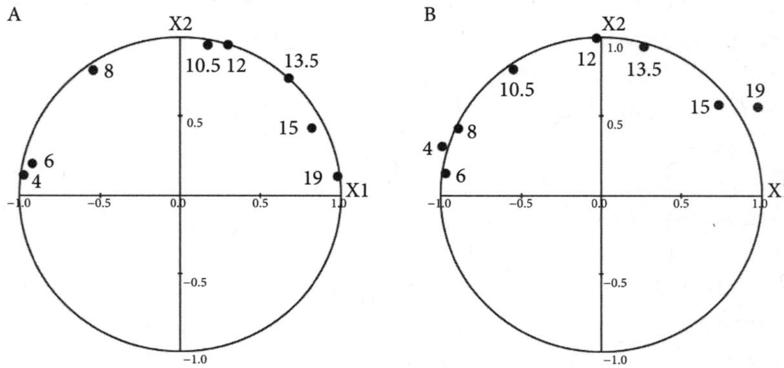

Figure 1.5 Two-dimensional achromatic visual space of the rabbit. (**A**) Sensory space for a single neuron in cortex. (**B**) Average space for 24 neurons in the lateral geniculate body. Data based on magnitude of spike trains in a 50- to 90-msec window following change in intensity of single-frequency light stimuli (4–19 Cd/m^2). (Modified from Evtikhin et al. 2008, with permission.)

space corresponded to activation of the darkness predetector. The horizontal axis consisted of two semiaxes. The right semiaxis corresponded to excitation of a *brightness neuron* and the left to activation of a contrast predetector, provisionally designated *black neuron*. Primary excitation of a *darkness neuron*, the darkness predetector neuron, corresponds to the color gray; primary excitation of the brightness predetector corresponds to the color white; and predominant excitation of the contrast, black neuron corresponds to the color black. All achromatic colors from white through gray to black are represented by selective intensity detectors located along the semiaxes of the achromatic colors. These detectors respond in accord with the intensity of color rather than with its spectral composition, its chromaticity, to form a two-dimensional space (Evtikhin et al. 2008; Polyanskiy et al. 2005, 2006, 2008).

Once it was shown that the responses of color detectors in visual cortex are determined by the input excitation vector of predetectors, the question arose as to the location of predetectors in the rabbit brain. A similar question concerned the origin of the early spike discharge in response to color difference. To answer these questions the firing patterns of neurons in the LGB of the rabbit were recorded in response to color changes (Polyanskiy et al. 2006). As in visual cortex, an early spike train was detected in these cells in response to a sudden change in the color of the stimulus, indicating that information about color difference was received at that level. Matrices of spike number in the early discharge of LGB neurons were analyzed by multidimensional scaling. A four-dimensional spherical color space emerged that matched the color space of the cortical neurons. The response of LGB neurons differed from that of the cortical color detectors in that their spike activity lacked an inhibitory pause. This indicated that they were not linked by inhibitory connections.

Another essential difference between LGB neurons and cortical color detectors was observed when the second stimulus was identical to the first. In this situation LGB neurons exhibited monotonic response functions instead of the selective color tuning that characterized detectors in visual cortex. These responses corresponded to blue–yellow, brightness, and darkness predetectors and also to response functions of red–green neurons that were reduced with regard to red. In addition to chromatic color predetectors in LGB, brightness and darkness predetectors generated prominent responses to achromatic stimuli. The brightness predetectors generated gradually increasing numbers of spikes with increasing intensity; correspondingly, the spike activity of darkness predetectors decreased as brightness increased. Factor analysis of matrices representing early spike trains to changes in achromatic stimuli resulted in a two-dimensional space, as did scaling of tonic activity to stimuli followed by the identical stimulus. This indicated that both tonic and phasic signals are received by the achromatic neurons of LGB in the rabbit.

Tonic signals determine the response characteristics of brightness and darkness predetectors, which serve as inputs for the selective intensity detectors located in the cortex. Phasic early discharges serve as a measure of the difference between changing achromatic stimuli. With color stimuli the early discharges correspond to stimulus differences in brightness. The phasic discharges are defined by the change of two-dimensional tonic excitation vectors. Analysis of a matrix of early spike trains to achromatic stimuli reveals a two-dimensional space, confirming that the phasic discharges actually depend on differences between tonic excitation vectors changing from one to another.

Based on these data one can conclude that the color predetectors that provide input to the color detectors of rabbit cortex are located in LGB. Achromatic predetectors of intensity are likewise located there. It is reasonable to assume, however, that the primary predetectors of color and brightness, as well as the early discharges representing differences recorded in neurons of the LGB and visual cortex, are located in the superior colliculi (Evtikhin et al. 2008) and in the retina (Chernorizov 1999; Chernorizov and Sokolov 2001, 2010).

That assumption was tested in experiments on the frog retina. Replacing one color by another evokes a b-wave in the electroretinogram recorded from the frog retina. The amplitude of the b-wave increases with increases in color difference. The b-wave is not recorded when the successive colors are identical. Multidimensional scaling of the matrix of b-wave amplitudes in response to color and luminance changes showed that they are represented by a sphere in four-dimensional space (Zimachev and Chernorizov 2001). The color space of the frog retina is determined by blue–yellow, reduced red–green, brightness, and darkness neurons. The coordinates of color stimuli derived from analysis of the matrix of b-wave amplitudes allow one to calculate color differences as the absolute values of the differences between excitation vectors. A highly positive correlation between the calculated color differences and the initial amplitudes of b-waves indicated that a mechanism within the retina computes color differences based on changes that occur in primary color predetectors located there (Izmailov and Chernorizov 2005; Zimachev and Chernorizov 2001). The fact that functional tonic primary predetectors exist at the retinal level is confirmed by a depolarizing shift in the constant potential that is accompanied by phasic responses in the form of b-waves. This shift reflects the overall activity of primary predetectors of color.

At the retinal level the four-dimensional spherical color space is represented by four types of tonic bipolar cell, which constitute the primary predetectors. The early spike train is presumably initiated by amacrine cells and generates the retinal b-wave, which occurs when Mueller glial cells are depolarized by the efflux of potassium ions associated with spike discharges. Amacrine cells of one type generate a burst of spikes with increasing excitation of predetectors. Cells of another type respond with spike discharges with reduced excitation of the bipolar predetector. These phasic responses are summed in phasic ganglion cells that connect to neurons of the LGB. Thus, there are two pathways from the retina to the LGB: a tonic pathway of primary color predetectors and a phasic pathway transmitting color differences. These paths converge on LGB neurons from which the signals are transmitted to cortical color detectors. A generalized, phasic early discharge representing color difference is initiated in those detectors. The phasic discharge is replaced in turn by color-selective, tonic activity of the color detector, which is associated with a specific color sensation. Changing one black–white stimulus to another elicits a b-wave. This suggests the possibility of a separate achromatic channel. To prove the existence of separate chromatic and achromatic channels at the retinal level, however, would require recording of neural activity that distinguishes the channels and the demonstration of tonic and phasic components in each.

Another question regarding the neural organization of color discrimination is as follows: How is the transition from three types of photoreceptors to four types of color predetectors accomplished? Trichromatic vision in humans and animals is associated with three types of cone, which absorb radiation in short-wave (B-receptor), medium-wave (G-receptor), and long-wave (R-receptor) parts of the visible spectrum (see Fig. 1.4). The value of each receptor's response is determined by the number of light quanta absorbed. The relationship between photoreceptor response and radiation intensity is represented by a logarithmic function. One can represent the combination of responses of the three types of photoreceptors by a vector whose length encodes radiation intensity and whose orientation encodes color tone. Because the spectral response functions of the photoreceptors overlap, the vectors corresponding to different combinations of photoreceptor activity represent a nonorthogonal coordinate system.

The mechanism of conversion to an orthogonal coordinate system was studied in the retina of carp, a fish with trichromatic vision. Recording the responses of three types of horizontal cell in the carp retina revealed that one type receives excitation from R-photoreceptors and inhibition from G-photoreceptors and hence was designated as R+G-. Illumination of the carp eye with white light did not evoke a response in such neurons. Another type of horizontal cell receives excitatory input from B-receptors and inhibition from R- and G-photoreceptors. Because appropriate mixing of red and green results in the color yellow, cells of this type were designated as B+Y-. Illumination by white light also did not evoke activity in these cells. The third type of horizontal cell, which receives excitatory input from R-, G-, and B-photoreceptors, is the only type that responds to white light. Such cells are called *brightness neurons* or L-cells (L for luminance). Different color tones, or hues, are represented by different combinations of responses of R+G-, B+Y-, and L-cells (Svaetichin and MacNichol 1958). For color stimuli of variable spectral composition but equal brightness presented to carp, the corresponding color excitation vectors are co-localized in a three-dimensional space, the orthogonal basis of which is formed by the responses of R+G-, B+Y-, and L-cells (Chernorizov 1995, 1999). Thus, the length of the vector encodes brightness and its orientation encodes a specific color (Latanov et al. 1997).

The next phase of color coding involves the formation of excitation vectors of equal length. This occurs at the bipolar cell level, where another type of neuron is found. Cells of this type exhibit spontaneous activity in darkness. Consequently, the color space becomes four-dimensional and the vectors encoding colors of different intensity become equal in length. Here color tone and brightness are represented solely by the orientation of the excitation vector. White and other achromatic colors are encoded by excitation of a combination of brightness (Br) and darkness (Da) bipolar neurons. Furthermore, duplication of color neurons occurs: R+G- neurons are split into R+G- and G+R- classes, and B+Y- neurons are split into B+Y- and Y+B- classes. Depending on the frequency composition of the stimulus, these neurons function according to the "either–or" principle. For example, if R+G- neurons are activated in response to a red color, then G+R- neurons are inhibited. When G+R- neurons are activated by a green color, R+G- neurons are inhibited. B+Y- and Y+B- neurons function similarly (Chernorizov 1999; Chernorizov and Sokolov 2001).

Constancy of radius is achieved by subtracting the responses of color neurons from the excitation of brightness and darkness neurons. Thus, the sum of excitation of these neurons remains constant for all combinations of spectral characteristics of light stimuli at the input. The *city-block metric*, in which normalization of vector length is determined by constancy of the sum of activated neurons, becomes equivalent to the *Euclidean metric* as the length of the vector becomes equal to the square root of the sum of the squares of its coordinates. This is attributable to neuronal adaptation, which limits the extreme values of neuronal excitation and results in an approximation of the Euclidean metric. Conformity with the Euclidean metric is confirmed by the constancy of the radius of the color hypersphere as determined from subjective evaluations of color differences and from the amplitudes of EPs in response to color changes.

We can conclude that color sensation results from the selective activity of color detectors in the visual cortex in response to stimulation of the retina by color stimuli. The responses of three types of retinal cones are transformed into excitation of four types of retinal bipolar cells, which generate equal-length vectors of tonic excitatory activity in primary predetectors. Phasic amacrine retinal cells are presumed to evaluate the differences in excitation of bipolar predetectors. Tonic responses of bipolar cells and phasic discharges of amacrine cells represent two parallel channels that converge on LGB neurons and thence to color detectors in the cortex. The tonic signals determine the color-specific responses of the detectors. The phasic discharges evoked by color changes serve as measures of color differences.

The set of selective color detectors in visual cortex constitutes a detector map represented by a hypersphere in four-dimensional space on which color sensations are distributed. When the color of a stimulus changes, the focus of excitation shifts across the hypersphere from one color detector to another, which leads to a change in color sensation. Color differences are measured by the absolute values of differences between the excitation vectors that represent the two colors. With substitution of one color stimulus by another, a color-difference signal arises in phasic neurons in the retina, which in turn is recorded in the LGB and visual cortex. The phasic color-difference discharge elicits a negative peak of EP in human visual cortex, the amplitude of which is directly proportional to the subjective difference between the colors.

A study of spike activity in neurons that encode color stimuli in rabbit visual cortex confirmed that such neurons respond to color changes with an early phasic discharge. The early discharge is followed by an inhibitory pause that is replaced by tonic spike activity if the stimulus is prolonged. The tonic discharge continues for the duration of the stimulation and reaches its maximum in a given color detector only if illumination of a certain color stimulates the retina. Other neurons are selectively sensitive to other color stimuli. Such selectivity of color-encoding neurons in visual cortex indicates that they form a *colorotopic map* on which certain colors occupy specific positions according to the kind of color

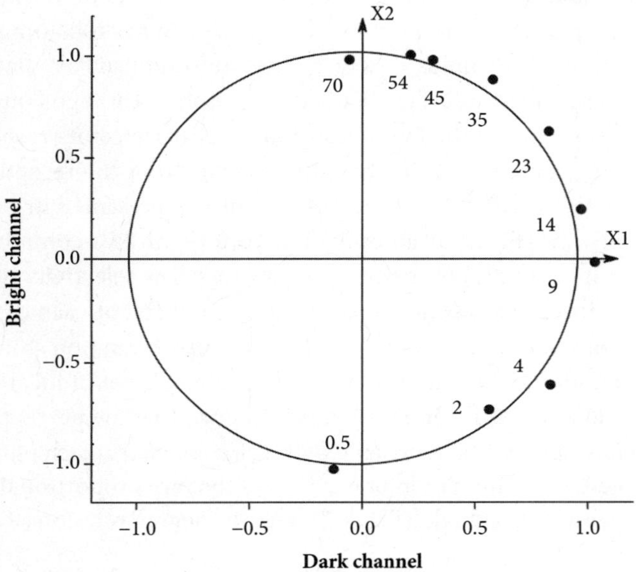

Figure 1.6 Spatial distribution of light stimuli of variable brightness (Cd/m^2) obtained by the method of multidimensional scaling of a matrix of ERG b-wave amplitudes in the frog. (From Izmailov et al. 2006, with permission.)

detector activated there. When the color of the input stimulus changes, maximal excitation passes from one color detector to another over the colorotopic map.

An analogous mechanism operates in the coding of light intensity. In this case, however, only two predetectors are involved: brightness and darkness predetectors. Therefore, the intensity detectors selectively tuned to stimuli of different brightness are represented by a two-dimensional space (Fig. 1.6).

In summary, the generalized psychophysiological model of color coding can be represented by a hypersphere in four-dimensional space. This model combines neuronal mechanisms and the psychological characteristics of color perception. The four Cartesian coordinates of the hypersphere correspond to excitation of four types of color predetector, and the three spherical, angular coordinates correspond to the three psychological characteristics of color perception: color tone, saturation, and brightness.

1.3. DETECTORS OF ORIENTATION AND SPATIAL FREQUENCY

Primary visual cortex constitutes a retinotopic map. In addition, it processes images with regard to orientation (the slope of a line) and spatial frequency (the standard distance between multiple lines). Individual neurons that respond selectively to a particular orientation are organized in microcolumns. The spatial frequency of the stimulus to which they are responsive is related to their distance from the cortical surface (Hubel 1990). Some years ago Fomin and colleagues (1979) proposed the hypothesis that a set of detectors responds selectively to the orientation of a line based on signals from the receptive fields of just two predetectors. The orientation of the line is represented in a local sector of the field of view (FOV) by an excitation vector with two components equal to the excitatory activities of the two predetectors. The selectivity of the detectors is determined by a specific set of synaptic contacts for each detector. As a line changes orientation in a local sector of the FOV, excitation shifts from one detector to another. Thus, the visual cortex contains a set of local orientation analyzers. Studies of visual orientation have shown that the perception of lines with different slopes can be represented by a circular space, each point of which is determined by a combination of excitations that are proportional to the sine and cosine of twice the angle (Fig. 1.7). (A 180-degree rotation of a line does

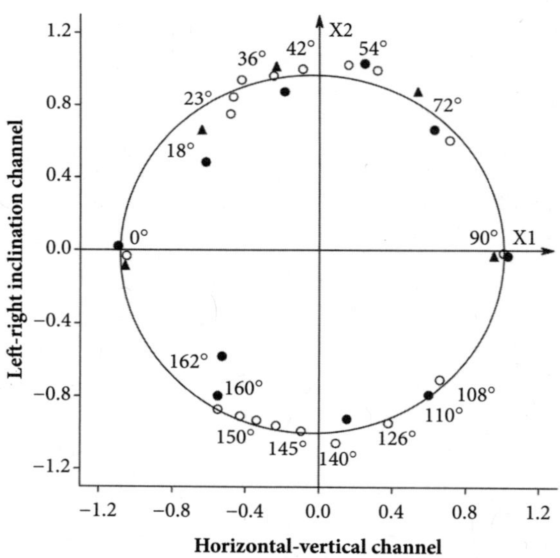

Figure 1.7 Two-dimensional space of perceived line orientation constructed from subjective estimated differences (*open and closed circles*) and from amplitudes of evoked potential responses (*closed triangles*) to substitution of one sloped line by another. Values in degrees represent the angles of lines relative to horizontal. The axes, X1 and X2, represent two channels of the neural slope-detection circuit. (Modified from Izmailov, Sokolov et al. 2004, with permission.)

not alter its slope.) It has been shown that the amplitude of EPs elicited by substituting one line for another of different slope is directly proportional to the subjective difference between the two slopes.

The spatial model of line orientation obtained by the psychophysical method (Izmailov and Sokolov 2004) and that obtained by the EP method coincide (Izmailov et al. 2004). Everson and colleagues' (1998) studies showed that such a vector model of coding line orientation applied to the processing of optical images in cat visual cortex. Using the same method it was found that spatial frequency was also encoded by two variables; that is, the set of detectors for spatial frequency was determined by the contributions of two channels, one of high frequency and the other of low frequency. In terms of predetectors, the entire primary visual cortex can be considered to be a set of local analyzers, each with two pairs of predetectors that encode orientation and spatial frequency respectively.

Now, let us imagine a part of cortex from which one obtains a photographic image of neuronal activity. Depending on the orientation and spatial frequency of the stimulus, different cortical neurons are excited to different degrees, and the activation of all of the individual neurons is determined by the activity of a common set of predetectors. Since the activity of the whole primary visual cortex is determined by one and the same set of excitation vectors, it potentially contains the information necessary to define the neuronal space. To extract this information one needs to collect comprehensive images of cortical activity in response to different stimuli and then to distinguish its basic components. Each image is represented by a vector whose components are the signals from individual elements of the image. The set of vectors representing different stimuli is converted to a correlation matrix, factor analysis of which provides the coordinates of the stimuli as they are represented in the neuronal space of the cortex. This procedure is based on the idea that the neuronal spatial model can be defined in terms of a limited number of dimensions, which is determined by the number of independent predetectors in each part of the visual cortex.

Such an approach was implemented in studies by Everson and colleagues (1998) as follows. The averaged photographic image of individual neuronal activity obtained from the surface of the visual cortex prior to the stimulus was subtracted from each image obtained in response to a certain stimulus, thus extracting from each image the contribution of the particular stimulus. Then, all of the some 10,000 images obtained for different stimuli were subjected to factor analysis. Each was represented by a vector, whose components were elements (pixels) in the image. Thus, each stimulus corresponded to a specific vector representing a particular distribution of activity in the visual cortex. Two identical stimuli generated two identical vectors. On the one hand, the scalar products of the vectors were equal to the sum of the pairwise products of signals of the respective pixels; on the other hand, they were proportional to the correlation coefficients between them. The matrix of correlations constructed from all of the images contained the data necessary to determine the number of independent variables determining the matrix.

When such a procedure was applied in a study using stimuli of different orientations (viz., slopes of 0, 45, 90, and 135 degrees), two basic factors emerged. This indicated that two coordinates uniquely defined the locations of lines in different orientations in a plane (i.e., in a two-dimensional space). Moreover, it turned out that the radial vector of the space was a constant. In short, stimuli of different orientation lie on a semicircle of 180 degrees, and with rotation through 180 degrees, a line returns to its original orientation.

If, instead of lines of different orientation, stimuli of fixed orientation but different spatial frequencies, 0.07, 0.14, 0.28, 0.57, 1.14, and 2.28 cycles/degree, are presented, a set of images of the visual cortex provides a matrix of correlations that is also defined by two factors. These factors represent the contributions of high- and low-frequency channels, from which the set of signals for different spatial frequencies is built.

With the presentation of complex stimuli involving a combination of orientation and spatial frequency features, two different results are possible. If orientation and spatial frequency are encoded independently, two two-dimensional spaces would be obtained. In that case, ignoring the contribution of spatial frequencies, the space representing the orientation of lines would be a circumference of double angle. On the other hand, a geometric model of the perception of spatial frequency that ignores the contribution of orientation would be a semicircle. Such results are probable based on examination of the primary projection of the visual cortex. In extrastriate cortex one would expect to find detectors of complexes characterized by selectivity for certain combinations of orientation and spatial frequency. The space of those detectors should be four-dimensional because of the summation of contributions of the four cardinal neurons that encode orientation and spatial frequency. In that case, the detectors of complexes would be represented by a spherical structure. This logical prediction as to a spherical structure in four-dimensional neuronal space to represent the combination of orientation–spatial frequency and its relationship to subjective space requires experimental verification.

Psychophysical validation of the spherical form of the neuronal model requires systematic presentation of stimuli of different orientations and different spatial frequencies for a comprehensive evaluation of the perceived differences between them. For a single spherical structure a combination of two coordinates for orientation and two coordinates for spatial frequency should produce a vector of constant length in a space of four dimensions. Physiological validation would involve the recording of EPs in response to changes in stimuli with a certain orientation and spatial frequency to stimuli of different orientation and spatial frequency. With identical stimuli, the EP should be absent. With increasing difference between the stimuli, the EP should increase in proportion to subjective judgments of difference. If the amplitude of the EP response is directly proportional to the subjective difference, the space representing EPs will coincide with the four-dimensional subjective space of orientation and spatial frequency.

The retinotopic organization of primary visual cortex suggests the existence of localized, independent analyzers for orientation and spatial frequency. Each such analyzer has either two predetectors of orientation or two predetectors of spatial frequency and generates inputs to appropriate detectors. In contrast to primary visual cortex, extrastriate cortex may contain detectors tuned to complexes of orientation and spatial frequency. Specific predetectors generate inputs to selective detectors of those complexes. The effective stimulation parameters for a given orientation–frequency detector are determined by the specific synaptic connections between predetectors and that detector. These connections are presumably genetically programmed. This proposed mechanism is open to experimental test by recording from individual cells in visual association cortex that respond selectively to certain combinations of orientation and spatial frequency.

The concept of local analyzers consisting of a few classes of predetectors and a set of detectors allows one to extract the response functions of the predetectors identified from the optical images of visual cortical activity mentioned above. Each stimulus evokes excitation in the selective detector of each local analyzer. This excitation is determined by just two orientation predetectors and two frequency predetectors. Thus, the image of visual cortex is represented by a set of localized excitation vectors. The brightness of individual pixels in the optical image of the cortex corresponds to the magnitude of the signal, which depends on local conditions. When processing the cortical images obtained with different stimuli, the contributions of different predetectors in each part of the cortex are determined. They include contributions to the perception of orientation, the perception of spatial frequency, and the integrated perception of stimuli involving orientation and frequency.

The analysis of optical images of the cortex to identify the response characteristics of predetectors can be extended to electroencephalographic (EEG) analysis with multiple electrodes distributed over a small region of the scalp. The EEG activity recorded by each electrode corresponds to a pixel of the optical image of cortical activity. By presenting stimuli of different orientations and spatial frequencies it is possible to obtain an analog of the optical image in the form of electric potentials. Now each stimulus is represented by a map of localized electric potentials that define a vector to which they contribute as components. Such maps are based on the excitation of the predetectors that encode the signals. Thus, if the optical images of visual cortex are adequately represented by two predetectors of orientation and two of spatial frequency, a similar four-dimensional space of orientation and spatial frequency can be expected using the EEG.

The matrix of spike discharges of detectors in response to different stimuli may serve as another approach to constructing the detector space. The response of each detector is determined by the scalar product of the predetectors' excitation vector and the synaptic weights vector of the given detector. Thus, the matrix of spike trains is the matrix of scalar products. Principal component analysis of such a matrix allows one to define the coordinates of the excitation vectors of the corresponding stimuli. Independent coding of orientation and spatial frequency by detectors in primary visual cortex should provide two two-dimensional spaces for orientation and spatial frequency respectively. Detectors in visual association cortex may reveal a four-dimensional space in which the detectors selectively responsive to different combinations of orientation and spatial frequency are represented.

1.4. DETECTORS OF ORIENTATION AND DIRECTION OF LINES IN MOTION

As described above, the responses of detectors are determined by the scalar products of incoming excitation vectors and the synaptic weights vectors of those detectors. The matrix of numbers of spikes elicited by a set of stimuli is a matrix of scalar products that contains information about the excitation vectors of the predetectors. Factor analysis of such a matrix allows one to reconstruct the excitation vectors of the predetectors.

A characterization of predetectors from a matrix of spike trains of the detectors associated with them was carried out by H. Vaitkevicius (Pleskaciauskas, Stabinyte et al. 1995; Stabinyte, Pleskaciauskas et al. 1999a,b; Satinskas, Stabinyte et al. 2000; Sokolov 2003; Sokolov, Satinskas et al. 2007). Analysis of the matrices representing the number of spikes in responses of detectors in areas V1 and V2 of visual cortex that were tuned to the orientation (i.e., the slope of line stimuli) revealed two basic predetectors. Their response functions coincided with the sine and cosine of twice the angle of slope of the line. A third, independent factor represented noise in the spike frequency independent of the slope of the line.

The same is true for neural coding of the direction of motion of a point. Thus, the orientation of a line and the direction of motion of a point are represented in areas V1 and V2 by independent, localized ensembles of predetectors. Each ensemble includes two predetectors representing sine–cosine characteristics of twice the angle of slope of the line and of the angle of direction of the moving point. The noise factor does not depend on the orientation or direction of motion but is determined by the difference between the intensity of the stimulus and the background. Considering only the sine–cosine predetectors, the geometric spaces of both orientation and motion detectors are circles in which the detector is represented by a vector of constant length with components $\cos 2\alpha$, $\sin 2\alpha$ for the orientation of lines and $\cos\varphi$, $\sin\varphi$ for the direction of motion, where α is the slope of a line and φ is the direction of motion of a point.

Neurons in the Clare-Bishop area of cat cortex, an analog of area V5 in primates, are characterized by large (45 degree × 45 degree) receptive fields and are selective for combinations of such features as orientation and direction of motion of stripes. Analyses of matrices of the number of spikes in response to different motion directions of stripes in a given orientation showed that the response of such a complex detector is determined by four predetectors with the following functions: $\cos 2\alpha + \cos\varphi$; $\cos 2\alpha - \cos\varphi$; $\sin 2\alpha + \sin\varphi$; $\sin 2a - \sin\varphi$. Each detector in visual association cortex is controlled by summing the outputs of local predetectors for orientation and for direction of motion.

Thus, the set of complex detectors of orientation and direction of motion is represented by a spherical surface in four-dimensional space, with each detector represented by a vector of constant length. This spherical map of complex detectors provides a means for displaying line segments of different orientation moving in different directions. When orientation and/or direction of motion change, the representation shifts across the detector map from one detector of the complex to another.

This example of the connection between orientation and direction of motion allows us to formulate a general principle of complex detector structure. The process begins with a combination of local predetectors that define a new space of complex detectors. The dimensionality of the space is equal to the number of types of predetectors. This fulfills the conditions for sphericity. The selectivity of the complex detectors is achieved by the combination of synaptic contacts, which is equal to or directly proportional to the respective contributions of the predetectors.

As in color vision, a hypersphere representing combinations of line orientation and direction of motion provides a psychophysiological model in which Cartesian coordinates represent the excitatory activity of predetector neurons and spherical coordinates represent psychological features of the stimulus.

1.5. COMPUTATION OF PERCEPTUAL DIFFERENCES: THE PERCEPTUAL EVOKED POTENTIAL

In geometry, the Euclidean metric is commonly used to measure the difference between two vectors. It is the absolute value of the square root of the sum-of-squares of the differences between coordinates. In the nervous system there is no specific mechanism for calculating squares and square roots, but mechanisms exist for the operations of addition and subtraction. Thus, in the nervous system, a given stimulus is represented by a corresponding excitation vector, the length of which is equal to the sum of excitations in individual channels. The operation of summation is also used in the nervous system to measure the difference between excitation vectors. In contrast to the Euclidean metric, this difference is computed as the sum of the absolute values of differences between coordinates of the excitation vectors being compared. In other words, a neural network uses the city-block metric. The empirically observed fit of experimental data to the Euclidean metric is related to neuronal adaptation, which limits the maximal values of differences.

Neural networks can accommodate more than three independent channels. Thus, they can form a vector space of more than three dimensions. The city-block metric and the Euclidean metric are particular cases of the universal *Minkowski metric,* in which the distance between two vectors is represented in multidimensional space. The absolute values of differences are raised to the power P and their sum is derived from the fractional exponent 1/P, where $P = 1, 2, \ldots, n$. The city-block metric corresponds to $P = 1$; the Euclidean metric corresponds to $P = 2$. Neural networks operate on the principle of city-block metrics by subtracting and summing the components of excitation vectors. Neural adaptation expressed in terms of the Euclidean metric can generate the scalar products of excitation vectors and synaptic weights vectors.

Psychophysical experiments involve quantitative evaluation of differences between stimuli. Such differences are equal to the absolute values of the corresponding vector differences. The excitation vectors that produce this difference cannot be determined from a single difference measurement. Using a sufficiently large set of stimuli and obtaining from them a matrix of differences, however, one can define the system of fundamental excitation vectors. This is possible because of the limited dimensionality of cognitive vector space. In its most general form the task is to derive from the matrix of subjective differences an orthonormal basis that is represented in the nervous system by independent neurons. Their responses to stimuli produce the excitation vectors that encode the input signals.

The Gram-Schmidt method of successive orthogonalization is considered a universal technique for revealing an orthonormal basis. In essence the procedure constructs an orthonormal basis through the sequential use of initial vectors. In the first step one of the primary vectors is taken to be basic. One finds a vector that is orthogonal to the first, and then finds a vector orthogonal to the first two. The dimensionality of the perceptual space is defined by the total number of orthogonal vectors. The remaining vectors are linear combinations of the basic vectors. They are located in the space whose dimensionality is defined by the basis. Further analysis of the vector space depends on the choice of origin of the coordinates. Because perceptual spaces are spherical, the origin should be defined such that the variation in distances from the center to points on the sphere (i.e., the vector lengths) is minimal.

A more complicated problem is to choose the orientation of the orthogonal axes. The preservation of perceptual specificity during adaptation suggests that experimental points are located near basal axes of the perceptual space. This concept is consistent with neurophysiological observations; when a stimulus acts on only one orthogonal channel without affecting others, the response retains its specificity. A final word regarding the orientation of orthogonal axes, however, needs to be confirmed at the neuronal level. The functional characteristics of the basis neuron should match characteristics of the corresponding basis axis. Checking that the basis obtained from the matrix of differences actually reflects the contributions of basis neurons involves the identification of nerve cells, combinations of whose activity (i.e., whose excitation vectors) coincide with vectors calculated from the experimentally determined perceptual matrix.

When an observer perceives two stimuli, one instantaneously replaced by the other, he perceives a difference and can assign it a numerical score. When one records from the observer's brain the EP that occurs in response to the stimulus change, one finds that its amplitude is directly proportional to the subjective difference as represented in the numerical score. Analyses of matrices of stimulus differences expressed in perceptual scores and matrices of the EP amplitudes evoked by stimulus changes lead to the same result. In both cases the stimuli can be represented as excitation vectors in spherical perceptual spaces that are coincident. These results raise a set of questions:

1. How are the numerical evaluations of subjective difference generated?
2. How are the EPs that occur in response to stimulus change evoked?
3. Why is the relation between subjective differences and EP amplitudes in response to stimulus change linear?
4. Why are the perceptual spaces obtained from matrices of subjective differences and EP amplitudes spherical?

To answer these questions, it is necessary to return to the principle of vector coding in neural networks. First let us consider the vector coding of stimuli at the input. Stimuli that arrive at sensory receptors act on an ensemble of monotonic neurons. The set of excitations occurring in the neural ensemble is represented by an excitation vector that is of constant length for all stimuli directed to the ensemble (Fomin et al. 1979). Normalization of the excitation vectors is achieved by adding to the neuronal ensemble a *noisy neuron*, which is active in the absence of stimulation. The activities of other neurons in the ensemble are computed from the activity of the noisy neuron such that the total excitation of the ensemble remains constant. Thus, the length of the vector is normalized in the city-block metric; the sum of the absolute coordinate values is constant. Neuronal adaptation limits the activity of monotonic predetector neurons at the extremes, converting the city-block metric to the Euclidean metric. The constant length of the excitation vectors means that stimuli are represented on the surface of a hypersphere in n-dimensional Euclidean space. The dimensionality of this space is determined by the number of monotonic predetector neurons in the ensemble. When one stimulus is replaced by another, one excitation vector is replaced by another. The difference between the stimuli is measured by the absolute value of the difference (chord length) between their excitation vectors (Fig. 1.8):

$$\mathrm{D}_{\mathrm{ij}} = \left|\vec{x}_i - \vec{x}_i\right|,$$

where D_{ij} is the difference between stimuli S_{i} and S_j, the chord distance between the intersection of vectors with the spherical surface, computed in the neuronal network;

$\vec{x}_i$ is the excitation vector evoked in the neuronal ensemble by stimulus S_{i};

$\vec{x}_j$ is the excitation vector evoked in the same neuronal ensemble by stimulus S_j; and

$\left|\vec{x}_i - \vec{x}_j\right|$ represents the absolute value of the difference between excitation vectors $\vec{x}_i$ and $\vec{x}_j$.

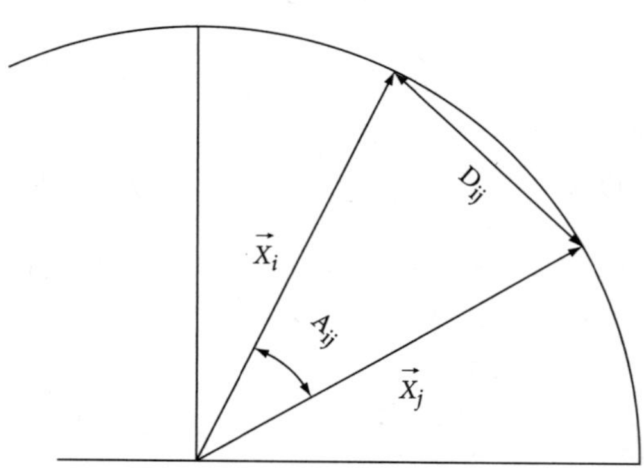

Figure 1.8 Computation of stimulus difference. Stimulus S_i is represented by excitation vector $\vec{x}_i$; stimulus S_j is coded by excitation vector $\vec{x}_j$. The difference between the stimuli is measured in the nervous system by the absolute magnitude of the vector difference $D_{ij} = \left|\vec{x}_i - \vec{x}_j\right|$. A_{ij} between the vectors is the angular measure of the difference between $\vec{x}_i$ and $\vec{x}_j$.

The differences are calculated in four steps:

> *Step 1.* A change in the activity level of one monotonic predetector neuron: with a change of stimulus excitation level X_{1i} changes to excitation X_{1j}.
> *Step 2.* The signal of change from X_{1i} to X_{1j} acts in parallel on phasic ON- and OFF-neurons through excitatory and inhibitory synapses that have different time constants. As a result, the ON-neuron generates spikes when $X_{1j} > X_{1i}$. The OFF-neuron generates spikes when $X_{1j} < X_{1i}$. ON- and OFF-neurons jointly register changes of excitation that are absolute in value in an individual monotonic predetector neuron.
> *Step 3.* Outputs of all ON- and OFF-neurons from the ensemble, including the noisy neuron, converge on a *summation neuron*. The signal of the summation neuron is subtracted from the background excitation of the noisy neuron, so that their total excitation is equal to a constant. In this case, the difference D_{ij} between the stimuli is coded by excitation vector Y in the city-block metric with Y_1 and Y_2 components; Y_1 represents activity of the summation neuron and Y_2 represents activity of the noisy neuron. Thus, $Y_1 + Y_2 =$ constant.
> *Step 4.* Neuronal adaptation transforms Y_1 into $Y_1{}^*$ where $Y_1{}^* = Y_1$ $(\exp(-kY_1))$ and transforms Y_2 into $Y_2{}^*$ where $Y_2{}^* = Y_2$ $(\exp(-kY_2))$.

As a result, with an appropriate choice of *k:* $(Y_1{}^*)^2 + (Y_2{}^*)^2 \approx$ constant.

Thus, the difference represented first by the scalar variable, excitation of the summation neuron, and now by the vector, normalized in the city-block metric, is approximated by the Euclidean metric. The difference between two specific stimuli is encoded by the vector $\vec{Y}^*$ of constant length in the Euclidean metric.

The excitation vector generated by the ensemble of monotonic predetector neurons for a specific stimulus acts on a pool of feature detectors in parallel. Each feature detector is characterized by a specific set of synaptic weights that define a vector of synaptic connection weights, or for brevity a *synaptic weights vector*. The synaptic weights vectors of all detectors belonging to a particular ensemble of monotonic predetector neurons are of equal length. The specific detector of a feature multiplies the presynaptic excitation by the synaptic weights and summarizes the products to "compute" the scalar product of excitation vector $\vec{x}_i$ and synaptic weights vector of connectivity $\vec{C}_k$ of detector *k*:

$$Y_{ik} = (\vec{x}_i, \vec{C}_k) = X_{1i}\, C_{1k} + X_{2i}\, C_{2k} + \cdots + X_{ni}\, C_{nk},$$

where $Y_{ik} = (\vec{x}_i, \vec{C}_k)$ represents the scalar product of the excitation vector $\vec{x}_i$ by the synaptic weights vector of detector $\vec{C}_k$;

$X_{1i}, X_{2i}, \ldots, X_{ni}$ represent the excitations of the ensemble's monotonic predetector neurons, components of the excitation vector $\vec{x}_i$; and

$C_{1k}, C_{2k} \cdots C_{nk}$ represent weights of the synaptic contacts of the detector, components of the synaptic weights vector.

The scalar product of two vectors can be expressed in terms of the lengths of the vectors and the cosine of the angle between them:

$$(\vec{x}_i, \vec{C}_k) = |\vec{x}_i||\vec{C}_k| \cos A_{ik},$$

where $(\vec{x}_i, \vec{C}_k)$ represents the scalar product of vectors $\vec{x}_i$ and $\vec{C}_k$;

$|\vec{x}_i|$ is the length of vector X_i; and

$|\vec{C}_k|$ is the length of vector $\vec{C}_k$.

The set of synaptic weights of a particular detector forms a vector of synaptic weights, $\vec{C}_k$. The detectors appear during a critical period in the development of the nervous system when the weights of the synaptic connections are tuned according to the intensities of presynaptic inputs, which are represented by excitation vectors of equal length. This determines the constant length of the synaptic weights vectors.

Since the lengths of the excitation vectors and the synaptic weights vectors are constant, the responses of the detectors depend only on the angle A_{ik} between the excitation vector $\vec{x}_i$ and synaptic weights vector $\vec{C}_k$. Thus, the detector of a specific feature with synaptic weights vector $\vec{C}_k$ is selectively configured for a specific stimulus S_i, which evokes excitation vector $\vec{x}_i$ in parallel with synaptic weights vector $\vec{C}_k$. The most excited detector represents stimulus S_i as the input. The set of detectors, having equal-length synaptic weights vectors $\vec{C}_k$, constitutes a spherical map of detectors. This detector map is a hypersphere in n-dimensional space, the dimensionality of which is determined by the number of different predetectors connected to the individual detector.

The detector map principle can be used to explain the subjective numerical estimates of stimulus differences. As shown above the stimulus difference D_{ij} is equal to the absolute value of the difference between the excitation vectors of the two stimuli:

$$D_{ij} = |\vec{x}_i - \vec{x}_j| = [(X_{1i} - X_{1j})^2 + (X_{2i} - X_{2j})^2 + \cdots + (X_{ni} - X_{nj})^2]^{1/2},$$

where $X_{1i}, X_{2i}, \ldots, X_{ni}$ represent components of the excitation vector $\vec{x}_i$ evoked in individual monotonic predetector neurons by stimulus S_i; and

$X_{1j}, X_{2j}, \ldots, X_{nj}$ represent components of the excitation vector $\vec{x}_i$ evoked by stimulus S_j.

Differences between individual monotonic predetectors arrive at a summation neuron Y_1. Vector encoding of the differences is based on the addition of the noisy neuron Y_2 to the summation neuron. (This process is similar to the normalization of the excitation vector for the specification of stimulus intensity.) Now $Y_1 + Y_2 = 1$ with the difference represented by the excitation vector $\vec{Y}$ in the city-block metric. Further, the difference due to adaptation is encoded by vector $\vec{Y}*$ in the Euclidean metric. The excitation vector $\vec{Y}*$ acts on a pool of difference detectors. The difference detectors are selectively configured for different stimulus differences. The mechanism involves specific synaptic weights vectors acting as described for detectors of intensity. The verbal, numerical estimate of stimulus difference is triggered by an articulation *command neuron* that receives its signal from a specific difference detector.

By what mechanism do stimulus differences influence the amplitudes of EPs? A change in the stimulus alters the activity of monotonic predetector neurons. First consider a change in one tonic monotonic predetector neuron. With a change in stimulus its level of excitation shifts to another level. Calculation of the shift occurs in phasic ON- and OFF-neurons. With an increase in excitation the monotonic predetector neuron sends to the ON-neuron two signals that create an excitatory postsynaptic potential (EPSP) and an inhibitory postsynaptic potential (IPSP). The EPSP and IPSP increase exponentially with different time constants:

$$EPSP = (X_{1i} - X_{1j})\ (1 - \exp(-k_1 t));$$
$$IPSP = (X_{1i} - X_{1j})\ (1 - \exp(-k_2 t)),$$

where $(X_{1i} - X_{1j})$ represents the increase in excitation;
t = time; and
k_1 and k_2 are exponential constants ($k_1 > k_2$).
When $t \to 0$ $(1 - \exp(-k_1 t)) \to 0$.
When $t \to \infty$ $(1 - \exp(-k_2 t)) \to 1$.

The same applies to the IPSP. The response of the ON-neuron is the algebraic sum of EPSP + IPSP:

$$ON = (X_{1i} - X_{1j})\ [(1 - \exp(-k_1 t)) - (1 - \exp(-k_2 t))].$$

At the onset and offset of a stimulus, the ON-neuron's activity level is zero. With onset of the stimulus, the excitatory effect grows faster than the inhibitory effect ($k_2 < k_1$), resulting in an early peak in excitation of the ON-neuron. As the level of excitation subsides, the EPSP decreases faster than the IPSP, creating an inhibitory peak in the ON-neuron. Spike discharges occur only during an excitatory peak. It is precisely this signal in the form of a train of spikes that is transmitted further. Thus, the ON-neuron identifies only excitatory processes.

But the same monotonic predetector neuron is also connected to a phasic OFF-neuron through excitatory and inhibitory synapses. Here the IPSP increase is steeper than that of the EPSP ($k_2 > k_1$). When the activity level of the tonic monotonic predetector neuron increases, the phasic OFF-neuron generates an inhibitory peak, while a reduction in the level of excitation of the OFF-neuron creates an excitatory peak. The ON- and OFF-neurons together compute the absolute value of change in excitation of each monotonic predetector neuron. The ON-neuron generates spikes with increasing levels of excitation and the OFF-neuron with decreasing levels of excitation. This happens for all monotonic predetector neurons, so that excitations of all ON- and OFF-neurons together measure the magnitude of stimulus differences.

ON- and OFF-neurons form a system that functions in parallel with the system of monotonic predetector neurons to provide two streams of spikes to the cortex. Monotonic predetector neurons specify the stimulus through selective activation of feature detectors. Phasic ON- and OFF-neurons transmit signals to all feature detectors through synapses that are equally weighted to all detectors, generating the initial difference discharge. The density of spikes in this discharge depends on the magnitude of the stimulus difference.

The initial spike train occurring in all feature detectors determines the negative peak of the EP. The negative peak results from the release of potassium into the intercellular environment, which depolarizes glial cells. The glial cell response is recorded as a negative peak in the EP. Feature detectors are linked by inhibitory connections (i.e., lateral inhibition). The difference discharge, occurring with some delay, causes an inhibition of spike generation in the detectors due to lateral interactions and, thus, decreases the release of potassium, which is recorded as a positive wave in the EP. On termination of the difference discharge, and following the inhibition of spikes, the detector produces a continuous stream of spikes in response to the stimulus specific to its synaptic weights vector. In summary, the detector's response to stimulus change includes an initial spike train determined by the magnitude of the difference, an inhibitory pause determined by lateral inhibition, and a continuous stream of spike activity determined by the stimulus.

The difference discharge, the negative peak of the EP, and the verbal estimate of stimulus differences are closely correlated in value. The positive correlation reflects their common origin in the differences in predetectors' excitation vectors. Therefore, the perceptual space derived from these data is a single spherical space defined by excitation vectors of equal length. The sphericity of the space is determined by normalization of the excitation vectors.

Studies of stimulus differences in the perception of colors (Izmailov and Sokolov 1991) and in the perception of emotion in facial expressions (Izmailov et al. 2000) have demonstrated the universality of the principles underlying the calculation of differences in neural networks. Subsequent studies have shown that the computation of semantic differences is based on the same principles as the computation of perceptual differences (Sokolov 2003).

The general, objective laws for defining stimulus differences are also confirmed by recording the responses of cortical neurons. When one color replaces another, detector neurons in primary visual cortex of the rabbit respond with an early, 40- to 90-msec delay, burst of spike discharges. As the difference between colors increases, the number of spikes in the burst increases. Multivariate analysis of a matrix of the number of spikes in the early discharge to color change produces a hypersphere in four-dimensional space with the exchanged colors distributed on its surface. The number of spikes in the early discharge of the cortical color detector correlates with the amplitude of the negative peak of the EP, N84, recorded from the cortical surface of the rabbit brain. Comparison of the number of spikes and EP amplitudes in response to color changes suggests that the EP is determined by the sum of early detector discharges. Therefore, the greater the number of activated color detectors per unit volume of brain cortex, the higher the amplitude of EP to be expected. Since the amplitude of the EP depends also on the magnitude of the color difference, the packing density of color detectors should influence the response to color changes.

How might one determine the contribution of the packing density of detectors to the response? One method would be to shift the recording electrode of the EP from the focus of neuronal activity in primary visual cortex to the periphery, specifically in the direction of the somatosensory and motor area. Such a move would reduce the probability of recording from color detectors and, thus, should reduce the total early spike train and the amplitude of the EP dependent on it. The recording of neural spike trains in response to color changes with a shift of recording site toward the sensorimotor area does in fact lead to a decrease in the probability of identifying color detector neurons and to reduced EP amplitudes in response to the most pronounced color differences (Polyanskiy et al. 2005). Investigation of EP amplitudes recorded in response to stimulus differences of varying magnitudes in different cortical areas may serve as a noninvasive method for estimating the distribution of detectors in the human brain. This approach is of particular interest in cases of central disorders of form perception.

2

From Detector Map to Maps of Memory and Semantic Units

2.1. THE VECTOR CODE IN MISMATCH NEGATIVITY

The spherical model of perceptual space is based on verbal scoring of differences between stimuli or on the amplitudes of evoked potentials (EPs) recorded in response to the change from one stimulus to another. Constructing a spherical model of memory requires the assessment of differences between memory traces by recording EPs associated with the replacement of one memory trace by another (Sokolov 2003). Let us start with a feature of the EP that reflects the formation of memory traces—namely, mismatch negativity (MN).

The term *mismatch negativity* was coined by Professor R. Näätänen of the University of Helsinki for a concept developed in his monograph "Attention and Brain Function" (Näätänen 1992). MN refers to a negative wave in cortical EPs that occurs in response to rare, nonstandard, differential stimuli. The experimental procedure for demonstrating MN involves presentations of two stimuli: one, the *standard stimulus*, has a high probability of presentation, and the other, the *deviant stimulus,* has a low probability of presentation. Deviant stimuli elicit EPs in human cerebral cortex that exhibit, in addition to an early negative peak of 100 msec latency, an additional negative wave in the range of 100 to 250 msec. The amplitude of the second wave is determined by the magnitude of the difference between the standard and deviant stimuli.

What is the basis for the increase in MN amplitude with increase in the difference between standard and deviant stimuli? To answer this question it is necessary to reconsider briefly the principles that govern the encoding of information in neural networks.

The excitation of receptors evoked by a stimulus is conveyed to an ensemble of predetector neurons representing a local area of the retina. One can think of predetector neurons as neurons located between the receptors and selective cortical detector neurons. An ensemble of predetectors is characterized by common inputs from the receptors and a common output, which acts in parallel on a population of selective detectors. A population of detectors constitutes a neural map on which the excitation vector of the predetectors produces a localized focus of activity. The combination of excitations of the predetector ensemble is represented by the excitation vector whose components are excitations of the individual predetectors.

The subjective difference between two stimuli acting sequentially on an ensemble of predetectors is defined by the absolute value of the difference between the excitation vectors encoding the two stimuli (Fomin et al. 1979; Sokolov and Vaitkevicius 1989). The validity of this statement was confirmed in the studies of color vision described in Chapter 1 (Izmailov and Sokolov 1991). Those studies showed that the entire set of color tones is distributed on a spherical surface in four-dimensional Euclidean space, such that each color corresponds to a specific four-component vector. Individual colors are represented by excitation vectors of equal length, and subjective color differences are measured by the absolute values of differences between the excitation vectors that encode the colors.

The components of the color vectors are identified by multivariate analysis. Those that encode monochromatic colors match the responses of four types of color-encoding neurons in the LGB: *red–green*, *blue–yellow*, *brightness*, and *darkness* neurons. The coincidence of neurophysiological data with the results of multivariate analysis of psychophysical variables allows us to conclude that in color vision the vector code is represented by the excitation of predetector neurons in the LGB. Considering the strong positive correlation between components of the color excitation vector and the corresponding excitations of red–green, blue–yellow, brightness, and darkness LGB neurons, one can assume that color differences are computed in the neural network as the absolute values of differences between those vectors.

How is the neural computation of color differences performed? The concept that color differences are defined by the absolute values of differences between excitation vectors in LGB color predetector neurons presupposes phasic subtraction neurons that compute the absolute values of changes in activity of individual predetectors as well as neurons, which compute the sum of those values as the absolute value of the difference between the excitation vectors.

Direct verification of this assumption has been achieved by recording the activity of single neurons in animals. Neurons found in rabbit visual cortex generate spike discharges in the interval of 40 to 90 msec in response to sudden changes in color stimuli. The density of spikes in these primary discharges increases with increases in the difference between the colors. The differences between colors as perceived by the rabbit were identified previously in behavioral instrumental conditioning experiments (Polyanskiy et al. 1999).

Indirect verification of the existence of neurons that compute color differences in humans comes from experiments showing that the amplitude of an EP is related to the duration of neuronal spike trains. Such a connection is consistent with the theory that the negative components of EPs result from glial cell depolarization due to the efflux of potassium ions from neurons in the generation of action potentials (Galambos 1971). The role of glia in generation of the EEG is highlighted in a review by Nicholls and colleagues (2001). From this perspective, the amplitude of negative components of EPs is directly proportional to the frequency of spike activity, and its duration is proportional to the duration of the spike train. Positive components correspond to inhibition of spike activity. Thus, one can assume that the amplitude of a negative peak in the EP is a measure of spike activity. With regard to neurons that compute color vector differences, it has been shown experimentally in humans that change from one color to another elicits an EP with a negative peak of 87 msec latency (N87). The amplitude of N87 in response to color change correlates closely and positively both with subjective color differences and with the absolute values of differences between the excitation vectors representing the two color stimuli (Izmailov and Sokolov 2004). The results of such studies allow the following conclusions:

1. The amplitude of the negative EP in response to color change is a measure of color difference.
2. The amplitude of the EP represents the absolute value of the difference in excitation vectors.

The concept that the amplitude of N87 equals the absolute value of the difference between color excitation vectors was subjected to further testing. When a matrix of N87 amplitudes in response to color changes was subjected to multivariate analysis, it was found that each color was represented by a four-component vector of excitation, which coincided with the excitation vector of LGB predetectors. Thus, the amplitude of N87 is a measure of difference between the excitation vectors of LGB predetector neurons. Indeed, the computation of such measures showed their coincidence with the initial N87 amplitudes, indicating parallels between subjective color differences, N87 amplitudes, and measures of difference between predetector excitation vectors. These results support indirectly the hypothesis that neurons compute the absolute value of vector differences.

Now let us consider the formation of excitation vectors in relation to memory. It is reasonable to suppose that repetition of a stimulus that produces predetector excitation vectors might produce traces in the form of memory excitation vectors. By analogy with perception, a trace in the form of a memory excitation vector is compared with a new excitation vector by computing the absolute value of their difference. With repetition of the stimulus the successive difference measures of the memory excitation vectors approach zero, and the EP consists only of an early peak that depends on the perceptual difference between the stimulus and background. If, however, two different stimuli are presented, two memory traces in the form of two excitation vectors are generated.

When two stimuli are presented with equal probabilities, the EP for each consists of the initial negative peak with a latent period of 100 msec, which depends on the degree of difference between the stimulus and background, and a second, later peak. The later negativity, which occurs with latency of about 200 msec, is presumably determined by the absolute value of the difference between the excitation vectors of the memory traces. This potential is the same for each stimulus, because its amplitude is equal to the absolute value of the difference from vectors of the short-term memory traces. To verify this assertion, one could deduct the value of the EP recorded in response to each stimulus independently from the value obtained when they are paired. One would expect that the difference between those potentials would reflect the absolute value of the difference between the memory excitation vectors. In practice, however, another method is used. One stimulus, the standard, is presented with a high probability, while the other, the deviant, occurs with a low probability. In this case, the differences between repetitive memory traces of the highly probable, standard stimulus decrease by subtraction, while the difference between memory traces of the standard and the deviant stimuli increases. The absolute value of the difference between the memory vectors is computed by subtracting the EP to the standard stimulus from the EP to the deviant stimulus.

By analogy with the computation of perceptual differences, the memory excitation vectors of standard and deviant stimuli are compared component by component in phasic ON- and OFF- subtraction neurons. These neurons compare the components of *memory trace vector*s. A combination of ON- and OFF-neurons computes the absolute magnitudes of vector differences and generates corresponding spike trains. The greater the difference between excitation vectors and memory traces, the higher is the frequency of spikes and, consequently, the greater the amplitude of the MN wave. The EP in response to a deviant stimulus consists of an early peak, which depends on the difference between the excitation vectors of background and stimulus, and the MN, which appears in the interval of 100 to 250 msec and which depends on the difference between the memory excitation vectors of the standard and the deviant stimuli. From this, we can conclude that the MN equals the absolute value of the difference between the memory excitation vectors of the standard and the deviant stimuli. It should be noted that the different stimuli occur at different intervals due to their probabilities of presentation; therefore, with an equal probability of presentation, the absolute differences between short-term memory traces are the same.

To detect MN experimentally one must increase the probability of presentation of the standard stimulus and reduce the probability of the deviant stimulus. When the standard stimulus is replaced by the deviant stimulus, the MN wave appears in the EP. It is equal to the absolute value of the difference between the excitation vectors. Since the memory excitation vectors are equal to the excitation vectors of the predetectors that encode the stimuli, the MN indirectly reflects the difference between the excitation vectors of the standard and the deviant stimuli by the difference between the memory traces. With a high probability of standard stimulus presentation, the MN component of the EP in response to the standard stimulus decreases, and the MN component in response to the deviant stimulus increases. The magnitude of the MN can be determined by subtracting the EP in response to the standard stimulus from the EP in response to the deviant stimulus.

By applying multivariate analysis to a matrix of MN amplitudes for different pairs of standard and deviant stimuli, one can determine the excitation vectors of short-term memory and the predetector excitation vectors which they equal. Thus, the method of computing the difference between excitation vectors in response to stimulus change can be used to compute the difference between short-term memory traces. In the case of perceptual differences one obtains the absolute value of the difference between vectors. In the case of memory differences one obtains the absolute value of the difference between excitation vectors representing traces in short-term memory. Thus, by analogy with perceptual EPs the mismatch negativity wave in the memory paradigm represents a brief mnemonic feature of the EP that reflects differences between traces in short-term memory. This raises the question of potential applicability of the EP model of short-term memory to the study of long-term memory.

2.2. RECOGNITION MEMORY: VECTOR TRANSFORMATION IN NEURAL NETWORKS

Long-term memory is associated with the functioning of neurons that hold traces of stimulation for an indefinitely long time. Konorski (1967) referred to such neurons as *gnostic units*. External stimuli elicit primarily perceptual EPs that reflect the difference between the stimulus and background with an MN wave that reflects the difference between short-term memory traces for standard and deviant stimuli. When long-term memory is involved, a similar EP reflects the difference between long-term traces. The vector encoding principle allows the computation of perceptual differences between traces of short-term and long-term memory, with EPs representing a combination of absolute values of three vector differences: predetector excitation vectors and memory vectors of short-term and long-term memory traces. In this case MN is determined by the absolute values of differences between not only short-term memory vectors but also long-term memory vectors, which preserve the traces of standard and deviant stimuli. Evidence in support of this mechanism comes from language studies of MN in relation to change in vowels, traces of which are held in long-term memory (Näätänen 1992).

The perception of a complex stimulus is associated with transformation of a combination of predetector neuron excitations to selective activation that determines the perception by a specific gnostic unit. The selective activation results from scalar multiplication of two vectors: a predetector excitation vector and a vector representing the synaptic weights of the gnostic unit. The predetector excitation vector is determined by the current stimulus. The synaptic weights of various gnostic units are formed in the course of learning. An excitation vector affects in parallel an entire population of gnostic units, generating in each of them a scalar product of the excitation vector itself and a vector representing the weights of synaptic contacts of the unit. A maximal response occurs in the gnostic unit whose vector of synaptic weights coincides with the current excitation vector.

New gnostic units emerge with the acquisition of experience and expand the range of perceived objects. The accumulation of long-term memory traces can be thought of as the establishment of new gnostic units that fix individual events in memory. Such units are created as follows. A nerve cell that is not fully differentiated, under the influence of a new excitation vector, acquires synaptic weights equal to the presynaptic excitations of the current excitation vector. The partially differentiated neuron becomes fully differentiated. The synaptic weights vector acquired by the neuron makes it potentially tuned to a certain excitation vector. Since the vector is determined by the current stimulus, the gnostic unit becomes selectively tuned to that stimulus. Subsequently the stimulus "finds" the respective gnostic unit among many others, because the scalar product of the excitation vector and the vector of synaptic weights is maximal in that particular gnostic unit.

Errors in the recognition of a stimulus occur when the synaptic weights of another gnostic unit are close to those of the current excitation vector. Difficulties in recognizing an object arise because the excitation vector does not act on the appropriate gnostic unit. Optimization of object recognition can be achieved by scanning the field of gnostic units with the "spotlight" of internal attention.

2.3. ASSOCIATION OF MEMORY TRACES BASED ON TIME AND SIMILARITY

The formation of gnostic units as a mechanism of long-term memory involves the development of linkages between gnostic units based on coincidence of the events they represent in time and space. A separate mechanism determines the association of events based on similarity.

The term *association* has many meanings. In one sense it refers to relations between image traces in long-term memory. At the level of the anteroventral temporal cortex, connections between traces based on coincidence in the time of occurrence are weakly expressed. This association mechanism is represented in perirhinal cortex at the next level of visual image processing. Neurons at the association level are *categorical neurons* that respond to a pair of associated images. The category for these neurons includes stimuli that are of different types but that coincide in time of occurrence. These associative-categorical neurons have descending connections with neurons of specific images. Activation of such a neuron by one image in the category enables it to represent other images of the category (Miyashita et al. 1991).

Associations based on similarity involve categorical neurons that are activated by inputs from one and the same set of predetectors. Such uniting of neurons within a single ensemble of predetectors can be conveyed to the next levels of predetectors to emphasize the similarity between clearly different objects. For example, consider the perception of emotional faces. Each emotional face is defined by the connectivity vector of synaptic weights of the respective gnostic unit, which is activated by coincidence with the excitation vector of emotion predetectors. The greater the similarity between the synaptic weights vectors of the two gnostic units, the more similar the emotional faces they encode. From this perspective, association on the basis of similarity between gnostic units is defined by the similarity of the synaptic weights vectors of their synaptic connections (Izmailov et al. 2003b).

2.4. CORRELATION BETWEEN PERCEPTS AND SEMANTICS

Sudden replacement of one stimulus by another evokes a characteristic EP, a sequence of negative and positive waves, in the human brain. With nonverbal stimuli the amplitude of the EP is directly proportional to their perceptual difference. The greater the amplitude of the EP, the greater is the perceived difference between the stimuli. If the second stimulus is identical to the first no EP appears, and no difference is detected. An example of a perceptual EP is the negative peak of 87 msec latency, N87, that occurs in response to sudden replacement of one color stimulus by another.

The EP in response to replacement of one verbal stimulus by another has a latency of 180 msec, N180, and is more complex. It consists of two subcomponents superimposed on one another. The subcomponents, one perceptual and the other semantic, can be analyzed separately. Let us take as an example the EP in response to replacement of the name of one color by that of another: the perceptual component reflects change in the "envelope" of the word, the visual pattern conveyed primarily by the different numbers of letters in the names of colors. The semantic component increases with increased difference between the meanings of the words.

One can construct an objective color space based on the amplitude of EPs in response to changes in color stimuli. The result is a geometric model of color space in which the distances between points representing individual colors correspond to the perceived differences between the colors. The model is generated from a matrix of N87 amplitudes by a multivariate analysis that identifies basis vectors and computes the coordinates of the color stimuli. As described in Chapter 1, multivariate analysis of a matrix like that in Fig. 1.3 has shown that the basis of perceptual color space is formed by four types of neuron, two chromatic (red–green and blue–yellow) and two achromatic (brightness and darkness) types. Each color stimulus is represented by a combination of excitations of such basic neurons, which are represented by color excitation vectors of equal length. The entire set of colors is distributed on a spherical surface, a hypersphere in four-dimensional space. Each color stimulus is represented by a vector whose components represent the excitation levels of the four basic neurons. Multivariate analysis allows one to obtain the coordinates of the vectors of individual colors and to compute the distances between the ends of their vectors, which represent the absolute values of their differences. From those values one can construct a matrix and compare it with the initial matrix of EP amplitudes. The coincidence of the model generated from matrices based on verbal report of color differences (Fig. 1.3) and the model generated from matrices based on EP amplitudes indicates that the computation of color differences in neural networks involves computing the absolute values of differences between the vectors that represent the two colors.

The change from one color stimulus to another elicits action potentials in phasic subtraction neurons of the retina. Their number of spikes is determined by the degree of excitatory change in each of the basic neurons. The summed excitations of the phasic neurons correspond to the absolute value of the difference between the excitation vectors generated by the change from one color to the other. The summed discharge of phasic neurons reaching the cerebral cortex leads to release of potassium ions into the intercellular space, which in turn depolarizes astrocytic glial cells to cause a negative peak in the EP. The greater the color difference, the greater is the number of action potentials generated by the phasic subtraction neurons, the greater is the efflux of potassium ions, and the greater is the negative peak, N87, of the EP that reflects the color difference. Identifying the connection between EP amplitudes in response to stimulus change and the number of spikes generated by phasic neurons opens new opportunities for the use of EPs in clinical diagnosis.

Matrices of the amplitudes of semantic EPs in response to replacement of one verbal stimulus by another contain information about both the perceptual component of the stimulus (namely, differences in the lengths of the words) and the semantic component (namely, differences in the meanings of the words). By applying multivariate analysis to such matrices, one can extract information reflecting the neural computation of differences in the letter sequence and in the semantic content of the words. The length of the words has been found to be encoded by excitation vectors of equal length with two components. They mapped to a two-dimensional space where they were distributed in order of increasing length along a semicircle. The meanings of the color terms also formed a two-dimensional space; they were located according to the colors they represented. Comparison of the spectral color circle in perceptual color space with the location of color names in the semantic color space shows close overlap of the two spaces.

The origin of the semantic EP can be explained by analogy with perceptual EPs. However, here the difference between color names is computed as the difference between the color memory traces that are activated when one word replaces another. The similarity between perceptual EPs and semantic EPs indicates that long-term memory neurons for color also activate phasic neurons whose discharges determine the amplitude of the semantic EP. The greater the difference between the verbally activated neurons of long-term color memory, the more action potentials are generated in the phasic subtraction neurons and the greater is the amplitude of the semantic EP. The overlapping of perceptual and semantic trajectories of color processing is explained by the fact that the long-term memory traces for colors are influenced by the processes that mediate color perception. The cognitive color space is a replica of the perceptual space.

To explain how the word's envelope acquires semantic content, it is necessary to postulate an associative process between the memory traces for color and the memory traces of the word's envelope. These links are bidirectional. When a color memory trace is activated "bottom-up," the color trace is turned on.

When the word symbol for a color is activated "top-down," the respective color memory trace is turned on. If one color name replaces another, one set of neurons of long-term color memory replaces another, which activates phasic subtraction neurons that compute the difference between the traces. The greater the difference in the set of color memory traces turned on by the color symbols, the greater is the amplitude of the semantic EP. If two names activate the same memory trace, the semantic component of the EP is absent, although the perceptual component (i.e., the response to the difference between the envelopes of the color terms) is retained.

The mechanism proposed to mediate the semantic EP has been tested experimentally. In a control experiment meaningless three-letter "words" in a consonant–vowel–consonant format were displayed on a computer screen. Evoked potentials were recorded as subjects observed one word replaced by another in all possible pairs. A matrix of the EP amplitudes was subjected to multidimensional scaling analysis. Since the words were all of the same length, no word length effect was expected or observed. The spatial model that emerged was highly noisy, although the vowels of the words made a detectable contribution. This control phase of the experiment was followed by a training procedure in which the subject learned to associate colors with the different three-letter combinations. The effectiveness of the training was tested by presenting the colors and confirming that the subject was able to name them by the appropriate artificial names (Izmailov and Sokolov, 1991).

The final phase of this study was to reevaluate the subject's semantic color space by the same protocol as before training. Now, two dimensions appeared in the structure of the semantic space. They represented the position of the three-letter color name on the color circle appropriate to the color it represented. Comparison with the perceptual color space indicated that the two spaces shared common axes: red–green and blue–yellow. This indicated that the memory traces for color names are arranged consistently with the perceptual characteristics of the colors.

In the next experiment the semantic color space was defined on the basis of "evoked potentials of discrimination" (EPDs) recorded in response to replacement of one artificial name by another (Izmailov et al. 2003a,b). Again two coordinates appeared. They defined the position of the color name on the color circle appropriate to the color it represented. Comparison with the perceptual color space showed common axes (red–green and blue–yellow), indicating again, this time by a neurophysiological measure, that the memory traces for color names are arranged consistently with the perceptual characteristics of colors.

Perceptual and semantic EPs are united by a common mechanism: the replacement of one excitation vector by another. The perceptual EP represents the replacement of one excitation vector by another. The semantic EP represents replacement of one memory trace vector by another. Memory trace vectors are activated by associations of verbal or other symbols with relevant memory traces. The generality of the mechanisms underlying the perceptual and semantic EPs illustrates the fact that, with the replacement of one symbol by another, the perceptual potential elicited by replacement of the word's envelope is superimposed on the semantic component elicited by its meaning. Multivariate analysis allows one to analyze separately the perceptual space and the semantic space. The first represents the envelopes of words. In the second the words are organized according to their meanings as defined by the memory traces associated with them. The common characteristic of perceptual and semantic potentials is their form, which is a sequence of negative and positive waves within a specific time window following the change of stimulus. The negative peak of the perceptual EP to change of color occurs with a latency of 87 msec. The combination of potentials in response to replacement of a word's envelope and semantic content is represented by a peak with latency of 180 msec.

In addition to the semantic potential in response to replacement of words with words of different meanings, changes of more complex groups of symbols elicit late semantic potentials with a latency of 400 msec (N400). For example, if a group of words belonging to a particular category, such as inanimate objects, is followed by words of a different semantic group, such as animate objects, a difference-dependent N400 appears in the EP. N400 amplitudes are determined by the magnitude of the difference between the semantic groups. If the group of words is followed not by words of a semantically contrasting group, but by words belonging to the same category, no N400 appears. Presumably N400 is a measure of difference between semantic categories (Bermeitinger et al. 2010; Kutas and Federmeier 2000; Kutas and Iragui 1998).

Generation of the N400 can be represented schematically as follows. When a group of semantically similar words is read orally and repeatedly to a subject, the memory traces associated with them are summated. Switching to a group of semantically different words elicits a different generalized memory trace. The difference between the traces determines the amplitude of the *late semantic potential*, which is a measure of the difference between the categories. A sequence of words is parsed into semantic groups and the magnitude of the differences between them is determined. As in the case of neuronal computations of other differences, phasic subtraction neurons are thought to play a role in the mechanism of late semantic potentials. The number of action potentials generated by a change is a measure of the categorical difference. The relationship between the number of spikes occurring in phasic neurons and the amplitude of the negative peak of the semantic EP is based on the same mechanism as for perceptual EPs. It includes the efflux of potassium ions associated with the generation of action potentials and the depolarization of glial cells. Thus, when one stimulus replaces another, the perceptual EP serves as a measure of the perceived difference; the early semantic potential represents the semantic difference between the words, and the late semantic potential is a measure of difference in category.

How does one explain the fact that the amplitudes of perceptual and semantic EPs are highly positively correlated with the subjective perceptual and semantic differences expressed verbally as numerical values by the observer? Let us go back to the mechanism mediating the perceptual EP to color change. The replacement of one color by another elicits a spike train in retinal phasic subtraction neurons the frequency of which increases with increasing magnitude of the difference between the colors. This phasic difference discharge is further transformed into a vocal response in the form of the name of the number. Let us consider the mechanism of this transformation, taking the coding of light intensity as an example. In that case two kinds of neuron are involved, a brightness neuron and a spontaneously active darkness neuron. Excitation of the brightness neuron is subtracted from the activity level of the darkness neuron such that the sum of excitations of the two remains constant for all values of the light stimulus. By this adaptive mechanism, the length of the vector reflecting the combined activities of the brightness and darkness neurons does not change. The vector that encodes the light intensity reaches a set of selective intensity detectors that have different sets of synaptic weights. Only the detector whose set of synaptic weights coincides with the incoming excitation vector is activated. In the course of training, the individual detectors become linked to the command neurons for specific verbal responses. Thus, a given intensity of light includes its appropriate verbal, numerical evaluation.

The mechanism of transformation from the perception of light intensity to its numerical evaluation is similar to the mechanism of numerical evaluation of any perceptual difference. A phasic difference discharge is obtained by subtraction from the activity level of a noisy neuron producing an excitation vector that consists of two components: a phasic discharge and the discharge level of the noisy neuron from which the phasic discharge is subtracted. The resulting excitation vector of constant length is addressed to selective difference detectors, one of which becomes activated. Since each difference detector is linked to its own command neuron, the detected difference specifies the appropriate verbal response. The key elements in this model are the neurons that detect the numerical values of excitations. Such detectors, which are particularly sensitive to the number of objects in the field of view, are found in the temporal cortex of monkeys (Nicholls et al. 2001). The amplitudes of perceptual and semantic potentials are determined by spike trains that represent the difference and that selectively initiate activity in command neurons. This, in turn, leads to an appropriate numerical scoring of the perceptual difference.

What are the functions of perceptual and semantic potentials? Let us consider three perceptual and cognitive operations: flicker fusion, differential threshold for detecting stimulus change, and segmentation of speech.

A light flashing at frequencies greater than 50 Hz evokes *flicker fusion*, a merged sensation of continuous light. Each individual flash consists of a light pulse and a subsequent dark period. At low frequencies, the replacement of the light pulse by a dark period evokes a difference signal that prevents flicker fusion. With a decrease in the dark period and an increase in the repetition frequency of the light pulse, the difference signal is reduced and ceases to separate the light flashes, which merge into a continuous sensation.

A *differential threshold* is the minimal detectable difference between two stimuli when one replaces the other. If no difference signal occurs, then the difference between the stimuli is characterized as *subthreshold*. Presumably the differential threshold is defined by a difference signal that is equal to the absolute value of the difference between excitation vectors. When this value fails to evoke a difference signal, the stimuli are not perceived to differ. This is the case when excitation is not transferred to a different detector.

Detector responses are determined by inputs from predetectors. The simplest case is a detector with two predetectors with sine–cosine response functions. Such detectors represent a two-dimensional space in the form of a circle. Another set of detectors with two other predetectors forms another two-dimensional space. The two sets of predetectors, summarized on detectors at higher levels, form a four-dimensional space of detectors responsive to complex stimuli.

Sudden replacement of one stimulus by another evokes a response to their difference that is manifested by a spike train followed by an inhibitory pause in cortical detector neurons. The frequency of spike discharge is positively correlated with an early negative peak in the EP. It is reasonable to suggest that the neuronal response to the stimulus change determines the perceptual segmentation and that the semantic difference signal determines the semantic segmentation.

2.5. COMPUTATION OF SEMANTIC DIFFERENCES IN NEURAL NETWORKS

The semantic difference between symbols, such as spoken or printed words, is the difference in their meanings. Mechanisms for computing semantic difference have been studied in experiments in which subjective semantic differences were compared with the amplitude of cortical EPs (Izmailov et al. 2003b). Two types of printed words were chosen as prototypes: the names of colors and the names of emotions.

A subject presented with the names of two colors can evaluate their difference in meaning (i.e., their semantic difference) and express it by a number. The semantic space for color names identified by multidimensional scaling of the difference scores is a hypersphere in four-dimensional Euclidean space. The space is isomorphic to the perceptual color space derived from the matrix of difference scores based on color stimuli (Izmailov and Sokolov 1991; Izmailov et al. 2003a).

The same results were obtained with the names of emotions. The semantic space of emotion names is also a four-dimensional hypersphere that is isomorphic to the space of perceived emotions based on subjective evaluation of differences between emotional facial expressions. Recordings of electrical activity of the brain in the same experimental paradigm have shown that a sudden change of color name on a computer screen elicits an EP consisting of two components: a perceptual component that depends on word length and a semantic component that is determined by the difference in the semantic content of words. These components are superimposed in the same time interval of the EP. Their independent contributions to the EP can be separated by multidimensional scaling of the matrix of EP amplitudes. Two two-dimensional spaces can be distinguished: a circle representing the distribution of color names and a semicircle representing the distribution of word lengths. The semantic color space based on EP amplitudes coincides with the semantic color space based on subjective evaluations of color names.

The sudden substitution of one emotion name for another also induces an EP whose amplitude depends on two variables: the semantic difference between the names and the perceptual difference between the lengths of the words (Izmailov et al. 2003b). The semantic space of emotions based on EPs in response to changes in emotion names coincides with the semantic space of the emotions based on EPs in response to sudden substitution of one emotional face for another (Fig. 2.1), as well as with the perceptual space of emotions derived from subjective evaluations of facial differences (Izmailov et al. 2000).

These observations raise two questions:

1. Why are the numerical scores for differences in color names and in names of emotions positively correlated with the amplitudes of semantic components of EPs elicited by sudden changes in the names presented?
2. Why are the semantic space of colors and the semantic space of emotions spherical?

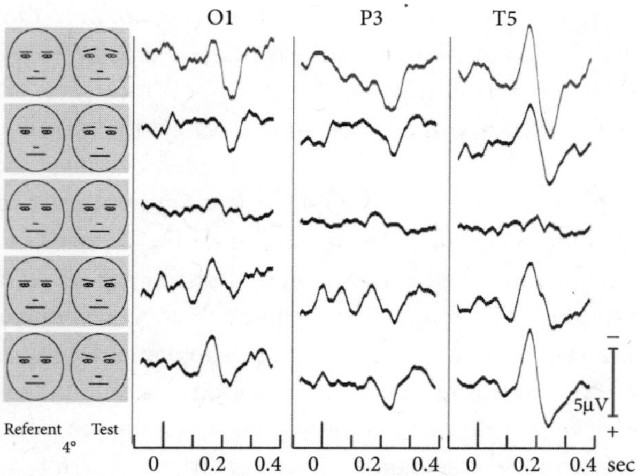

Figure 2.1 Evoked potentials in response to sudden change from one (Referent) emotional face stimulus to another (Test). The greater the subjective difference between the faces, the greater is the amplitude of the negative upward wave 0.18 sec after the change, N180. O1: occipital lead #1; P3: parietal lead #3; T5: temporal lead #5. (Modified from Izmailov et al. 2005, with permission.)

To answer these questions it is necessary to transpose the principle of vector coding from the perceptual domain to the semantic domain. Let us start with conversion of the memory map to the map of semantic units in the processing of color information. The first step is the generation of excitation vectors in an ensemble that consists of four predetector neurons. The excitation vectors are equal in length and form a hypersphere in four-dimensional space. Color detectors have four types of synaptic contacts with four types of predetectors. The contacts are represented by synaptic weights vectors of equal length. Thus, the set of color detectors also forms a hypersphere. A color stimulus creates a predetector excitation vector that evokes a pattern of excitation in the detector map with maximal excitation in the detector whose synaptic weights vector coincides with the currently active vector.

During ontogenesis the output signals of detectors reach the memory neurons from which is formed a map of units selectively tuned to specific colors. Endogenous activation of color memory neurons is the basis of color representations in consciousness. With the development of an association between a color concept and a color symbol, specific memory neurons are linked to the neurons representing specific color symbols. The semantic neuron representing the color symbol, in turn, forms synapses with memory neurons that correspond to the excitation value of each. The connections between color memory neurons and color symbol neurons are bidirectional. This makes possible two cognitive operations: symbolization of the color (i.e., naming the color stimulus) and recall of the color when its name is presented.

The recall of a color results from the color symbol's induction of an excitation vector in the color memory map. When one color symbol is suddenly replaced by another, the excitation vectors in the color memory map change accordingly. Excitations arising in color memory neurons in response to color changes are directed to *subtraction neurons* that compute the changes of excitation in individual color memory neurons. The excitations of subtraction neurons are combined in *summation neurons* that compute the overall value of the semantic distinction. The summation neurons are supplemented by *noisy neurons* that are most active when the summation neurons are silent. The combination of excitations of these neurons is represented by a two-component excitation vector, which encodes the semantic difference. It provides input to difference detectors. The numerical scoring of the semantic difference is achieved by the difference detectors associated with the semantic neurons representing the names of numbers, which are further linked to command neurons of the verbal response.

The amplitude of an EP in response to a change of color names is determined by two factors: the perceptual difference in the configuration of the symbols (i.e., the difference in word lengths) and the semantic difference between the meanings of the symbols. Both are represented in the EP; they are superimposed, coinciding in time. One can separate the two sources of influence on the EP by multidimensional scaling of the matrix of EP amplitudes. Two two-dimensional spaces are distinguishable. One, the perceptual two-dimensional space, represents the color names distributed on the basis of length. The other, the semantic two-dimensional space, represents the color names distributed on the Newtonian color circle. (The contributions of the brightness and darkness channels to the four-dimensional color space may not be evident if the number of color names used in the experiment is small.)

In summary, a color name, as the symbol for a given color, reaches the level of semantic neurons and activates a population of color memory neurons via a system of top-down links. This creates an excitation vector in the memory map. The next color name generates another excitation vector in the memory map. Corresponding components of these two vectors create excitation differences in phasic subtraction neurons. Together, the subtraction neurons compute the absolute value of the vector difference, which is represented by excitation of a summation neuron. The vector difference represents the semantic difference between the color names and determines the semantic component of the EP. At the same time the change in configuration of the symbolic stimulus, a sensory event dependent on variation in the length of the words, determines the perceptual EP. Occurring together, the semantic and perceptual EPs create overlapping negativities, which can be separated in a multidimensional scaling matrix of their amplitudes.

Similar mechanisms are involved in the naming of emotions. Let us consider the results of experiments involving sudden changes in images of faces representing different emotions and of experiments involving changes in the presentation of the names of the respective emotions. The features of visual inputs are encoded by line orientation detectors in area 17 of visual cortex. Combinations of line orientation detectors create four predetector neurons that represent the slopes of eyebrows and angles of the mouth, as well as their summed characteristics. Categorical detectors of specific emotional expressions known as *gnostic units* are located in the visual area of temporal cortex, where they form a memory map of emotions. Through learning, specific facial expressions of emotion become associated with their symbolic representations (i.e., the names of emotions). Memory neurons of emotional facial expression are connected with neurons representing the symbols through bidirectional links. The emotion names activate semantic neurons and through top-down links excite emotion memory neurons associated with the names of the respective emotions. This is the basis for emotional recall. With the sudden substitution of one emotion name for another, two excitation vectors are generated and, component by component, are subtracted in subtraction neurons. The differences are added together in summation neurons, generating spike trains proportional to the absolute value of the difference of excitation vectors on a memory map of emotions. The spike train in the summation neurons is a measure of the semantic difference between the emotion names. This correspondence is achieved by the formation of a difference vector with subsequent excitation of the difference detector and the command neuron for articulation of the name.

At the same time, the sudden change of emotion name elicits a semantic spike train from the summation neurons that creates a negative peak in the EP. The amplitude of the EP contains information about the semantic difference between the names of the emotions. The EP representing the semantic difference is complicated by a contribution from the perceptual difference resulting from the different configurations of the words and evokes an independent EP that coincides in time with the semantic EP. The total amplitude of the combined EP is equal to the sum of its semantic and perceptual components. Separation of the semantic and perceptual contributions to the combined EP is achieved by multidimensional scaling, which identifies two two-dimensional spaces: a circular semantic space of emotions and a semicircular space of word lengths.

Thus, electrophysiological experiments suggest a model for the computation of semantic differences in neural networks. The computation of subjective differences and the amplitudes of EPs in response to sudden change in symbols can be represented in generalized form by the following operations.

1. Selective Tuning of Detectors

$$d_{ij} = (\vec{F}_i, \vec{C}_j) = |\vec{F}_i||\vec{C}_j| \cos A_{ij}$$

where d_{ij} represents the excitation of the j-th detector, which is equal to the scalar product of the i-th excitation vector $\vec{F}_i$ multiplied by the synaptic connections vector $\vec{C}_j$ of the j-th detector.

External stimuli are coded as predetector excitation vectors of equal length. The excitation vector of the predetectors acts on detectors together with synaptic weights vectors, also of constant length, to evoke a detector response that is equal to the scalar product of the active excitation vector and the vector representing its synaptic connections.

The detector whose synaptic connections vector coincides in direction with the excitation vector is most activated and represents the external stimulus on the detector map.

2. Computing the Perceptual Difference with a Sudden Stimulus Change

$$dif_{ij} = |\vec{F}_i - \vec{F}_j|,$$

where dif_{ij} represents the perceived difference between stimuli S_i and S_j;
$\vec{F}_i$ is the excitation vector evoked in predetectors by stimulus S_i;
$\vec{F}_j$ is the excitation vector evoked in predetectors by stimulus S_j; and
$|\vec{F}_i - \vec{F}_j|$ is the absolute value of the difference between the excitation vectors.

The difference between stimuli that are spatially separated but that coincide in time is equal to the absolute value of the difference between the predetectors' excitation vectors that represent them. The change of excitation in each predetector is measured by subtraction neurons.

3. Calculating the Perceptual Difference Between Sequential Stimuli in Phasic ON- and OFF-Neurons

$$ON_p = \left|f_{ip} - f_{jp}\right|\left[(1-\exp(-k_1 t)) - (1-\exp(-k_2 t))\right], \quad k_1 > k_2$$

$$OFF_p = \left|f_{ip} - f_{jp}\right|\left[(1-\exp(-k_1 t)) - (1-\exp(-k_2 t))\right], \quad k_1 < k_2$$

$$p = 1,2,\ldots,n,$$

where ON_p and OFF_p represent phasic subtraction neurons in the p-th predetector responding to the difference between stimuli S_i and S_j.

The difference between sequential stimuli is computed by phasic subtraction neurons. The change in excitation of each predetector is measured by two phasic neurons. An ON-neuron generates spikes when the excitation of a predetector increases, and an OFF-neuron responds with a spike train in response to a reduction in the level of excitation of the predetector. The distribution of responses of ON- and OFF-neurons following a change of stimulus is a bell-shaped curve. ON- and OFF-neurons function according to the "or–or" principle, together measuring the absolute value of change in excitation of the predetector.

4. Calculation of Net Difference by a Summation Neuron

$$SUM = \sum_{p=1}^{n} (ON_p + OFF_p),$$

Where *SUM* represents the total number of spikes generated in all ON- and OFF-neurons of a predetector ensemble in response to the replacement of stimulus S_i by stimulus S_j.

The phasic ON- and OFF-neurons that measure changes in the excitation of each predetector converge on a summation neuron, which measures the total change of excitation in all predetectors. The sum of changes in predetector excitation represents the absolute value of the difference of predetector excitation vectors computed in a city-block metric.

5. Generation of the EP Is Determined by the Sum of Spikes of ON- and OFF-Neurons Measured by the Summation Neuron

$$amp = C \cdot Sum,$$

where *amp* represents the amplitude of the negative peak of the EP;
C is the transformation coefficient relating spikes to the negative wave of the EP; and
Sum is the total number of spikes in the train from the neuron, which combines the contributions of the phasic ON- and OFF-neurons of the predetector ensemble.

The output of the phasic ON- and OFF-neurons is input to the summation neuron whose spike train is determined by the change in the predetector excitation vector in response to the stimulus change. The spike train of the summation neurons in response to the stimulus change determines the amplitude of the EP.

6. The Verbal Score of Perceptual Difference Involves Transformation of the Scalar Value of the Sum of Excitations from the Summation Neuron into a Vector Representation of Difference

This transformation involves a spontaneously active *noisy neuron*, whose excitation is subtracted from the excitation of the summation neuron:

$$\vec{G} = (sum, 1 - sum),$$

where $\vec{G}$ is the difference vector;
sum represents the excitation level of the summation neuron; and
1 – *sum* represents the residual excitation of the noisy neuron.

Thus, the difference *Sum* is transformed into the difference vector $\vec{G}$, which is normalized in a city-block metric. The transformation to a Euclidean metric is implemented physiologically by neuronal adaptation.

7. The Perceptual Difference Vector $\vec{G}$ Acts on the Set of Difference Detectors that Have Variable Synaptic Weights Vectors that Are of Equal Length

The selective difference detector, D_i, computes the scalar product of the difference vector and the synaptic connections vector of a given difference detector, d_{ij}:

$$Dif(d_{ij}) = (\vec{G}_i, \vec{H}_j),$$

where $\vec{G}$ is the difference vector;

$\vec{H}_j$ is the synaptic connections vector of the difference detector; and

$Dif(d_{ij})$ represents the excitation level of the j-th difference detector.

The perceptual difference specifies the maximally excited difference detector. Through training each difference detector becomes linked to a particular semantic neuron, which represents the difference in symbolic, numerical form. Semantic neurons representing different numerical values are potentially associated with various command neurons, but with training the semantic neuron comes to activate the command neuron for articulation of the number that is appropriate to the perceived perceptual difference.

Let us now turn to the computation of semantic differences and the semantic EP.

8. Mechanism for Generating the Excitation Vectors of Detectors

The computation of semantic differences requires long-term memory. Thus, it is necessary to consider properties of the detector map. Eliciting an excitation vector in predetectors, a stimulus creates in the detector map an excitation vector whose components are the excitations of individual detectors.

$$\vec{D}_i = [(\vec{F}_i, \vec{C}_1), (\vec{F}_i, \vec{C}_2), \ldots, (\vec{F}_i, \vec{C}_n)],$$

where $\vec{M}$ represents the excitation vector of detectors evoked by stimulus S_i; and

$(\vec{F}_i, \vec{C}_j)$ is the excitation of the j-th detector, which is equal to the scalar product of the excitation vector $\vec{F}_i$ and the synaptic connections vector $\vec{C}_j$.

9. Transformation from the Detector Map to the Long-Term Memory Map

Memory neurons develop under the influence of detector excitation vectors. Memory is laid down in the form of synaptic contacts whose weights are directly proportional to components of the excitation vector of the detectors.

$$\vec{K}_i = \vec{D}_i$$

where $\vec{K}_i$ represents the vector of synaptic connections on the *i*-th long-term memory neuron; and
$\vec{D}_i$ represents the excitation vector of the detectors evoked by the *i*-th stimulus.

The memory neuron stores information about a stimulus in the form of a vector of weights of its synaptic connections. The memory map is composed of neurons with different synaptic weights vectors.

10. The Recording of a Stimulus Trace Is Determined by the Reserve Memory Neuron that Is Maximally Activated by the Input

$$M_i = D_i \Rightarrow K_i,$$

where M_i represents the memory neuron that has acquired synaptic weights vector $\vec{K}_i$ under the influence of stimulus S_i as mediated by excitation vector $\vec{D}_i$ of the detectors.

11. Response of the Memory Neuron to Presentation of a Stimulus

After a memory neuron has been established, it participates in recognition of the stimulus. A stimulus at the input generates a *detector excitation vector* that coincides with the synaptic weights vector of the neuron.

$$M_i = (\vec{D}_i, \vec{K}_i),$$

where M_i represents the excitation of the memory neuron established to stimulus S_i;
$\vec{D}_i$ represents the detector excitation vector established by repeated presentation of stimulus S_i;
$\vec{K}_i$ represents the synaptic connections vector of memory neuron M_i on first presentation of stimulus S_i; and
$(\vec{D}_i, \vec{K}_i)$ is the scalar product of the detectors excitation vector and the synaptic connections vector of memory neuron M_i.

12. Elicitation of an Excitation Vector on the Long-Term Memory Map

A detector excitation vector acts not on a single memory neuron but on the population of neurons that constitute the neural memory map. The presentation of a stimulus S_i evokes in the memory map an excitation vector whose components are activated memory neurons.

$$\vec{M}_i = [(\vec{D}_i, \vec{K}_1), (\vec{D}_i, \vec{K}_2), ..., (\vec{D}_i, \vec{K}_n)],$$

where $\vec{M}_i$ represents the memory excitation vector evoked in the neuronal memory map by stimulus S_i;

$\vec{D}_i$ represents the detector excitation vector evoked by stimulus S_i;

$\vec{K}_j$ represents the synaptic connection vector of the j-th memory neuron, $j = 1, 2, \ldots, n$; and

$(\vec{D}_i, \vec{K}_j)$ is the scalar product of the detector excitation vector evoked by the i-th stimulus and the synaptic connections vector of the j-th memory neuron.

13. Formation of Bidirectional Connections Between Semantic and Memory Neurons

The weights of synaptic contacts on a semantic neuron are equal to the excitations of neurons in the memory map. The synaptic contact on each memory neuron that connects it with a semantic neuron equals the excitation of that memory neuron at the time the synapse was formed. Thus, excitation of a semantic neuron creates an excitation vector in the memory map that is equal to the initial excitation vector of neurons in the memory map:

$$\vec{W}_{ij} = \vec{M}_i,$$

where $\vec{M}_i$ represents the excitation vector in the memory map; and

$\vec{W}_{ij}$ represents the synaptic connections vector formed by the memory excitation vector $\vec{M}_i$ on the j-th semantic neuron.

At the same time, vector $\vec{W}_{ij}$ represents the set of synaptic contacts that connect the j-th semantic neuron with long-term memory neurons, which in turn form the memory excitation vector $\vec{M}_i$. Thus, the memory excitation vector can be evoked bottom-up by stimuli at the input through the predetector excitation vector and detector excitation vector. It can also be evoked top-down by the symbol that activates the corresponding semantic neuron.

14. Bottom-Up Formation of an Excitation Vector in the Neural Memory Map

$$\vec{M}_i = [(\vec{D}_i, \vec{K}_1), (\vec{D}_i, \vec{K}_2), ..., (\vec{D}_i, \vec{K}_n)],$$

where $\vec{M}_i$ represents the memory map excitation vector evoked by the i-th stimulus;

$\vec{D}_i$ represents the detector excitation vector evoked by stimulus S_i; and

$\vec{K}_j$ represents the synaptic connections vector of the j-th memory neuron, $j = 1, 2, \ldots, n$.

15. Top-Down Formation of an Excitation Vector in the Neuronal Memory Map

$$\vec{M}_i = (I_j, \vec{W}_{ij}),$$

where I_j is the excitation level of the j-th semantic neuron;

$\vec{W}_{ij}$ represents the synaptic weights vector of the j-th semantic neuron to memory neurons; and

$\vec{M}_i$ represents the excitation vector of memory neurons evoked by excitation of the i-th semantic neuron.

16. Calculation of the Semantic Difference Between Symbols Due to a Change of Excitation Vectors in the Memory Map

The semantic difference between symbols equals the absolute value of the difference in memory excitation vectors evoked by the change in stimuli:

$$d_{ij} = \left|\vec{M}_i - \vec{M}_j\right|,$$

where d_{ij} is the semantic difference between the i-th and j-th symbols;

$\vec{M}_i$ represents the memory excitation vector evoked by the i-th symbol; and
$\vec{M}_j$ represents the memory excitation vector evoked by the j-th symbol.

17. Computation of the Semantic Difference Between Successive Symbols Involves Phasic ON- and OFF-Neurons

Presentation of the i-th symbol evokes excitation M_{ip}, where p is the number of an individual memory neuron. Presentation of the j-th symbol evokes excitation M_{jp} in the same neuron. The individual memory neuron is connected with an ON-neuron through parallel activating and inhibiting synapses in such a way that the rate of exponential increase in excitation is greater than that of the inhibitory increase:

$$ON_p = (|M_{ip} - M_{jp}|)[(1-\exp(-k_1 t)) - (1-\exp(-k_2 t))], \quad k_1 > k_2,$$

where ON_p represents the p-th individual ON-neuron;

M_{ip} is the excitation of the p-th memory neuron in response to the i-th symbol;

M_{jp} is the excitation of the p-th memory neuron in response to the j-th symbol;

$|M_{ip} - M_{jp}|$ represents the absolute value of the difference in excitations of the p-th memory neuron in response to replacement of the i-th symbol by the j-th symbol;

$(1-\exp(-k_1 t))$ represents the exponential increase in the excitatory postsynaptic potential on the p-th ON-neuron; and

$(1-\exp(-k_2 t))$ represents the exponential increase in the inhibitory postsynaptic potential in the p-th ON-neuron.

$$OFF_p = (|M_{ip} - M_{jp}|)[(1-\exp(-k_1 t)) - (1-\exp(-k_2 t))], \quad k_1 < k_2$$

where OFF_p represents excitation of the OFF-neuron;

M_{ip} is the excitation of the p-th memory neuron in response to the i-th symbol;

M_{jp} is the excitation of the p-th memory neuron in response to the j-th symbol;

$(1-\exp(-k_1 t))$ represents the exponential growth of the excitatory postsynaptic potential; and

$(1-\exp(-k_2 t))$ represents the exponential growth of the inhibitory postsynaptic potential.

Thus, the ON-neuron generates spikes when excitation of the memory neuron increases. The OFF-neuron generates spikes when excitation of the memory neuron decreases.

18. Transformation of Spike Trains Generated by ON- and OFF-Neurons into Wave Amplitudes of the Semantic EP

The outputs of ON- and OFF-neurons are combined in summation neurons whose spike trains are measures of semantic difference. The spike trains of summation neurons are associated with release of potassium from the neurons into the intercellular space, which leads to the depolarization of adjacent glial cells. The degree of glial depolarization determines the amplitude of the negative peak of the EP. Thus, the EP in response to a change of symbols is a measure of the semantic difference between the symbols:

$$Sum = \sum_{p=1}^{n} (ON_p + OFF_p),$$

where *Sum* represents the total number of spikes in ON- and OFF-neurons, which determines the discharge of the summation neuron.

$$A = C \cdot Sum,$$

where *A* is the amplitude of the semantic EP; and

C is the coefficient for converting the number of spikes in the difference signal into the amplitude of the EP representing semantic difference.

It is necessary to take into account the EP in response to the difference between the configurations of the two stimuli. Thus, the numerical evaluation of semantic differences and the amplitudes of semantic EPs in response to sudden symbol changes are based on differences in the memory excitation vectors elicited by the two stimuli. The latter are elicited top-down by semantic neurons acting on the map of memory neurons. Spike trains generated by ON- and OFF-neurons are combined in summation neurons whose discharge is determined by the semantic difference. The spikes are translated into a negative peak in the EP by the depolarization of neighboring glia. The spherical structure of the semantic space is determined by the normalization of excitation vectors at the predetector level.

The subjective numerical scores of semantic difference correlate with the amplitudes of EPs in response to substitution of one word for another of different meaning because both are determined by the same summation neurons. Those neurons measure the absolute magnitude of the difference between excitation vectors that are generated by semantic neurons in the long-term memory map.

The spherical structure of semantic spaces is based on the equal lengths of perceptual excitation vectors that determine the sphericity of detector maps. The latter, in turn, determine the sphericity of the memory maps in which semantic neurons form the excitation vectors that determine semantic differences.

3

Vector Encoding in Response Conditioning

3.1. SYNAPTIC MECHANISMS OF THE CONDITIONAL RESPONSE

The spherical model of cognitive processes is based on the concept of vector encoding in neural networks. In this context a *neural ensemble* is a group of nerve cells that receive a common input signal and that converge on at least one neuron. An external stimulus induces one or another intensity of excitation in each neuron of the ensemble. As a result, the ensemble as a whole exhibits a particular combination of excitations, which constitutes a representation of the current stimulus in the nervous system. In the spherical model this combination of excitations is represented by an excitation vector. This differs from other models in that an external stimulus is represented in the nervous system not by a scalar value but by an excitation vector whose components are the excitation intensities of the individual neurons in the ensemble.

The neural ensemble concept extends to groups of receptors having common inputs and converging on a single neuron. In this case, one speaks of the "excitation vector of the receptors." A particular feature of a receptor ensemble is overlapping response sensitivities of the individual receptors. Thus, mathematically a receptor ensemble represents a nonorthogonal basis. The combination of receptor signals represents the neural ensemble at the next level in an orthogonal system based on activity at excitatory and inhibitory synapses. Here the external stimulus is also represented by a vector, but in an orthogonal coordinate system. The length of the vector is determined by the intensity of the input stimulus, and the orientation of the vector represents its specific quality. Thus, stimulus intensity is encoded in quite a different way than other features of the stimulus: it is encoded in the length rather than the direction of the excitation vector. This aspect of the difference between stimuli is eliminated at the next level by normalizing the excitation vectors, after which the intensity of the stimulus is also represented in the orientation of the vector.

The normalization of excitation vectors is achieved by the inclusion of a special *noisy neuron* in the ensemble—that is, a neuron that is active in the absence of external input and that is inhibited by the stimulus. If a vector has two components, each stimulus intensity value is associated with a pair of neurons in the ensemble, one excited by the stimulus and the other inhibited by it. Generally the constancy of the excitation vector length is obtained by subtracting the excitations of other neurons in the ensemble from the activity of the noisy neuron. In the absence of input, the length of the excitation vector is determined only by the spontaneously active neuron. The combined excitations of other ensemble neurons inhibit the noisy neuron, so that the sum of excitations of the total ensemble of neural units remains constant. In other words, the length of the excitation vector is equal to the sum of excitations of units in the neural ensemble.

The vector length measure is somewhat different from the usual measure in Euclidean metrics. As mentioned earlier, the metric is commonly referred to as the *city-block metric*. Application of the city-block metric is appropriate only to neural networks that summarize excitations algebraically (i.e., which are not organized structurally for computing a square or extracting a square root). Since experimental findings indicate approximation to the Euclidean metric, one must assume a process of neuronal adaptation that limits maximal responses so as to approximate the results obtained in city-block metrics (i.e., results obtained in the Euclidean metric).

Neurons receiving input from receptor neurons through inhibitory synapses exhibit excitatory and inhibitory phases in their activity. In normalization, a pair of units emerges for each of the neurons in which the inhibitory and the excitatory phases of the response are inverted. These paired neurons function according to the "or–or" principle. Any stimulation of the neural ensemble generates a vector all of whose components are excitatory. The transformation from overlapping receptor response functions to the orthogonal characteristics of neurons in the next layer incurs, because of the inhibitory synapses, inhibitory phases during which generation of spikes is not possible. Signal transmission during the inhibitory phases is enabled by duplication of neurons and their serial excitation. Thus, without increasing the dimensionality of the model, the signal encoding vector always has only excitatory components.

The next layer of the model is a layer of detector neurons, which differ from each other in the weights of their synaptic contacts. These weights form a synaptic weights vector of constant length. This can be achieved through evolution by screening for mechanisms that constrain the optimal values of the weights of those connections. The detector sums the pairwise products of excitations coming from the predetectors by the weights of their synaptic connections. Formally, this represents computation of the scalar product of the predetector excitation vectors by the synaptic weights vector. Selective activation of a specific detector is achieved when the direction of the detector's synaptic weights vector coincides with the incoming excitation vector of the predetectors. The set of detectors represented on the surface of a hypersphere encodes stimuli by the location of maximal excitation on the surface. Information from predetectors and detectors can be transmitted to the command neurons of executive mechanisms activated during the formation of conditional responses. Let us consider the details of that process.

Pavlov's classic experiments showed that a behaviorally indifferent stimulus repeatedly followed by a reinforcer, such as food or pain, comes to elicit the response previously elicited only by the reinforcer itself. The same *conditional response* is also elicited by stimuli with features similar to those of the *conditional stimulus*. This effect of *conditional stimulus generalization* was traditionally attributed to irradiation of an excitatory process. More recently, intracellular recording techniques have provided an opportunity to analyze the mechanism of conditional response formation and generalization at cellular and synaptic levels.

The hippocampus plays an important role in the establishment of conditional responses. Novelty neurons located in the hippocampus are involved in memory trace formation. The level of hippocampal activation can be monitored indirectly by recording skin resistance to electric current, the *galvanic skin response*. Interaction between the hippocampus and the prefrontal cortex is important for the improvement of learning abilities. One can significantly improve learning and memory for school subjects in children by the presentation of complex visual stimuli when hippocampal activity is optimal (Mangina and Beuzeron-Mangina 2004; Mangina and Sokolov 2006). Direct evidence for the enhancement of memorization by hippocampal activation has been obtained in experiments with local electrical stimulation of the brain in patients during exploration for foci of epileptic activity (Mangina and Beuzeron-Mangina 1996). And a concomitant increase in the amplitude of negative waves in EPs from both prefrontal cortex and hippocampus is seen with the optimization of cerebral cholinergic function (Sokolov and Nezlina 2003a,b).

The control of behavioral responses involves command neurons. A *command neuron* is a neuron that is directly associated through its axon with a specific pool of motor neurons to control a corresponding behavioral response. Direct stimulation of a command neuron evokes a complete behavioral act or a fragment thereof. The command neuron receives sensory information provided by the excitation vectors of individual neural ensembles via synapses on

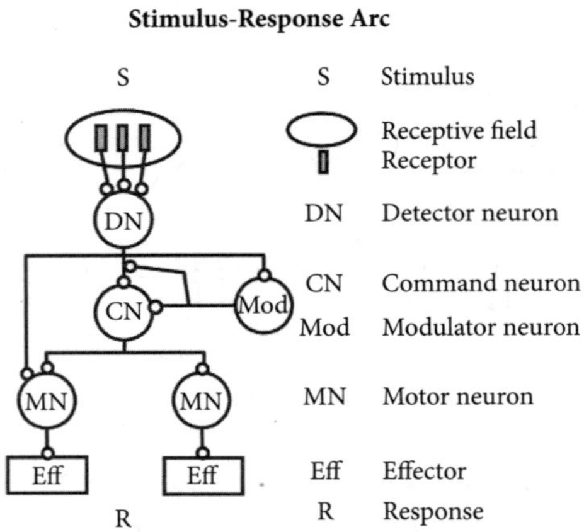

Figure 3.1 Conceptual model of stimulus–response arc. See text for description of neuronal elements. Not shown: predetector neurons located between the receptor and detector elements.

its dendrites (Fig. 3.1). It has both plastic and nonplastic synapses. During the formation of a conditional response, the effect of the conditional stimulus is directed to plastic synapses, and nonplastic synapses represent the reinforcement (Sokolov and Nezlina 2007).

Let us confine the analysis of command neuron activation to inputs from a single neural ensemble. Remember that excitation vectors are vectors of fixed length whose ends lie on a spherical surface and that every external stimulus, producing its own combination of excitations, has its own excitation vector. The set of weights of plastic synaptic contacts, which are affected by the excitation vector, is also represented by a vector (viz., a synaptic weights vector). The presynaptic excitation at each synapse is multiplied by the synaptic weights, which is presumably determined by the density of receptors in the postsynaptic membrane. An elementary postsynaptic potential occurs at each synapse. The command neuron summarizes these elementary potentials and generates a complex postsynaptic potential equal to the sum of pairwise products of the presynaptic excitations and synaptic weights. This sum represents the scalar product of two vectors: an excitation vector that encodes the stimulus and a synaptic weights vector that represents the set of plastic synapses.

So far we have expressed the scalar product of vectors in terms of its components, but it can also be represented as a product of the lengths of these vectors and the cosine of the angle between them. If the length of the vectors is fixed, the scalar product depends only on the angle between them. When an excitation vector and a synaptic weights vector coincide in direction, their scalar product is maximal (cosine = 1). When the excitation vector is orthogonal to the synaptic weights vector, the scalar product is zero (cosine = 0).

The excitation vector that occurs in response to an external stimulus affects in parallel a wide variety of command neurons without eliciting an unconditional response because of the weakness of their plastic synapses. If the excitation vector is followed by reinforcement, which is addressed to the same command neuron controlled by the unconditional response, the plastic synapses increase their weights in proportion to the incoming presynaptic excitations. The greater the presynaptic excitation, the greater is the increase in weight of the synapse. If, on the other hand, the presynaptic excitation is less than the initial synaptic weights, the latter is reduced to equal the level of the presynaptic excitation. Thus, a synapse that does not receive presynaptic excitation during reinforcement is weakened.

The mechanism of tuning synaptic weights to the magnitude of presynaptic excitations can be thought of generally as follows. Postsynaptic receptor molecules are found in two states: phosphorylated and unphosphorylated. Presynaptic transmitters attaching to phosphorylated receptors open ion channels associated with those receptors. The sum of currents in the channels constitutes an elementary postsynaptic current. At the same time, the association of the transmitter with the receptor protein makes it insensitive to the action of phosphatase. Active molecules that are not affected by the transmitter are dephosphorylated. Transmitter molecules that fail to open the channels of inactive, dephosphorylated receptors render them sensitive to protein kinases. Reinforcement leads to transfer of calcium into the cell, which activates protein kinases. Under their influence, the dephosphorylated molecules become phosphorylated and, thus, active. Some of the phosphorylated receptors are dephosphorylated by the phosphatases. The more intense the presynaptic effect, the greater is the number of protein kinase molecules induced by the transmitter. In synapses where the presynaptic effect is weaker, phosphatases dominate, and the number of active receptors decreases. Thus, the weights of synapses that receive intensive presynaptic input increase, and the weights of synapses with weak presynaptic input decrease. The result is an adjustment of the synaptic weights vector corresponding to the presynaptic excitation vector.

With repeated reinforcement of a conditional stimulus, the synaptic weights vector of the command neuron comes to coincide with the excitation vector evoked by that stimulus. The scalar product of the presynaptic excitations vector and the synaptic connections weights vector of the command neuron approaches maximum. This elicits the maximal response of the command neuron to the conditional stimulus. Differential stimuli evoke a stronger response the closer their excitation vector approximates the excitation vector of the conditional stimulus. In other words, the greater the similarity between differential stimuli and the conditional stimulus, the greater is the postsynaptic potential evoked. The degree of generalization of the response to differential stimuli is determined by the degree of similarity between the excitation vectors of the conditional and the differential stimuli.

When the postsynaptic potential of the command neuron reaches threshold for an action potential, it evokes spikes that pass down the axon and its branches to the pool of motor neurons that control behavioral actions. Because the threshold for generating action potentials fluctuates, the behavioral response to the conditional stimulus occurs with a certain probability depending on the amplitude of the postsynaptic potential. The probabilities of responses to differential stimuli are lower the greater the difference between their excitation vectors and the synaptic weights vector of the command neuron. This means that as the conditional response is established, a synaptic weights vector of the command neuron is formed. This vector coincides with the excitation vector of the conditional stimulus. The probabilities of responses to the conditional and differential stimuli are equal to the scalar products of their excitation vectors and the synaptic weights vector formed to the conditional stimulus.

By repeated conditioning of a response using various differential stimuli as conditional stimuli, it is possible to construct a confusion matrix whose cells contain the probabilities of response that are represented by the scalar products of the excitation vectors and the corresponding synaptic weights vectors associated with the different stimuli. Such a matrix contains information about the excitation vectors of the set of stimuli that can be computed by factor analysis. Loadings on the individual factors correspond to the individual components of the excitation vectors—that is, to the activation of units of the ensemble elicited by the corresponding stimuli. Once the excitation vectors representing the stimuli in geometric space are determined, the sphericity of the space is confirmed. The criterion for sphericity is equality of length of the excitation vectors. The coincidence of the scalar products of the excitation vectors and the synaptic weights vectors with the probabilities of response is tested. The scalar products are calculated from the computed excitation vectors, taking into account the fact that the synaptic weights vectors are equal to the excitation vectors of the conditional stimuli. Finally, the correlation coefficient between the original matrix of response probabilities (i.e., the confusion matrix) and the matrix of scalar products is computed.

The general scheme of response conditioning includes vector encoding of the stimulus and the restructuring of the plastic synapses of command neurons based on the combination of the presynaptic effects of the conditional signal and the reinforcement. As a result, a synaptic weights vector is formed that coincides with the excitation vector representing the conditional stimulus. The value of the postsynaptic potential of the command neuron in response to the conditional stimulus reaches its maximum, which translates into maximal probability of the conditional response. The degree of generalization of the response to other stimuli is determined by the degree of approximation of the excitation vector of the differential stimulus to the excitation vector of the conditional stimulus. Thus, the vector representing the excitation complex evoked by the stimulus in conjunction with the vector representing the combination of synaptic contacts of the command neuron encompasses both conditional response formation and stimulus differentiation.

A key feature of the conditional response is plasticity: if the conditional stimulus ceases to be reinforced, the response undergoes extinction. The recruitment of "sleeping" receptor molecules is terminated, because the protein kinases involved in the phosphorylation of the receptors cease to be activated. At the same time, the effect of phosphatases on active molecules does not decrease, and the number of inactive receptor molecules increases with dephosphorylation of the active molecules. Decreasing the density of active molecules means weakening the synaptic connection. The greater the presynaptic excitation, the greater the reduction of synaptic weights. This is reflected in the vector model by a change in orientation of the synaptic weights vector of the command neuron due to nonreinforcement of the conditional stimulus. With alternation of the reinforced conditional stimulus and nonreinforced differential stimuli, the pattern of synaptic contacts to the conditional stimulus is intensified, because the nonreinforced differential stimuli shift the synaptic weights vector of the command neuron in the direction of coincidence with the excitation vector of the conditional stimulus. Thus, the vector model of information coding in the nervous system is able to explain the formation of conditional responses by the reorganization of synaptic connections in individual command neurons.

In general terms, the model implements response conditioning as follows. Each command neuron is acted on by an excitation vector that includes components f_1, f_2, f_3, and f_4. By summing the pairwise products of presynaptic excitation vectors that are of equal length, by the synaptic weights c_1, c_2, c_3, and c_4, it computes the scalar product of the excitation vector by the synaptic weights vector. During conditioning the weights of the synaptic connections are modified by the arrival of reinforcement signals via nonplastic synapses. The mechanism of synaptic weights modification involves the phosphorylation–dephosphorylation of a portion of the postsynaptic receptors, which leads to their activation–inactivation. As a result, the command neuron becomes selectively tuned to the conditional stimulus that generates an excitation vector coincident with the synaptic weights vector. The closer the orientation of the excitation vectors of differential stimuli D_1 and D_2 to the excitation vector of the conditional stimulus, the greater is the excitation they evoke in the command neuron.

The vector model has been confirmed in studies of conditional responses to color stimuli in monkeys, rabbits, and fish. In all cases factor analysis of the matrix of probabilities of conditional responses yielded a four-dimensional spherical color space (Latanov et al. 1997). In rabbits it was also shown that the four-dimensional spherical color space obtained by the conditioning coincides with the spherical color space obtained from the matrix of EPs to color stimuli.

Recordings from cortical neurons in the rabbit revealed further that the amplitude of the EP is governed by an early spike train, which corresponds to the absolute difference between the excitation vectors as one color replaces the other. Thus, the spherical model of color vision covers not only perceptual and semantic processes but also the process of conditional response formation (Polyanskiy et al. 2005).

The mechanism of conditioning considered thus far involves predetectors at the thalamic level; however, cortical detectors can also be involved. These two pathways have been examined with the conditioning of defensive responses in response to acoustic stimuli. One pathway from the thalamus to the amygdala mediates conditioning of responses to simple sound stimuli. Another pathway connects the amygdala with the auditory cortex to mediate conditioning of defensive responses to complex acoustic stimuli (Ledoux 1991).

Detectors of sound intensity play an important role in the auditory cortex. Studies of neurons in the middle layers of primary auditory cortex (area A1) of rats demonstrated, in addition to specialized detectors tuned to the spectral and temporal aspects of acoustic stimulation, detectors of intensity. As with other kinds of detectors, excitation of these cells is enhanced at a specific intensity. Thus, the selectivity and magnitude of response of intensity detectors can be enhanced in the same way as for detectors generally (Polley et al. 2004).

3.2. CORTICOFUGAL AND CENTRIPETAL MODULATION OF DETECTOR MAPS

Detectors that distinguish certain features of the stimuli presented to receptors have rather stable selective response functions. Their responses are usually not altered by repetition of a stimulus. A repetitive train of stimuli, however, leads to sharpening of the poststimulus histogram of cortical neuron firing. This indicates on the one hand that excitation of the central area of the neuron's receptive field is enhanced, while on the other the peripheral inhibitory process is intensified. The combination of these effects leads to narrowing of the area of excitation in the poststimulus histogram. Such sharpening is the opposite of habituation, in which the peak amplitude of the poststimulus histogram is reduced and action potentials appear during inhibitory phases.

Detectors do not show full habituation. Partial habituation is seen there and also in EPs recorded in the human. Consider the N100 wave, which consists of specific and nonspecific components. With repetition of a stimulus, the nonspecific component of the N100 attenuates similarly to attenuation of the galvanic skin response, while the specific component remains unchanged. The coincidence of dynamics of the nonspecific component of the N100 with the dynamics of the galvanic skin response indicates involvement of the orienting response mechanism, the arousal component of which disappears with the loss of signal novelty (Sokolov 2003). Comparison of attenuation of the nonspecific N100 component with partial attenuation of the spike response suggests a common mechanism for the termination of activation.

The relation of EP dynamics to the sharpening effect in the poststimulus histogram is more complex. But here also one can envision a common mechanism involving long-term potentiation of both excitatory and inhibitory components. This mechanism is particularly evident in that the critical flicker fusion frequency and the electroencephalographic (EEG) response to lights flickering at high frequency are both greater in the light than under dark conditions (Sokolov 2003). Thus, one can postulate that the narrowing effect in the poststimulus histogram represents facilitation of the arousal response to high-frequency stimuli.

Some recent reports have developed the concept of local retuning of detector responses (Suga 1990). Of particular interest is the modification of detector response functions in the course of conditioning. A sound stimulus of a certain frequency, the conditional stimulus, followed by reinforcement in the form of mild electrical stimulation of the animal's feet, leads to a change in the frequency-specific response of the detector—namely, its characteristic frequency shifts in the direction of the frequency of the conditional stimulus and simultaneously the response amplitude increases. This does not occur if the difference between the characteristic frequency and the frequency of the conditional sound stimulus exceeds a certain critical value or if the reinforcement precedes the conditional stimulus. The modification of detector response functions persists for at least three hours.

Suga (2008) proposes the following model for the selective retuning of frequency-specific detectors. The acoustic and electrocutaneous signals reach primary auditory and primary somatosensory cortical areas respectively. From there the signals pass through association cortex to the amygdala. The author suggests that the association of sound stimuli with electrocutaneous reinforcement involves the excitation of cholinergic nuclei in the forebrain.

The release of acetylcholine in the auditory cortex in response to the conditional stimulus induces a restructuring of detector response functions. These changes are transmitted through efferent tracts from the cortex to subcortical auditory nuclei. Thus, the detector map adapts to the conditional stimulus. This adaptation, which has been referred to as *egocentric selection*, consists of an increase in the number of detectors along the transmission pathway of the conditional stimulus that are selectively tuned to the conditional stimulus, while detectors whose best frequencies do not coincide with that of the conditional stimulus are partially inhibited. Focal electrical stimulation of the cortex also evokes a characteristic frequency shift, which is similar to that observed with the pairing of sound and electrocutaneous stimulation. Application of an agonist for the inhibitory transmitter gamma-aminobutyric acid (GABA) to the auditory cortex results in attenuation of responses of both cortical and subcortical neurons. Furthermore, their responses to cortical stimulation and conditioning cease to change. The attenuation of responses of neurons in the inferior colliculi indicates that the cortex ceases to strengthen their responses via corticofugal pathways.

In summary, one can say that, in addition to evoking generalized activation–inactivation effects on the entire detector map, a conditional stimulus induces selective retuning of individual neurons. This takes the form of a shift in frequency characteristic toward that of the conditional stimulus, if its best frequency is close to the frequency of the conditional stimulus, or partial inhibition if its best frequency is significantly different from that of the conditional stimulus. As a result of such local restructuring of the detector map, the number of detectors with frequency characteristics similar to that of the conditional stimulus increases. The responses of neurons with frequencies that differ significantly from that of the conditional stimulus are reduced. The result is a learning-induced contrast between the effects of the conditional and differential stimuli.

Experiments in bats by Suga and colleagues (1997) demonstrated shifts in the frequency response functions of neurons in primary auditory cortex toward the frequency of the conditional stimulus. The shift occurred only when the difference between the original best frequency of the neuron and the frequency of the conditional stimulus did not exceed a certain value. Otherwise, the neuronal responses faded. Thus, the conditional stimulus frequency recruits neurons of similar frequency characteristics. Such recruitment can be explained by the fact that while afferents from a broad area of the thalamus converge on frequency detectors, only some are involved in conditioning, namely those that influence the frequency response function of the cortical detector. Reinforcement activates sleeping afferents that shift the frequency characteristics of detectors toward the frequency of the conditional stimulus. The functional significance of increasing the number of detectors that represent the conditional stimulus is a sharp increase in the effectiveness of learning. This is achieved by increasing the contribution of the conditional stimulus to initiation of the response that is driven by the command neuron on whose synapses the outputs of the additionally mobilized detectors are concentrated.

Continuing the study of the reorganization of the acoustic detector map, Ma and Suga (2001) turned their attention from the detectors that distinguish the frequency characteristics of the ultrasonic calls of bats to detectors that are selectively tuned to the time interval between the call and arrival of the echo signal reflected from a target, such as a flying insect or an obstacle. Each timing detector is selectively tuned to a certain duration within the range of 1 to 13 msec, with discriminable steps of 1 msec. Time detectors do not respond to a single sound signal, whether it be a call or an echo. Their excitation requires two signals, a call and its echo. To distinguish the call–echo sequence from a random sequence of sounds, the call is frequency modulated and contains second, third, and fourth harmonics. The echo also contains these harmonics, which are attenuated to variable degree by differential absorption.

The harmonic composition of the echo defines sound reflective properties of the target or obstacle. But, in addition, neurons respond selectively to the delay between the first and later harmonics. The auditory cortex of the bat contains three groups of neurons selectively responsive to the combinations $H_1 \rightarrow H_2$, $H_1 \rightarrow H_3$, and $H_1 \rightarrow H_4$, where the subscript represents the harmonic number. The first harmonic corresponds to the call, while the second, third, and fourth harmonics correspond to the returning echo. Thus, the delay between the call and the echo is measured simultaneously in three frequency bands. These three classes of neurons are detectors of the duration of time intervals between call and echo. Each responds only to a specific time interval.

Time detectors are distributed in an anterior–caudal direction in the cortex of the bat. They form a map in which each detector corresponds to a certain distance from the target. Electrical stimulation of neurons in different cortical areas evokes different effects. In areas where the neurons are packed tightly, electrical stimulation produces a shift in the frequency characteristics of neighboring neurons away from the frequency of the stimulated neuron. Such a change can be called a *centrifugal shift*. As a result, the contrast between the neurons increases. In areas where neurons are packed loosely, the change is a *centripetal shift*. There, nearby neurons acquire the frequency characteristic of the stimulated neuron. The difference in organization of the detector map based on the packing density of the detectors is determined by the number of inhibitory interneurons. In the more densely packed areas interneurons are more numerous, so the application of GABA-receptor antagonists to a densely packed area of detectors converts a centrifugal frequency shift to a centripetal shift in which neighboring neurons acquire the frequency response function of the stimulated neuron. Centripetal modulation increases the effectiveness of response to the conditional stimulus by increasing the number of neurons responsive to it. The centrifugal effect on neurons, whose best frequency is initially different from that of the conditional stimulus, becomes even more different, thus intensifying the discriminative function.

Retuning the detector map is an important mechanism in the differentiation of conditional stimuli. If centripetal retuning increases the effectiveness of the conditional signal, centrifugal retuning ensures the effectiveness of differential stimuli, which together lead to stabilization of the conditional response.

3.3. FLUCTUATION OF THE PACEMAKER POTENTIAL

One of the factors determining the effectiveness of the conditional stimulus is the regular, endogenous fluctuation of membrane potentials commonly referred to as *pacemaker potentials* (Alving 1968). These fluctuations of potential are sinusoidal and range widely in frequency from 0.1 to 200 Hz. The presence of pacemaker potentials in cells throughout the brain makes them one of the principal distributed systems of the brain.

The ionic mechanisms of pacemaker activity involve the interaction of potassium and calcium ion channels with the level of the cellular membrane potential. When the membrane potential shifts toward a depolarization value close to the threshold for the opening of calcium channels, the most sensitive channels open. This leads to an influx of calcium ions and further depolarization, which results in the opening of less sensitive calcium channels. Thus, the depolarization caused by the opening of calcium channels is a positive feedback process that feeds on itself. When the intracellular calcium concentration reaches a certain value, activation of calcium-dependent potassium channels triggers a switch to negative feedback. The release of cellular potassium leads to hyperpolarization, which, in turn, terminates the opening of calcium channels. This interrupts the calcium current, reinforcing the hyperpolarization effect evoked by potassium release.

Reducing the intracellular calcium concentration leads to the closure of calcium-dependent potassium channels and increases depolarization to the level at which the reopening of calcium channels initiates a new cycle. In considering the ionic mechanism of pacemaker activity, the mechanism that maintains the constancy of calcium and potassium levels must be taken into account. This mechanism operates by the export of excess calcium from the cell and the import of potassium ions. These processes require energy, which is stored in the form of mitochondrial ATP. Thus, the maintenance of pacemaker activity requires a continuous supply of energy to the cell. The resource of ATP is renewed by the delivery of glucose and oxygen by the bloodstream. The dependence of pacemaker activity on the levels of blood oxygen and glucose makes it particularly sensitive to hypoxia and hypoglycemia.

The pacemaker potential is unusually sensitive to the level of the membrane potential. A slight depolarization of the pacemaker neuron by an influx of cations or by the action of a neurotransmitter produces an acceleration of the ascending phase of the pacemaker wave and a phase shift of subsequent fluctuations that constitute the reset mechanism of pacemaker activity. Such a reset also occurs with termination of the hyperpolarization current or disappearance of an inhibitory postsynaptic potential. The reset effect is crucial for the integration of neural activity. If a sensory signal reaches several nerve cells that are out of synchrony, a reset of their pacemaker activity brings them into phase, synchronizing their spike activity. On termination of a stimulus the pacemaker waves of the neural population desynchronize and the activity of the neurons returns to the initial level. By creating synchronized bursts of spikes, the pacemaker potential enhances and extends the sensory effect.

Earlier we considered the case in which the frequency of fluctuation of pacemaker potentials of different neurons was the same but out of phase. Shifting the phase of activity by a reset brought them into phase for a period of time. This suggests a new explanation for the synchronization described by some authors with regard to fluctuations of focal potentials and spike trains in different brain areas when the detector response functions of the neurons share certain features. Usually this effect is interpreted in terms of interneuronal connections. In the context of a distributed pacemaker mechanism where each unit has its own pacemaker, a reset brings all neurons that receive the signal in parallel into phase for some period of time. The result of simultaneous neuronal activity is an increase in potassium release, which leads to depolarization of glial cells in the neighborhood of the neurons working in phase. As a result, the amplitude of the focal potential, which is determined by the frequency of the pacemaker, increases. Such a relationship is consistent with the fact that extracellular recording from a given neuron shows spikes that occur in phase with fluctuations of the focal potential.

With different frequencies of pacemaker fluctuation in different neurons, two variants are possible. The first is that, as a result of reset and synchronization, the frequency and phase of pacemaker potentials remain the same. In that case statements made with regard to pacemaker neurons of the same frequency hold true. In the second variant, which requires special analysis, the frequency of pacemakers is variable and unchanged by a reset. A reset, however, causes a common initial phase of fluctuation. As a result they are superimposed, producing a complex focal potential whose shape depends on the component frequencies of the pacemaker fluctuations. If those frequencies are very close, the focal response, as in the case of equal frequencies, is determined by the degree of synchrony of the fluctuations. The greater the frequency difference between the separate fluctuations, the more complex is the form of the focal potential. In addition, the shape of the focal potential depends on the individual amplitudes of the component frequencies.

Now we proceed from description of the focal potential, which depends on the initial phase of pacemaker fluctuations of different frequencies, to characterization of the EP. From the outset we accept the premise of delta-, theta-, beta-, and gamma-oscillators as the basic frequency types mediating pacemaker oscillations in nerve cells. One can consider focal potentials and EPs to result from the summation of these frequency components after reset of pacemaker fluctuations. If that is so, spectral analysis of the EP should detect those frequency components. Assuming that the frequencies of pacemaker oscillations remain the same with changes in phase relations, the spectrum of the EP should coincide with the spectrum of the background EEG, which represents the summation of pacemaker oscillations with varying degrees of synchronization. Basar (1998) has demonstrated precisely such coincidence of background EEG spectra with EP spectra.

Endogenous pacemaker fluctuations may be present in receptors, detector neurons, and command neurons. The distribution of the pacemaker potentials to a variety of individual neurons makes each cell an independent oscillator. Independent oscillators can, however, form *functional ensembles* of neurons by phase reset of pacemaker potentials. The synchronization of activities in a functional group of units is not sufficient to form a gestalt. That occurs only if phasing-in amplifies particular inputs that converge on a gnostic neuron (Sokolov 1996).

The shape of an EP is determined by involvement of specific cells, including receptors, detectors, gnostic units, and command neurons, in the response and by rhythmic units that organize their excitation. Here again we encounter the issue of the relation between the excitation vector, which represents the stimulus in the nervous system, and the rhythmicity of excitation, which determines the effectiveness of such a vector by resonant mechanisms during synaptic transmission. The combination of neuronal excitations represented by the excitation vector, which contains information about the stimulus, and the oscillation frequency determines the effectiveness of that vector.

3.4. THE PACEMAKER POTENTIAL IN RECEPTORS, DETECTORS, AND COMMAND NEURONS

As an endogenous rhythmic process, the pacemaker potential serves as an amplifier of excitatory postsynaptic potentials (EPSPs). This is seen at receptor, effector, and central levels. At the receptor level, hair cells in the organ of Corti provide an example of pacemaker potential involvement in receptor function. There the pacemaker mechanism increases selectivity for sound frequencies. An example at the effector level is provided by cells in the pancreas, where insulin secretion is controlled by pulsatile calcium influx set by the cells' pacemaker activity. The hippocampal theta-rhythm provides an example of a central pacemaker mechanism. There, the pacemaker potential determines the theta-rhythm in terms of spike trains separated by silent intervals. In this case, the pacemaker potential controls quanta of information.

The pacemaker mechanism is seen particularly vividly in the selective frequency tuning of hair cells in the organ of Corti in the internal ear of mammals. When the frequency of a sound stimulus coincides with the pacemaker frequency of the hair cell, their resonance leads to increased amplitude of the cellular response. The frequency selectivity of hair cells is determined by their location on the basal membrane of the organ of Corti. With increases in sound frequency, the site of maximal excitation moves through the population of hair cells. The increase in response amplitude of hair cells triggered by a specific sound frequency gives rise to an increase in spike frequency in the auditory nerve fibers leading from synaptic contacts with those cells.

The pacemaker potential plays an important functional role in color detectors. Color-selective neurons in visual cortex respond with tonic spike discharges during the color stimulus to which they are sensitive. How does the tonic response of the color detector relate to its high color selectivity? One possible mechanism is commonly regarded to involve an endogenous *latent pacemaker potential.* A latent pacemaker potential is not apparent in the normal resting potential of the cell but appears and is stably maintained with the membrane depolarization evoked by an EPSP. One can imagine that a synaptically launched pacemaker potential serves as a source of rhythmic spike activity in the color-selective detector. The detectors are connected with each other by lateral inhibitory connections mediated by the inhibitory transmitter GABA. The maximally activated color detector inhibits the potential pacemaker activity of neighboring detectors through its collaterals, thus assuming dominance in coding of the color. Such participation of the pacemaker potential in determining the selectivity function of the detector supplements the monotonic vector code with a sensitive sharpening of detector selectivity as a generator of action potentials.

Pacemaker potentials are found in many of the command neurons that control behavioral acts. Receiving excitation from predetectors or detectors, they generate pacemaker oscillations that reinforce and prolong the effect of EPSPs by generating the sequence of action potentials that mediates the behavioral response. Hyperpolarization of the command neuron maintaining an EPSP suppresses the waves of pacemaker potential, prevents the generation of spikes, and blocks the behavioral response ordinarily mediated by the neuron.

The pacemaker mechanism is involved in other neurophysiological control processes as well. Sensitivity of a pacemaker mechanism to temperature or light is involved in the switching on and off of circadian activity and seasonal rhythms. A launch mechanism for pacemaker waves is involved in the anticipation of rhythmic stimuli. The EPSP evoked by activation of a *time interval detector* anticipates repetition of a stimulus; it triggers pacemaker waves and action potentials in the command neuron that mediates the anticipatory behavioral response.

The pacemaker potential of command neurons also is involved in the mechanism of dominant neuronal circuits. A focus of elevated excitation occurs in a command neuron that exhibits greater pacemaker activity than other neurons. Subthreshold EPSPs, which boost the amplitude of those waves to exceed the threshold for generation of an action potential, evoke the behavioral response specific to the command neuron. Such a command neuron becomes an attraction center for subthreshold stimuli that, but for the background pacemaker activity of the command neuron, would remain ineffective.

Background pacemaker waves are controlled by an unconditional stimulus. Thus, a feeding command neuron is activated by a low blood glucose level. When the level of blood glucose is low, even unrelated stimuli that would not evoke a feeding response in a sated animal become effective. Activation of the feeding command neuron in a hungry animal is accompanied simultaneously by inactivation of the command neuron for defensive behavior. With emergence of the feeding command neuron as dominant, a conditional stimulus that would ordinarily evoke a defensive response can evoke feeding behavior. Gradual satiation of the animal is accompanied by an increase in blood glucose concentration and inactivation of the feeding neuron. The amplitude of pacemaker oscillations decreases, and the dominant effect of the feeding circuit disappears.

Thus, the pacemaker potential functions as an allocator of response priorities. EPSPs of equal amplitude induced in different command neurons will only activate those where the amplitude of the pacemaker potential, which is below action potential threshold, is maximal.

PART TWO

The Neural Screen of Consciousness

4

The Modular Organization of the Brain

4.1. THE MODULAR ORGANIZATION OF CORTICAL NEURONS

Recordings of spike activity from individual cortical neurons shows that those in the primary sensory projection areas detect specific features of external stimuli, while those in the cortical association areas respond selectively to complex stimuli. For example, neurons in the primary area of visual cortex are tuned to simple features such as the slope of lines (Hubel and Wiesel 1979), and neurons in the association areas of visual cortex represent *gnostic units* (Konorski 1967), which detect such complex stimuli as emotional facial expressions (Ehrenstein et al. 2003; Rolls 2000).

How do gnostic units relate to detectors? Considering that damage to association cortex does not disrupt the function of detectors in the primary projection areas, one can assume that a set of functionally nonidentical neurons are combined into a system that is organized hierarchically in a pyramid. [*Note that in this model the author refers to neurons in the primary projection areas as detectors of simple stimulus features, such as line orientation and color. They are the same neurons referred to as predetectors in the models described earlier. (Eds.)*] At the base of the pyramid are thalamic neurons, which, as predetectors, provide a base for detectors in the primary projection areas. At the top of the pyramid is a gnostic unit, which determines the holistic perception of the complex stimulus acting on predetectors at the base of the pyramid. The gnostic unit at the top of the hierarchy may be referred to as a *gestalt detector* and the neural pyramid itself as a *gestalt pyramid* (Sokolov 1996). One needs to keep in mind that a number of similar pyramids rest on the same base of predetectors. Each is topped by its own gnostic unit, which responds to excitation of a specific set of predetectors. Thus, a certain emotional facial expression activates a specific combination of line orientation detectors that represent the slopes of the eyebrows and corners of the mouth, which in turn selectively activates the gnostic unit at the top of one of the pyramids. The total set of neural pyramids with their gnostic units constitutes a *neural module*, such as the module for emotional facial expressions in the example above. The tops of the pyramids in a neural module are separated by a distance that increases with the difference between the stimuli that activate them. The tops of the pyramids can be represented formally in a geometric space the dimensionality of which is determined by the number of independent predetectors (Izmailov et al. 2005).

The modular principle of organization extends to other neural modalities, including a color information processing module, a face identification module, a module for detecting direction and speed of motion, as well as a module for analyzing spatial relations. These modules form two cognitive systems: a ventral system for determining "what" and a dorsal system for determining "where." While they receive common inputs, the two systems function in parallel and independently of each other.

Let us consider the sound source localization module of the "where" system and the phoneme perception module of the "what" system. The auditory system receives information about the location of a sound source based on the binaural intensity difference and the phase shift of acoustic oscillations reaching the two ears. Predetector neurons represent the first stage of processing after the cochlear receptors. They provide the neuronal basis for the encoding of sound direction. The perception of the direction of sound propagation is determined by direction detectors located in the auditory cortex. Damage to those neurons leads to an inability to identify the source of sound stimuli. The perceptions of loudness and pitch are not changed because they are mediated by other modules. The perception of phonemes is also not disrupted. It is represented by a special module in Wernicke's area of the auditory cortex. Damage to the phonemic module leads to disruption of speech perception, a form of sensory aphasia, without affecting either the tone perception module or the sound source direction module. Thus, the pyramidal structure of auditory modules is reflected in the fact that damage to neurons at higher levels does not impair functioning at lower levels of the module (Spillmann 1999).

Study of the brain in talking birds has shown that their auditory system contains neurons that acquire phonemic selectivity in the course of learning to mimic human speech (Nicholls et al. 2001). Phonemic gnostic units have also been recorded in the auditory cortex of the human brain. Destruction of those units results in sensory aphasia (Creutzfeldt 1993).

The modular organization of neurons explains the absence of strict anatomic localization of functions. Neurons belonging to different modules can overlap anatomically but may operate independently. Damage to the overlapping areas of modules leads to complex patterns of functional disorder (Luria 1970, 1973). The independence of neural modules is confirmed by observations that localized brain damage can eliminate the functions of one with total preservation of others (Luria 1973). This has been shown in extensive research on lesions of the association areas of human cerebral cortex caused by strokes (Spillmann et al. 2000). Analyses of patients' fields of vision and introspective reports suggest that a stroke in cortical association areas of the right hemisphere does not affect speech and intellectual functions. No detectable changes were found in the primary visual projection areas. While black–white, achromatic vision remained intact, there was a total loss of color vision. Functional disruption at the highest level of the face identification module was apparent. The patient was unable to recognize a familiar person, a loved one, even though the perception of individual facial details was not lost. Recognition of people by their voices also remained intact.

The example of impaired holistic face perception with intact perception of individual facial features supports the pyramidal gestalt principle. Loss of gnostic units, *gestalt neurons*, at the top of the pyramid of the face identification module can occur with preserved integrity of lower levels of the pyramid where the detection of basic features, such as the slope of lines, occurs. The hierarchical organization of the color identification module is confirmed by the preservation of achromatic vision, for which a lower level of the pyramid, area V1, is responsible, with total elimination of chromatic perception, which is mediated by a higher level of the visual system, area V4.

A further indication of the independence of the color module from the face recognition module is that restoration of color vision can occur with persistent impairment of facial recognition. It should be emphasized that impairment of face recognition, prosopagnosia, usually does not extend to the recognition of other objects, such as houses and tools, which are represented by other specific modules. Moreover, impairment of face recognition does not extend to the identification of emotional facial expressions, which are represented by their own module.

The modules considered thus far belong to the ventral, "what" system for identifying objects. Damage to the *spatial module* with neurons located in the parietal cortex leads to inability to perceive spatial relations, even though the perception of individual items is not impaired (Spillmann et al. 2000). One can assume that the topographic module of the "where" system constitutes a spatial frame of the visual field where modules of the "what" system are located.

The integration of modular contents from the "what" and "where" systems can be attributed to the prefrontal cortex where neurons of working memory are found. Those neurons respond selectively to specific combinations of qualitative and spatial attributes (Nicholls et al. 2001). Such integration is made possible by *topographic neurons*, which have giant receptive areas covering the entire field of vision (Rolls 2000). Expansion of the receptive area of neurons at progressively higher levels of the gestalt pyramid allows the brain to integrate the modular contributions of neurons of the "what" system to reflect the whole scene in an individual neuron.

Microelectrode studies of inferotemporal association cortex in monkeys have revealed neurons that are selectively responsive to a specific face, such as that of a particular animal caretaker (Rolls 2000). A neuronal response selective for a specific stimulus associated with the animal's experience indicates that the external environment is involved in the development of such selectivity. It suggests that life experience is recorded into long-term memory through the formation of gnostic units that fix events (Sokolov and Nezlina 2003a,b). This hypothesis is based on experiments by Miyashita and colleagues (1991) in which monkeys were trained to distinguish between 90 random visual patterns. When appropriate responses had been established, extracellular unit activity was recorded in the temporal cortex during the presentation both of patterns used in the training and of new random visual patterns. Neurons were found that responded selectively to one of the stimuli reinforced during training, not to others and not to the control stimuli. This indicated that during learning, neurons selective for individual patterns in the learning set were formed. Similar results have been obtained in rabbits and rats. New neurons were found that responded selectively to certain feedboxes used in the training sessions (Svarnik et al. 2001). According to a hypothesis of Shvyrkov (1995), neurons are recruited during training from a pool of reserve neurons. Recent research on neurogenesis in adult organisms suggests that such a pool consists of stem cells that differentiate and are embedded into neural networks during the learning process (Sokolov and Nezlina 2003a,b).

The animal experiments revealing new long-term memory cells have been confirmed in humans in the course of diagnostic clinical studies to identify epileptic foci (Kreiman et al. 2002). Neuronal spike activity was recorded from neurons in the medial temporal cortex of seizure patients as they were shown portraits of well-known faces. Cells were identified that responded selectively to a particular face. A neuron that responded selectively to the portrait of President Bill Clinton was studied in detail. This cell did not respond to any of 49 portraits of other individuals. It responded, however, to different photos of the president, which demonstrated invariance of a particular human perception. An advantage of this study was that it involved presentation of stimuli to the two eyes independently. This allowed the investigators to test for suppression of the primary perception by presenting a competing image to the other eye. They showed that a neuronal spike train that lasted as long as the president's portrait was presented ceased on presentation of a competing stimulus. Thus, spike activity of a specific gnostic neuron lasts for the full duration of presentation of a familiar face. Spike activity of the gnostic neuron ceases simultaneously with change in the visual object by presentation of a different figure to the contralateral eye.

In summary, it bears repeating that the brain involves a system of semi-independent modular processes that perform different operations. One can distinguish cognitive and executive modules. Cognitive modules include two subsystems for "what" and "where." In vision the "what" subsystem participates in the identification of faces, objects, and words. It is proposed that the cortical modules operate automatically and possess innate specificity for different classes of image. Visual recognition is a process in which the retinal image of an object is sequentially translated into a more abstract image that is compared with a set of visual representations of objects stored in memory (Fodor 1983). The visual "what" channel involves a vast area of ventral occipitotemporal cortex of the right hemisphere. It is more strongly activated in tasks that involve face identification than in tasks comparing the positions of stimuli. The "where" subsystem, which occupies the occipitoparietal cortex, is more strongly activated in tasks that involve comparison of stimulus positions than in tasks involving face comparisons. The left medial extrastriate visual area is more involved in word and pseudoword processing as compared with tasks that involve visual fixation on a point, a sequence of consonants that do not form a pseudoword, or a sequence of pseudoletters. This area constitutes a zone of visuoverbal form recognition. The inferior temporal and fusiform gyri represent possible objects, and bilateral areas of inferolateral cortex are associated with the analysis of visual forms.

Developing further the principle of modular organization of the brain, we should give special attention to the processes of categorization and differentiation of categories. Specific neurons have been found in the prefrontal area, the temporal gyri, and the hippocampus that respond to objects of one category and not to objects of another. Such categorization is usually explained in terms of sensitivity to a wide range of perceived signals. That begs the question, however, of why objects of another category are ineffective.

Let us consider examples of categorical differentiation at the neural level. Two types of neuron have been found in studies of color vision: several varieties of predetector and a set of color-selective detectors (Izmailov et al. 2004). A color detector responds selectively to a particular color and in varying degree to other colors, but never to stimuli of a different visual category (e.g., to movement of an object). Another example is the perception of emotional facial images, which involves a limited number of predetectors and a large number of gnostic units (Izmailov et al. 2005). While they responded in varying degree to different emotions, gnostic neurons of the emotions were "dumb" with regard to other categories, such as color. Apparently the distinct separation between neurons that respond to different object categories can be attributed to the different ensembles of predetectors that provide input to them.

Responding to input from a given predetector ensemble, gnostic units completely ignore stimuli addressed to other predetector ensembles and other gnostic unit populations. This was verified in a study of color vision and emotions. Matrices of EPs representing the discharges of gnostic units of each type were subjected to multidimensional analysis. It was shown that color detectors are based on four types of color predetectors, and gnostic neurons of emotional expression receive information from four predetector types that encode the slopes of eyebrows and mouth. Thus, a distinct separation of neurons into categories of encoded objects is explained by the modular organization of predetectors. Stimuli that do not affect a given predetector ensemble do not have the capacity to influence its detectors or gnostic units. Such a mechanism of categorization is consistent with the modular organization of cognitive processes.

4.2. ARE ALL NEURONS ASSOCIATED WITH CONSCIOUSNESS?

Consciousness can be defined as the flow of subjective states that includes perceptual, emotional, and cognitive processes in the human brain. In recent years an experimental approach has been developed that is designed to bring the study of consciousness into the realm of the natural sciences (Edelman 2003). Schrödinger (2000) posed the fundamental question with regard to consciousness: What are the physical processes directly associated with consciousness? Dualistic concepts attribute a particular kind of substantiality to consciousness. Consciousness is added as a special element to the physical structure of the brain. An example of this concept is found in the theory of John Eccles in which free will is seen as the influence of a spiritual entity on the physical, neural structure of the brain (Eccles 1993). According to Eccles, the sites of such influence are the synaptic contacts of pyramidal neurons in human cortex. Changes in the probability of release of quanta of mediator are proposed as a mechanism for a nonphysical effect on neural activity. Based on the connection between the excitation of neocortical neurons and sensory experience, Eccles postulated that consciousness emerged through development of the neocortex in the course of mammalian evolution. From this perspective he further postulated that a fundamental act of consciousness, the cognitive unit or *psychon*, results from the activation of a set of dendrites of neocortical pyramidal cells, a *dendron*. According to Eccles's theory, a given psychon and dendron are unambiguously linked.

The consciousness theory proposed by Eccles was a subject of heated debate at a conference at Radford University (Pribram 1993). Karl Pribram emphasized in his conclusions that the theory proposed by Eccles excluded the concept of consciousness as emergent from neuronal processes. By entertaining the possibility of mental influence on neuronal processes, Eccles failed to consider the emergence of consciousness from the functioning of neurons. Pribram, for his part, proposed examination of the relationship between physiological and cognitive processes as descriptions in two languages of the same phenomenon, analogous to descriptions of the same computer functionality in machine language versus an abstract programming language (Pribram 1991).

A unified theory of physiological and cognitive processes at the neural level, *psychoneural activity*, was proposed by I. S. Beritashvili (Beritov 1961). According to that theory subjective images occur as the result of activity in cortical stellate cells. Depending on the cortical area involved, subjective phenomena can be elementary, if in the primary projection areas, or complex, if in the cortical association areas. Comparing the concepts of Eccles and Beritashvili, one notes an obvious difference in the cell populations proposed as the substrate of consciousness by the two authors: large pyramidal cells according to Eccles versus small stellate cells according to Beritashvili. Perhaps the difference derives from the fact that Eccles was concerned with the mechanism of voluntary actions, whereas Beritashvili focused on the mechanism of subjective imagery.

G. M. Edelman (1987) has applied the evolutionary theory of *natural selection, selection theory*, or *neural Darwinism* to explain the evolving complexity of function of individual neurons. He has suggested that the combination of variation and selection basic to Darwin's theory of the origin of species could be the basis for evolution of physiological systems within the individual organism. As an example he considers the immune system, in which the repertoire of antibodies is brought into accord with the population of foreign antigens by the cloning and selection of cells.

Applied to the nervous system, the question in most general terms concerns the growth and selection of synaptic neuronal contacts in the course of individual development. The selection of synapses and the formation of neural groups appropriate to external demands is based on *reentrant connections* (i.e., return of signals from higher to lower levels). As a metaphor of such repeated entry, Edelman considers the musicians in a quartet. The individual musicians continuously exchange signals with each other during the performance of a musical piece, which leads to correlation among the sounds of the performers, even though they operate independently of each other. Reentry has been proposed by A. M. Ivanitsky as a mechanism for consciousness (Ivanitskiy 2005; Ivanitskiy et al. 1984). He regards it as a basis for unifying the participation of independent neurons in acts of perception or behavior. Taking a similar position, E. R. John (2002) has introduced the idea of a *critical mass* of neurons necessary for the emergence of consciousness. While supporting the reentry principle, he emphasizes the role of coherent oscillations in neural activity.

Pursuing the evolutionary approach to the neural substrate of consciousness, Edelman introduces the notion of *primary consciousness*, which he relates to the role of thalamic nuclei, modulated by the reticular nucleus of the thalamus as well as to the corticothalamic reentry mechanism and corticocortical connections (Fig. 4.1; Edelman 2003). Primary consciousness, which exists also among the higher animals, can create an image or scene. Humans possess a higher order of consciousness, which is based on symbolic constructs. One cannot help but notice a similarity between Edelman's notion of primary imagery and symbolic consciousness and Pavlov's (1947) concept of *first* and *second signaling systems.*

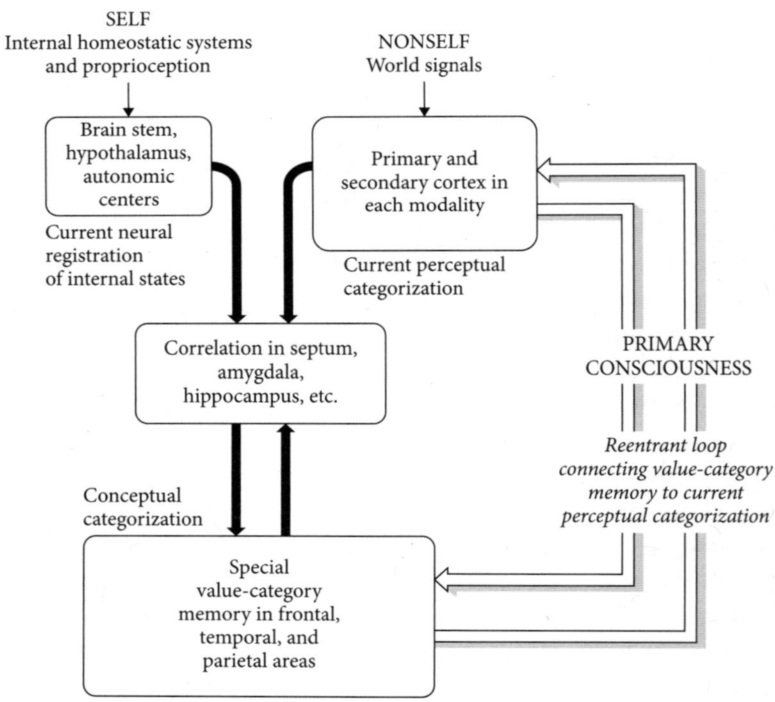

Figure 4.1 The neural mechanism of primary consciousness is the reentrant loop of reciprocally interactive corticothalamic and corticocortical circuits (*heavy arrows right*), which link the posterior cortical sensory systems that mediate *perceptual categorization* of currently incoming signals (*box top right*) with more anterior cortical structures that are the substrate of *conceptual categorization* based on memory of past experience (*bottom box*). (With permission from Edelman 2003, copyright National Academy of Sciences, U.S.A.)

Considering the origin of consciousness in evolutionary perspective, one must acknowledge that the simplest forms of consciousness are present even in early stages of phylogenetic development where external stimuli are represented in specific combinations of plastic synaptic connections on gnostic neurons.

The materialist approach requires a search for mechanisms of consciousness in the functioning of brain structures (i.e., in neurons, synapses, and intracellular molecular mechanisms). John Eccles, focusing on the relation of neocortical pyramidal cells to consciousness, raises the question of whether all of the neurons of mammalian neocortex are related to consciousness. In response we have proposed the hypothesis that subjective phenomena are mediated by the activity of a distributed subsystem of specific consciousness neurons. From this perspective the stream of consciousness represents the sequence of excitatory activity in different consciousness neurons (Sokolov 2004).

The *consciousness neuron hypothesis* postulates the existence of two types of neuron: neurons directly related to consciousness and neurons that simply support their function. Consciousness neurons form modules that are represented in different areas of the brain. Destruction or functional disruption of such a module leads to a loss of a certain area of consciousness without damaging other areas. An example of such modular organization is found in the mechanisms of color perception. Color vision is represented in area V4 of the cerebral cortex. Damage to this area in humans leads to loss of color vision with total preservation of achromatic (i.e., black–white vision). A person suffering from achromatopsia, the loss of color perception, sees all things in different shades of gray, like "dirty snow" (Tootell et al. 2003).

Experiments in monkeys have shown that when area V4 is temporarily cooled to disrupt normal function, the animal does not distinguish one color stimulus from another, yet shows normal behavior otherwise (Tootell et al. 2004). Neurons in the V4 color module exhibit the properties of selective color detectors. They are organized in color columns analogous to the organization of neurons of visual cortex that respond selectively to specific line orientations. Another example of the modular organization of consciousness is found in prosopagnosia, loss of the ability to recognize the faces of familiar people as a result of focal damage to temporal cortex. In such cases the recognition of other objects (e.g., houses, instruments, furniture, etc.) is not disrupted. Furthermore, the ability to distinguish the emotional significance of facial expressions remains intact in prosopagnosia, even with total inability to identify the person. In this area of temporal cortex one finds neurons that are selectively tuned to recognize individual persons, regardless of perspective.

Having considered neurons associated with consciousness, we should turn our attention to examples of brain activity that are not associated with the awareness of events. Under certain conditions, emotional facial expressions can serve as stimuli eliciting an unconscious response. Williams (2003) has shown that, depending on the degree of involvement of the defense system, a face expressing fear can evoke activation in different parts of the brain. If there is a galvanic skin response (GSR), a sign of defensive activation, the fMRI shows increased blood flow in the amygdala and in the medial prefrontal cortex. If a GSR is not present, areas of increased brain activity are detected in the hippocampus, cerebellum, fusiform gyrus, and lateral prefrontal cortex. The first has to do with resonance between the perception and the emotion of fear, while the second simply reflects recognition of the fear expression itself.

The perceptual system for fear is more sensitive among women and is somewhat less subject to habituation. Unconscious discrimination between a neutral face and a fearful face is nevertheless detectable in GSR and fMRI responses. Expressions that are not recognized consciously as fearful but that evoke the GSR appropriate to fear expressions create foci of activity in the thalamus and in the superior and middle temporal gyri. This indicates that there exist pathways unassociated with consciousness neurons that include the neural mechanism of the fear response without conscious perception thereof. Thus, the mechanism of the fear response can be triggered even before the conscious perception of the emotional state. In terms of the spherical model of cognitive processes, predetector neurons are not associated with consciousness. They do not produce subjective phenomena themselves, but only feed necessary information to detectors.

The designation of a class of consciousness neurons allows us to approach the mechanisms of loss of consciousness from a new perspective. Current advances in neurosurgery permit the saving of lives of many patients with severe brain damage. In some cases, however, it is impossible to ensure a return of normal mental activity. Many patients remain for several months or even years in an unconscious state, the neurophysiological mechanism of which is not yet fully understood (Sharova et al. 2001).

In terms of the consciousness neuron hypothesis, long-term unconsciousness is associated with the shutdown of neurons associated with awareness, while the functioning of neurons not directly associated with consciousness is preserved. The hypothesis also provides an explanation for the gradual recovery of consciousness (Dobrokhotova et al. 1985). The stages of recovery from vegetative status and coma proceed in accord with an expansion of the range of cognitive functions and the localized neuronal responses that support them. Thus, akinetic mutism gives way to akinetic mutism with emotional reactions, which in turn proceeds to mutism with speech comprehension. With further recovery confusion, disordered speech and cognitive impairment give way to normalization of consciousness. These stages in the recovery of consciousness can be considered to represent the sequential activation of individual modules of consciousness neurons. Future progress in understanding recovery from longstanding coma can be expected to result from study of specific intracellular mechanisms of activation of individual consciousness neurons.

The hypothesis as to the existence of consciousness neurons is also supported by the results of focal electrostimulation of human cerebral cortex. Such stimulation has revealed both zones associated with subjective feelings and *silent areas*. Electrical brain stimulation in an area of right prefrontal cortex, where evoked potentials are recorded in response to emotional facial expressions, elicits hallucinations in the form of visual images of faces. Lesions in this area disrupt the perception of emotional facial expressions (Marinkovic et al. 2000).

Some loci of human cortex are "dumb" (i.e., do not respond to electrical stimulation). Stimulation there does not evoke subjective experiences or motor responses. It provides only a modulating influence, activation or suppression, on responses evoked by the stimulation of areas that do mediate such responses (Ojemann 2003). Presumably such modulating loci represent projections from the ascending activating and synchronizing systems of the brain stem reticular formation and reticular nuclei of the thalamus to the cerebral cortex (Creutzfeldt 1993). A characteristic of consciousness neurons is their dependence on neurons of activating and inactivating systems. Neurons of those systems themselves do not generate conscious events. However, switching off neurons of the activating reticular system leads to the loss of consciousness associated with disrupted functioning of consciousness neurons in the neocortex. Intensification of activity in the synchronizing system also leads to loss of consciousness due to the inactivation of consciousness neurons, as in slow-wave sleep.

4.3. CONSCIOUSNESS AND SLEEP

It is difficult to compose an unambiguous definition of consciousness, primarily because the term is applied to two different characteristics of the mind. One meaning of the term refers to knowledge—that is, the aggregate of individual experience that can be communicated to other people. In this case, "consciousness," *soznanie* in Russian, is equivalent in both its Russian and Latin roots to the *co-knowledge* that is exchanged through verbal communication. The second meaning relates directly to the brain function of a given individual. Because we have no independent objective measure of a person's subjective experience beyond his verbal description thereof, this interpretation of the concept is easier to convey in terms of a negative characteristic: loss of consciousness. What happens during a sudden loss of consciousness, as in fainting? The person loses the image of his surroundings and the sense of his own self and emotions. The recording of current events in memory ceases; images are not retrieved from memory; and voluntary, purposeful actions, speech, and cognitive operations disappear. At the same time, certain automatic motor functions may continue, the autonomic nervous system continues respiratory and cardiac functions, and certain motor automatisms may occur.

Accepting the hypothesis regarding specific neurons of consciousness, it is important to recognize the dependence of consciousness neurons on the activating and synchronizing systems of the brain. With that in mind, loss of consciousness can be thought of as a global shutdown of activity in consciousness neurons and the return of consciousness as an accompaniment of their global recovery.

Loss of consciousness can be induced by any of a number of factors, including hypoxia, hypoglycemia, physical trauma, and exposure to specific chemicals. There is, however, a naturally occurring loss of consciousness with the onset of slow-wave sleep. The switching on and off of consciousness was studied in the laboratory of A. R. Luria (Luria 1982; Rusalova 1990). He and colleagues studied the performance of voluntary movements, such as finger flexion by electromyogram (EMG) and key presses, together with EEG responses to sound stimuli as a subject fell asleep and awoke. During wakefulness the sounds evoked a depression of alpha rhythm with latency of about 100 msec. With the onset of drowsiness the EEG slowed, the latencies of EEG and EMG responses increased, and some of the sound stimuli, which evoked only weak EEG depression, were accompanied by attenuated EMG and ineffective motor responses. The onset of slow-wave sleep, which corresponds to the switching off of consciousness, interrupted the EMG and motor responses altogether. Increasing the volume of the sound reinduced wakefulness. The slow waves were replaced by the alpha rhythm, which again was suppressed in response to the sound stimulus. The voluntary motor response recurred against the background of alpha-rhythm suppression.

It should be emphasized that, in the switching off of consciousness, the switch occurs only with the slow-wave phase of sleep. In the fast-wave phase, paradoxical sleep, a different change in consciousness occurs in the form of dreaming. This phase of sleep is recognized by suppression of slow-wave EEG activity, rapid eye movements, and significant loss of muscular tone, as manifested in decreased EMG amplitude of the neck muscles. The content of dreams includes images, words, and emotions. Other functions of waking consciousness, such as voluntary movements and the recording of external information in memory, are not operational.

The involuntary combinations of images, emotions, and thoughts in dreams are amazing in their diversity. Of particular interest is the phenomenon of involuntary problem solving during sleep. A problem abandoned after several failed attempts to find a solution during wakefulness may be resolved during sleep.

Such a change of consciousness in paradoxical sleep represents the involuntary functioning of cognitive systems. This limited activity of cognitive systems coincides with the high-frequency EEG of paradoxical sleep. The apparently uncontrolled flow of events characteristic of dreams, however, is not necessarily totally free of determination by the dominant conscious state. Analyzing the role of the unconscious in mathematical creativity, Adamar (1970) has emphasized that the emergence of a new idea as insight is preceded by a phase of intense conscious work on the problem. If a solution is not achieved, a *dominant state* is created, which is focused on the problem. Thus, the solution found in a dream emerges involuntarily but is prepared for during a stage of active conscious effort. This solution is further subject to verification, which takes place again on a conscious level. Puankare (1983), reasoning on the basis of introspection, concluded that a solution reached in the unconscious state is an intermediate result: it is preceded by conscious work on the problem, and it is completed by a process of verification and final formulation, again on a conscious level.

Thus, one approach to understanding loss of consciousness is to study the mechanisms of slow-wave sleep. Slow-wave activity has usually referred to fluctuations of EEG potentials in the range of 0.75 to 4.50 Hz. Recently, however, spectral analysis of slow-wave sleep has revealed even slower frequencies. These fluctuations recorded from the surface of the scalp are in line with the frequencies of fluctuation in membrane potentials of thalamic and cortical cells. In the waking state the brain stem reticular formation has a depolarizing, stimulating effect on thalamic neurons. The cells show a tonic effect in the form of irregular spike activity. With the onset of slow-wave sleep the influence of the activating system is reduced, and thalamic and cortical cells become hyperpolarized. Waves of depolarization appear against the background of hyperpolarization, which generates bursts of spikes followed by deep waves of hyperpolarization. Under these conditions sensory signals become ineffective. They are lost both in the spike discharge phase and in the hyperpolarization phase. The cortex is functionally disconnected from the sources of sensory signals.

Moruzzi (1954) proposed the hypothesis that, with activation of the neurons and synapses responsible for consciousness, substances are released that lead to their inactivation. According to his theory those elements are switched off not accidentally, but under the influence of a mechanism common to them, the triggering of a synchronizing, inactivating system. Indeed, the onset of sleep occurs suddenly in such a way that the event is not recorded in one's memory. The sudden switching off of consciousness with the onset of slow-wave sleep is not so much the result of switching off the activating system as a threshold effect of switching on an inactivating system.

A microelectrode study of thalamic neurons showed that the level of the membrane potential determines the frequency of endogenous pacemaker potentials (Llinas 1998). With a depolarizing shift simulating that seen in active wakefulness, the fluctuation frequency increases to 40 to 80 Hz. Simultaneously the source shifts from the cell body to the dendrites. These fluctuations in the gamma range (i.e., greater than 35 Hz) are determined by a particular set of calcium channels. Measurements of calcium concentration in the dendrites have shown sharp increases after episodes of gamma oscillation. With a shift to hyperpolarization of the membrane potential the gamma oscillations disappear, and slow oscillations localized in the cell body are observed. One possible mechanism of such oscillations is a reset of the depolarizing wave following the pulse of hyperpolarization. The inactivation system involves interneurons that evoke inhibitory postsynaptic potentials in thalamic neurons, and consequently, as an aftereffect of the inhibition, launch a wave of depolarization. Comparison of brain function with EEG fluctuation in the slow-wave and gamma ranges indicates that loss of consciousness correlates with the termination of gamma oscillations. This suggests that the mechanism underlying gamma oscillation is related to conscious functioning.

One function of the gamma rhythm that relates to consciousness is as follows. Consciousness involves the integration of sensory processes with memory traces and the recording of incoming information in long-term memory. These processes involve thalamic neurons that connect to cortical neurons, which in turn transmit excitation back to the dendrites of thalamic neurons. Gamma oscillations create high-frequency stimulation to the thalamic-cortical-thalamic loop that supports posttetanic potentiation of the corresponding synapses and the subsequent structural fixation that is necessary for the formation of long-term memory traces. Apparently this mechanism also operates in dreams, which can be fixed in long-term memory, but which are distinct from the memory traces formed in the waking state.

From this vantage point let us consider the mechanism of the *dominant state* and its role in the involuntary selection of information during paradoxical sleep. Rusinov's (1987) classic experiment demonstrated the formation of a cortical dominant by the application of a polarizing current to an area of motor cortex. He showed that after cessation of the current the dominant state continues and "attracts" sensory excitatory inputs. Previously indifferent sound stimuli now elicit movement of the limb represented in the area of motor cortex that is in a state of dominant activity induced by the polarizing current. Presumably the dominant focus is maintained by circulation of activity at the gamma frequency. A dominant focus determines the content of dreams. Thus, in a state of hunger, dreaming is evoked by the feeding dominant. A similar explanation is reasonable with regard to erotic dreams. A dominant evoked in the process of creative effort activates memory traces associated with the problem being solved.

The thalamocortical system acts as a frequency filter that is tuned to input signals of different frequencies depending on the level of membrane potentials controlled by the balance of activating and inactivating systems. This accounts for the appearance of high and low harmonics or even substitution of a harmonic for the main signal frequency during photostimulation. Thus, when the spectrum of background EEG activity shifts toward slow-wave frequencies, a flicker frequency of 9 Hz evokes oscillations of 6 and 4.5 Hz, whereas with a shift in the EEG toward high frequencies, the same flicker frequency elicits higher harmonics of 18 and 27 Hz. A frequency filter reinforces the frequencies in the signal to which it is tuned. By varying the filter frequency through shifts in the membrane potential of thalamic and cortical cells, a nonspecific system selects from a complex spectrum the components that are in its frequency range. Increasing the resonant frequency enhances the transmission of information about subtle and transient but distinctive characteristics of the signal. This is analogous to the enhancement of spatial discrimination where a corrective lens enables one to read small text that merges together in the absence of such a correction.

Note that in paradoxical sleep access to images and cognitive functions is lost to voluntary control. The complexity of images, emotions, and thoughts during paradoxical sleep is associated with inability on the part of the dreamer to manage those processes, rather like a spectator who cannot control the movie he is watching. In the waking state the observer can control the input of sensory information by changing the focus of attention or the line of sight, by adjusting head and body positions. Moreover, the program for such control is largely determined by the task. This was shown convincingly in an analysis of eye movements by Yarbus (1965). Depending on the task, for example to determine relationships among characters or objects in a picture, the sequence and loci of visual fixation points followed a regular pattern, highlighting the portion of the image that potentially contained information relevant to the task.

Such task-oriented scanning also occurs in mental decision making, but in that case the search field is the screen of long-term memory. Scanning conscious memory may prove unsuccessful. However, unsuccessful attempts define and narrow the field of search, setting the conditions for an involuntary solution in the form of insight during a break in conscious effort. The dominant continues to function even when work on the task moves outside the field of consciousness to the level of unconscious operations, similar in part to its function in consciousness. Whereas in the waking state the focus of attention can be moved across the memory screen to emphasize certain events, in sleep such voluntary control is lost. The lack of voluntary control in paradoxical sleep extends to spontaneous myoclonic limb movements and saccadic eye movements. However, the currently active dominant can apparently continue to function during paradoxical sleep, developing a solution that was not found during wakefulness.

While the screen of long-term memory may function during paradoxical sleep, it is inactive during the slow-wave phase of sleep. How can this be explained? One of the mechanisms by which the activating system of the brain maintains wakefulness is by acting on neurons in the locus ceruleus, which releases norepinephrine at synapses widely distributed throughout the brain. Norepinephrine in turn stimulates the expression of genes early in the chemical pathway that mediate the neural recording of long-term memory. During slow-wave sleep, spike activity is reduced in these neurons, thereby reducing the release of norepinephrine at their synapses. Thus, at the molecular level, slow-wave sleep is characterized by a decrease in expression of early genes that are important elements in the formation of long-term memory. The correlation between loss of consciousness in slow-wave sleep and the decrease in expression of early genes necessary for long-term memory suggests that the lack of memory trace formation during slow-wave sleep may be linked specifically to this effect. In addition during slow-wave sleep, brain metabolism, the energy production of which is linked to mitochondrial function, decreases by some 30 percent. Again, the expression of genes involved in the synthesis of mitochondrial enzymes decreases during slow-wave sleep compared to active wakefulness.

Thus, research on slow-wave sleep suggests that the state of consciousness is functionally determined. Nevertheless, the basic question remains: Does a particular population of neurons determine the state of consciousness, or does consciousness depend on appropriate activation of a general system of neurons? Data obtained by the Canadian neurosurgeon W. Penfield (1958) support the concept that specific neuronal populations are responsible for the conscious perception of complex images and scenes. During surgical operations for epilepsy, Penfield tested systematically the effects of electrical stimulation of focal brain areas on conscious experience. In this setting, the patient treated with local cutaneous anesthesia to prevent pain at the site of incision was fully conscious and able to describe the sensations resulting from stimulation.

Stimulation of the primary visual projection area of the cortex evoked localized phosphenes (i.e., flashes of light in the visual field). Stimulation of the primary auditory area produced elementary auditory sensations, such as a cracking sound or noises. Only stimulation of temporal cortex at its borders with visual and parietal areas evoked complex scenes from the past. Thus, only certain areas of cortex are responsible for the conscious perception of integrated scenes. The holistic images and scenes evoked by electrical stimulation are similar, on the one hand, to hallucinations and, on the other, to dreams. Or they can be integrated into the perception of reality, combining to form "chimeras" by integration of the activated memory traces with the current situation. Focusing on conscious perception in the human, one cannot ignore the processes of categorization and integration of images, including verbal encoding. Appropriately interpreted, a dream or a scene evoked by electrical brain stimulation differs from the actual perceived situation. A perceptual hallucination includes within itself the inappropriate interpretation of an event. The consideration of consciousness should not be limited to phenomena involving language or perception; consciousness is an alloy of perceptual, mental, and verbal operations.

The categorization of neurons into classes related and not related to consciousness allows one to address the issues of global versus focal loss of consciousness from a common perspective. A simple example of global loss of consciousness is slow-wave, dreamless sleep. At first glance, such a global loss of consciousness appears contradictory to the concept of consciousness as distributed among a set of independent consciousness neurons. But the contradiction disappears upon recognition that consciousness neurons operate only within a certain range of activation by input from the midbrain reticular system. Moreover, such a view clarifies the observation that certain neural spike activity is maintained during slow-wave sleep. Only consciousness neurons are disabled during this phase of sleep, while neurons that are not related to consciousness and that are not dependent upon activating input from the reticular system continue to function.

The transition to slow-wave sleep occurs as a step function; that is, a person is not aware of the moment that consciousness switches totally off. To understand the sharp transition to unconsciousness, it is necessary to recognize the function of the synchronizing system centered in the pons and medulla of the lower brain stem. Synchronization accelerates the switching off of consciousness neurons. Damage to the midbrain reduces the activation effect and results in slowing of the resting EEG, just as stimulation of certain lower regions of the brain stem reticular system results in increased synchronization of the EEG. The combination of reduced activation and increased synchronization disables consciousness neurons without affecting neurons unrelated to consciousness.

The dominance of the EEG by slow waves in the delta band of frequencies, 1 to 4 Hz range, is closely correlated with loss of consciousness in the human. Anesthesiologists use this transition as a criterion in dosing for anesthesia. An incremental increase of high frequencies in the EEG with increasing wakefulness may be due to an increase in the number of activated consciousness neurons, while a reduced frequency of EEG oscillations is associated with a progressive decrease. A testable hypothesis in this context would be that activity in the high-frequency channel is associated with increased release of norepinephrine, including nonsynaptic release from locus ceruleus neurons, and activity in the low-frequency channel, involving inhibitory neurons, increases levels of the inhibitory transmitter, GABA.

Unlike slow-wave sleep, paradoxical sleep involves a high level of activation from the brain stem reticular activating system. Mediators such as epinephrine and serotonin play an important role in this activation. Paradoxical sleep is characterized by rapid eye movements, blockade of motor output (muscle atony), and disabling of sensory input. At the same time phasic potentials are seen in pontine structures, the lateral geniculate nucleus, and visual cortex. Under these conditions dreaming can occur, its contents determined not by the short-term memory associated with hippocampal function but by the activation of neurons involved in long-term memory. The capricious stream of images is determined by endogenous sources through the activation of consciousness neurons. One such source is the PGO signal (pons-geniculate-occipital wave), which substitutes in paradoxical sleep for the sensory sources available during wakefulness. At the same time, paradoxical sleep involves increased activity of the emotional centers. Thus, dominance of amygdalar excitation is associated with scenarios involving the emotions of fear and anger. Simultaneous inactivation of the prefrontal cortex leads to the paralysis of will and logical judgment that interrupts the control of dreams and evaluation of their content. The transition from the paradoxical phase back to slow-wave sleep represents the switching off of the activating input and switching on of inhibition involving GABAergic neurons. Dreaming terminates with switching off the PGO generator. The subsequent transition from slow-wave sleep to wakefulness is associated with switching on the brain stem reticular activating system and the reticular thalamus, together with the functional disabling of inhibitory neurons.

A common feature of consciousness in both paradoxical sleep and active wakefulness is that in both states information can be recorded in long-term memory. Thus, the content of emotionally significant dreams can be recalled multiple times. The source of the images remains in memory. More complex is the emotional substrate of the dream, which may continue into the state of wakefulness as a determinant of mood.

5

The Mosaic Nature of Consciousness

5.1. THE CONCEPT OF DISTRIBUTED CONSCIOUSNESS

In contrast to holistic conceptions, the concept of *distributed consciousness* is that of a mosaic of individual specialized neurons. In this concept, based to some extent on a theory proposed by John Eccles (1993), consciousness is a collection of separate mental elements, *psychons*, that correspond to individual dendritic bundles, *dendrons*, on pyramidal cells in neocortex. We have proposed that the functions that Eccles attributed to dendrons are performed by specific *consciousness neurons* organized into specialized *modules*. Each module consists of a *screen of detector neurons* in which specific sensations occur and an ensemble of predetector neurons that are not directly associated with consciousness but that constitute the link between receptors and detectors (Sokolov 2004).

Evidence for the pointillistic structure of consciousness is found in the highly specific nature of missing elements thereof. For example, impairment of stereoscopic vision occurs only in the portion of the visual field associated with loss of *depth detectors* in the limited part of area V4 of visual cortex that is responsible for perceiving the distance of objects, while monocular space perception remains intact. The mechanism for stereoscopic vision constitutes a separate module consisting of predetectors not directly associated with consciousness and a screen of consciousness neurons, in this case depth detectors, representing external space. The mechanism of binocular space perception overlaps the mechanism of monocular perception. Monocular consciousness neurons, responding to different combinations of input from an overlapping set of predetectors, maintain visual awareness of that aspect of the visual field despite loss of binocular depth detectors. The loss of stereopsis in a certain part of the visual field reflects localized destruction of a particular part of the depth-representing screen. Neither the perception of motion nor the perception of color is affected.

Impairment of motion perception restricted to a section of the visual field can occur in the same way, that is, as a result of focal loss of detectors selectively tuned to different directions and velocities of motion there. A lesion of the whole motion perception module in area V5 results in inability to perceive the movement of objects across the entire visual field, with no effect on color perception or stereopsis. Impairment of color vision limited to certain portions of the visual field can be similarly selective. In some cases the perceptual loss is limited to specific colors. With suppression of the entire color module of area V4, the human perceives all objects in shades of black and white with no loss of either stereopsis or motion perception.

Thus, focal absences of conscious awareness can occur both at the level of individual detectors and at the level of individual modules. In the latter case, the selective shutdown of one module does not affect modules representing neighboring modalities. The loss of individual consciousness neurons within a given module results in loss of perception of specific features of the sensory field without affecting the perception of other features.

The modular organization of consciousness extends also to the perception of complex objects. Thus, two modules are involved in the perception of faces, a module for the perception of emotional expressions and a module for face identification. These modules also consist of predetectors not directly associated with consciousness and screens of consciousness consisting of gnostic units (i.e., detectors of complex attributes). A lesion of the module for face identification results in inability to identify faces, even of close relatives and friends (prosopagnosia). The perception of emotional facial expressions remains unaffected. A person with a disorder of the module for perception of emotional facial expressions cannot, for example, distinguish a joyful expression from a sad one, whereas the mechanism for identifying individuals by their faces operates normally.

Modular organization also applies to aural perception, for example in the perception of phonemes, particularly vowels. The screen of consciousness for the perception of vowels is represented by detector neurons for vowels that are fed signals from vowel predetectors that are not directly associated with consciousness but that support the activity of those selective units. A total lesion of the vowel detectors or predetectors leads to sensory aphasia, but the perception of individual tones remains intact.

Thus, the modular organization of the brain involves two neuronal levels of information processing: the predetector level, where conscious perceptions have not yet occurred, and the level of selective detectors and gnostic units that constitute the screen of consciousness, where conscious perceptions occur.

Disorders of function at the two levels lead to different results. Damage to predetector neurons results in inability to perceive all input signals addressed to the module. However, direct electrical stimulation of consciousness neurons that are part of the module still evokes sensory images. On the other hand, a disorder of the individual detectors that constitute the screen of consciousness leads to the loss of the corresponding perceptions, despite normal functioning of predetectors. The loss of a specific perception due to a focal defect in the screen of consciousness cannot be reversed by electrical stimulation of other parts of the screen of consciousness.

One argument for a mosaic organization of consciousness in which neurons participate as relatively independent units is the possibility of evoking the subjective effects by direct stimulation of neurons. Such effects can be achieved by transcranial stimulation directed at the neurons responsible for certain states of consciousness. Although it is not yet possible to stimulate selectively a single neuron, focal stimulation of a specific neuronal population has been quite successful. An example is the stimulation of area V5 in the human, where neurons respond selectively to stimuli moving in the visual field. Individual neurons in area V5 possess detector properties such that they respond to specific combinations of direction and velocity. Transcranial magnetic stimulation of this area in the human produces the appearance of moving phosphenes, subjective perceptions of visual motion, without other features of a visual image (Crick and Koch 2002). This suggests that the population of V5 neurons determines the visual perception of motion without involvement of other consciousness neurons. Moreover, the fact that individual neurons are specific with respect to rate and direction of motion suggests that each perceived moving phosphene may be determined by a single individual consciousness neuron in area V5. Focal damage to this area leads to selective loss of perception of movement of visual objects, while the perceptions of form and color are not affected.

Similar selectivity of lesions affecting the perceptions of shape and color testifies further to the selective properties of consciousness neurons, at least with respect to their specific populations. Considering the detector properties of individual neurons in these populations, it is logical to assume that such selectivity leads to a mosaic of consciousness as a whole.

Returning to the psychon concept proposed by Eccles (1993), one will note a similarity between the concepts of the psychon and the consciousness neuron. The difference is that Eccles links the psychon to a dendron (i.e., a bundle of pyramidal cell dendrites in neocortex). Consciousness neurons, in contrast, constitute a separate class of cortical neurons, each of which is linked to an individual cognitive act. Therefore, the loss of a single consciousness neuron leads to loss of the cognitive experience associated with it. Damage to a significant number of consciousness neurons in a population leads to loss of the type of perception associated with it, which produces, for example, achromatopsia, akinetopsia, and prosopagnosia (loss of perception of color, motion, and facial identity respectively).

5.2. PERCEPTION

The input to a color module is provided by three types of cones, which absorb light in the ranges of long, medium, and short wavelengths. A visual stimulus is transformed into a combination of excitations of the three types of photoreceptors. From there color information is transmitted through several levels of retinal cells to the LGB, a predetector system, which consists of four types of neurons: *red–green, blue–yellow, brightness, and darkness* neurons. Of particular interest are the darkness neurons, which are spontaneously active in the dark. When a light stimulus is presented they undergo inhibition that depends on the degree of excitation of the red–green, blue–yellow, and brightness neurons. Thus, at the predetector level a light stimulus is converted into a combination of excitations of the four types of neuron. That combination can be represented as a color vector of excitation.

A key feature of the vectors whose directions correspond to different color stimuli is that they are equal in length. In terms of a geometric model representing the quantitative relations between the physical stimulus for color and the color perception, that means that the excitation vector resulting from any change of a color signal terminates on a spherical surface in four-dimensional cognitive space. The inputs to detectors of color stimuli are encoded by the orientations of color excitation vectors of equal length (Izmailov and Sokolov 1991; Leonov and Sokolov 2005, 2008; Sokolov 2003). These vectors represent the excitations of the color predetectors that form the basis of the color module. While predetector neurons determine the responses of color detector neurons, they do not themselves belong to the category of consciousness neurons.

The transformation of the color signal from predetectors to detectors that determine the perception of specific shades of color is based on a synaptic mechanism. Each color detector has four types of synapses that receive excitations from corresponding predetectors: red–green, blue–yellow, brightness, and darkness neurons. The effectiveness of the synapses varies such that the pattern of contacts of the color detectors can be represented by synaptic efficacy vectors of variable direction but equal length. Excitatory signals from color predetectors arrive in parallel at the synapses of all color detectors. The excitation from a given predetector as it arrives at the different detectors is multiplied by the efficacy of the synapses on the detectors, and the products of transmission from different predetectors combine to produce an excitatory postsynaptic potential in the detector. Thus, the response of the color detector can be represented as the scalar product of two vectors: a vector representing the excitation of predetectors and a vector representing the efficacies of synaptic contacts of the detector. The predetector excitation vectors as well as the synaptic weights vectors of the color detectors are of equal length. Therefore, the maximal response to a given stimulus will occur in the detector whose vector of synaptic weights coincides in direction with the excitation vector of the current predetector. This corresponds to the display of a local maximum of excitation on the spherical surface representing color stimuli. When the color of a stimulus and the corresponding predetector excitation vector change, the maximal focus of excitation on the spherical color screen shifts to another color detector whose vector of synaptic weights coincides with the new predetector excitation vector (Sokolov 2003). Thus, individual loci on the spherical screen correspond to the specific color detectors excited selectively by different color stimuli.

Damage to the color detectors in a certain section of the color screen only eliminates sensation of the colors associated with them. Neighboring sections of the color screen, which are associated with intact detector neurons, are not affected. The situation is different if the predetectors are deactivated. In this case, the defect blocks all color detectors, resulting in complete loss of color vision. The screen of color detectors, however, remains intact. Electrical stimulation of area V4 in humans lacking color vision elicits phosphenes that are colored. These observations indicate that the color module consists of two components. A color predetector component transmits color information from photoreceptors to the color screen, but it is not directly associated with consciousness. The color detector component forms the screen of consciousness. When the predetector component is damaged, the consciousness neurons normally activated by the predetectors can be activated only by direct electrical stimulation.

The existence of neurons that are directly related to consciousness and neurons supporting them is confirmed by the study of neuronal activity in cortical perceptual modules when an observer is presented with stimuli that are subjectively invisible (Moutoussis and Zeki 2002). Invisible images of faces and houses were created by the binocular fusion of monocular contrast stimuli. For example, the image of a contrast face contour on a red background was presented to one eye and the contour of the same face on a green background to the other eye. Because of binocular fusion the face contour was suppressed and the background appeared yellow. Functional MRI was used to detect the brain areas activated by two modes of stimulation: one in which the facial contour was represented by the different contrast images to the two eyes so that it was not perceived and the other in which the same image was presented to both eyes in such a way that the observer perceived the facial contour. The experiments showed that the fusiform gyrus, which is responsible for the perception

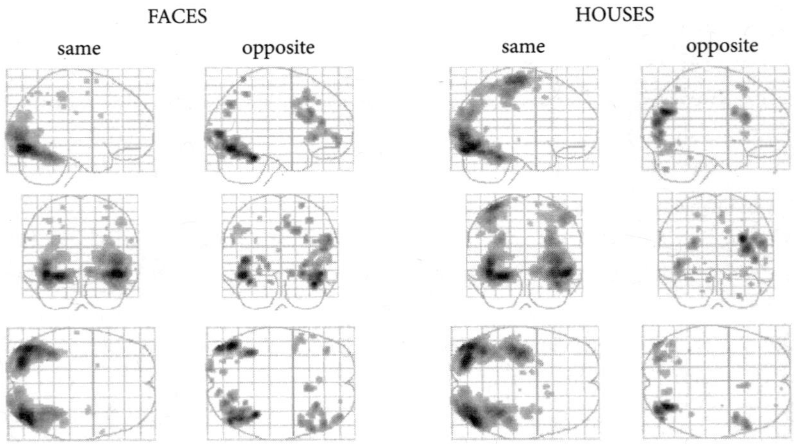

Figure 5.1 "Glass-brain" presentations of group results of the activation produced by the same and opposite dichoptic stimulation with pictures of faces and houses. Same: image presented against same-color background to both eyes; Opposite: image presented against backgrounds of contrast colors. FACES: For faces, fusiform activity is greater when the backgrounds are the same than when they are different. HOUSES: For houses, parahippocampal activity is greater when the backgrounds are the same than when they are different. (With permission from Moutoussis and Zeki 2002, copyright National Academy of Sciences, U.S.A.)

of faces, is activated by both visible and invisible images of faces (Fig. 5.1). But activation of that area by a visible face image is significantly greater than with an invisible image. Similar results were obtained with visible and invisible images of houses, but in this case the parahippocampal gyrus, which is involved in the perception of the positions of objects, was activated.

These results indicate that the module for the perception of faces, which is located in the fusiform gyrus, contains both consciousness neurons and predetector neurons that serve them but that are not associated with consciousness. With the binocular fusion of contrasting facial contour images (i.e., the condition in which the contours are invisible), only neurons not related to consciousness are activated. In the absence of binocular fusion of contrasting images (i.e., the condition in which the contours are visible), the neurons that detect faces are linked to them, increasing the overall activation of the fusiform gyrus. The same occurs with the perception of house images by the module that detects the position of inanimate objects in the parahippocampal gyrus. This module also consists of a component of predetector neurons that are not connected with consciousness and object location detectors that are directly associated with consciousness. When both predetectors and localization detectors are stimulated by a visible image, the overall activation of the parahippocampal gyrus increases. Thus, the concept of modular organization of the brain and the mosaic organization of consciousness is supported by studies of the perception of complex objects. Mosaics of consciousness can be located in different parts of the brain. This allows us better to understand the relations between subjective phenomena and anatomic structures.

5.3. MEMORY AND SEMANTICS

A symbol is any sensory event that functions as a substitute for another sensory event, including another symbol. Pavlov referred to substitution of abstract signals for other signals as the *second signaling system.* If the *first signaling system* involves the neural signals representing the unconditional stimuli that trigger unconditional responses, signals in the second signaling system pertain to stimuli that do not have fixed biological significance. The term "second signaling system" emphasizes that symbolic encoding is involved primarily in communication. Besides its communicative function, the second signaling system performs an information processing function. It allows operations on symbols instead of real objects.

In communicative tasks symbols provide the basis for cognitive operations in which real objects are replaced by their symbols. Thus, it facilitates generalizations about phenomena that are not necessarily similar in sensory characteristics. Spoken, written, and gestural body languages all represent symbolic codes. Written language has the particular advantage of enabling the documentation of events. In the modern era this function is performed in computer languages residing on magnetic and optical media. The power of computerized information technology rests on computational operations involving mathematical and verbal symbols.

Symbols are different from complex stimuli, or gestalts. In gestalt formation two or more sensory stimuli form an integrated perceptual phenomenon in which the individual sensory events are equal parts of the gestalt; they do not signalize separate sensory events. Signals in the second signaling system occupy a higher hierarchical position than gestalt neurons, which are hierarchically subordinate. Complex visual stimuli are represented by gnostic neurons in inferotemporal cortex. *Semantic neurons* or *symbolic neurons* of the left prefrontal cortex are linked to the gnostic units by bidirectional connections.

The psychophysiology of symbolic encoding involves a hierarchical system of neural maps. First, the stimulus is represented on a certain detector map regardless of whether it is to function as a symbol or not. Representation on the detector map is of short duration, because its retention requires another level of processing, namely generation of a long-term memory map. A familiar signal that has emerged on a detector map activates the corresponding cell in a long-term memory map, which identifies the stimulus. If the stimulus is novel, a new neuron is established to fix it in long-term memory. This expansion of the volume of long-term memory is presumably accomplished by neurogenesis—that is, through the differentiation of stem cells, which ultimately become integrated into the neural network through the formation of input and output synapses with other long-term memory neurons.

The organization of long-term memory is remarkable for the sheer volume of information that it is able to record. Not only is a concrete event recorded, but the time of its occurrence is noted as well. With repetition an event is recorded with linkage to the memory of the initial occurrence—in other words, a continuous record is formed, which can be reproduced in the same sequence. It is not always possible to achieve such reproduction voluntarily, but as was shown by the neurosurgeon W. Penfield, fragments of past experiences can be evoked by electrical stimulation of the temporal region of the brain. The completeness and intensity of the evoked memory make such an experience as vivid as the actual event.

It is reasonable to assume that the mechanism that mediates dreaming involves excitation of the image storage system without voluntary control. A dream is recorded into long-term memory together with actual events but is tagged as received in a special state. Such a tag may appear at first to be quite an artificial, hypothetical construct. Considering the phenomenon of *state-dependent learning* (the observation that information learned under a particular set of environmental and physiological conditions is most effectively recalled under the same conditions), however, one need not be too skeptical of the concept that additional state-dependent tags are involved in the recording of events in long-term memory. Indeed, each memory episode, or *frame*, recorded into long-term storage has a time-stamp that allows the ordering of event recordings in temporal sequence.

Integrating this phenomenon with Penfield's activation by electrical stimulation of past images stored in temporal cortex, one can understand why hallucinations occur under the influence of specific chemical substances and in certain diseases where neural excitation occurs uncontrolled by voluntary processes. Here again we have to take into account the annotation mechanism. The hallucinatory image is recorded into long-term memory as an episode with the tag of a special state. If the tagging mechanism is impaired, the hallucination becomes embedded in long-term memory as a real event, which leads to distortion of the content of consciousness.

Considering dreams as a form of long-term memory activation, one needs to account for the emergence of synthetic images (images that cannot be reduced to a simple combination of elements from past events). One must recognize that the rewriting of events is embedded in the mechanisms of long-term memory at a subconscious level as a means for creating new images. Once included in long-term memory, these combinations come under voluntary control and are once again written into long-term memory as a product of conscious creativity. If long-term memory were a perfect copy of actual events, new images would be limited to combinations of previously recorded elements. Variability in the recording of events into long-term memory creates the possibility of creativity (i.e., the generation of new images that serve as material for creative solutions). Along with expansion of the image content of long-term memory based on original images, the symbolic base expands, fixing the new content.

An important role in the annotation of contents of long-term memory is played by working memory, the *screen of consciousness*. The entire immense capacity of long-term memory is not accessible to consciousness; only certain portions of long-term memory, those recorded to the *working memory screen*, become conscious. The content of the working memory screen becomes incorporated into long-term memory as new content, as conscious fact. The fact that long-term memory is self-enriched by the participation of working memory suggests that working memory makes its own contribution to the recognition of external stimuli. Such stimuli are represented on the detector map, the screen of working memory; they are fixed in the repository of long-term memory and on the semantic map as well. The working memory screen can accommodate both current perceptions and images from the past. Working memory neurons are located in the prefrontal cortex. They are active through the full duration of the visual image. Their inputs to long-term memory neurons activate a certain portion of the content of past experience.

Now let us consider the language mechanism for naming stimuli. The perception of a stimulus involves its projection onto the working memory screen, which activates the neuron in the semantic map associated with the image. The semantic map determines the categorization of the stimulus and the activation of the command neuron for the speech response. Transformation of the stimulus image into an appropriate verbal response involves *intention neurons*, whose excitation precedes activation of the command neuron for the spoken response. The phase of intention neuron activation allows search through different response variants before the final decision. The variant selected is that of maximal coincidence with the stimulus image.

Another operation that involves interaction among long-term memory, working memory, and semantic memory mechanisms is the selection of objects based on their names. Experimentally, the instruction to the subject specifies a keyword by which he should choose a stimulus presented in the visual field—for example, by pointing at the color designated by the word. The color name, as an element of the semantic map, activates the corresponding subset of long-term memory neurons displayed on the working memory screen. Coincidence of the color name with one of the elements of the working memory screen triggers the command neuron for the act of pointing at the appropriate color sample.

The projection of excitations from the semantic screen to the long-term memory map suggests the following mechanism to be responsible for semantic discrimination. The symbols to be compared are represented by different elements on the long-term memory map. Each symbol activates its own set of neurons on the map. The difference between the long-term memory traces activated by the symbols represents their semantic difference. Support for such a mechanism has been obtained by recording EPs in response to the sudden replacement of one color name in the visual field by another. The negative component of the EP, N180, represents information both about the change in the visual shape of the word and about the semantic difference between the words. Multivariate analysis of the matrix of EPs in response to changes in color names presented on a monitor identifies two spaces: one perceptual, the other semantic. The perceptual space can be represented by a semicircle along which the color names are placed in accord with the lengths of the words. The semantic space is a circle, where the names of the colors are placed in accord with their hue, Newton's circle. This indicates that the color names generate cognitive differences in accord with the contents of two memory domains.

A further operation that involves interaction among the semantic memory, long-term memory, working memory, and detector screens is the identification of a stimulus to match a sample. The sample stimulus is displayed on the working memory screen. It is held in working memory for comparison with different parts of the detector map. Coincidence of the sample with a certain element of the detector screen leads to identification of the stimulus. Instead of the sensory sample one can use its symbolic designation. In that case the symbol activates long-term memory elements, which are displayed on the working memory screen. Coincidence of the sample on the working memory screen with excitation of the corresponding detector allows identification of the target with a specific area of external space. This allows tracking of a target by a series of compensating commands to controllers of the process, in particular to the neurons that control eye and head positions. Such a mechanism can detect the location of a target, designated by a sample or a symbol. The sample is held on the working memory screen and is compared with the contents of the detector map in the same area of the visual field. If the difference is greater than a certain value, an eye movement command follows, and the detector map is moved to another area in the field of vision. If the difference from the sample still exceeds threshold, the detector map shifts again. Coincidence of the sample with an element of the detector map signals identification of the target location.

The semantic map of the positions of symbols, words for example, in accord with the elements of long-term memory is represented mathematically by a spherical surface in n-dimensional space. The semantic differences between symbols are defined by the measured differences between the combinations of long-term memory neurons excited by them. If the combinations for two different symbols coincide, the two symbols are synonymous. The lower the degree of coincidence between the combinations of neuronal excitation evoked by the symbols, the greater the semantic difference. By analogy with perceptual space, semantic space can be reconstructed from a matrix of semantic differences. The semantic space is isomorphic to a certain part of long-term memory space to the extent that the long-term memory space is isomorphic to the perceptual space that determines the contents of the memory. The working memory space is determined by representation of a part of the long-term memory space on its screen.

The neurons of working memory are located in the prefrontal cortex. In the *match-to-sample* task they maintain a spike train throughout the delay between termination of the sample stimulus and onset of the stimulus or set of stimuli to be compared. Some neurons are specialized to preserve a trace of the position of the stimulus in space. Others preserve the trace of the image. Of particular interest, however, are the working memory neurons: they preserve a trace of both the position and the image of the object. Long-term memory neurons for visual neurons are located in the temporal cortex. They are established through learning, have selective reactivity toward specific patterns of stimulation, and preserve those traces chronically. Semantic neurons located in frontal cortex are excited by certain categories of symbolic stimuli generating verbal responses through command neurons.

Studies using positron emission tomography (PET) in combination with fMRI have shown that speech can be generated in two ways. One way is based on well-learned responses; the other involves the conscious choice of a response based on the value of the signal (Posner and Raichle 1994). Automatic responses to words presented visually are mediated by extrastriate visual cortex, insular cortex, and motor cortex. Involvement of Broca's area in the left inferior frontal cortex and Wernicke's area in the left posterior temporal cortex is not necessary. Semantically determined responses, as in the selection of a verb in response to presentation of a noun, involve, in addition to the extrastriate area, Broca's area and Wernicke's area, the anterior cingulate gyrus, and the right cerebellar cortex.

A disadvantage of PET studies is the low temporal resolution of the method. Combining PET with recordings of EPs to verbal stimuli in tasks of varying complexity, however, has revealed that three peaks in the EP relate to semantic encoding. The first peak, with a latency of 200 msec, is maximally expressed in the left inferior frontal cortex, Broca's area. The second peak, with a latency of 700 msec, occurs in the left temporal area, Wernicke's area. The third, "late" component, with latency of 1,000 to 1,500 msec, is localized to the insula, where PET recordings indicate that semantic tasks are associated with decreased blood flow. Thus, the distribution of electrical activity in different brain areas indicates a sequence of localized activities not detected by PET but by EPs in EEG recordings. Analysis of the sequence of activity in different brain structures during the performance of cognitive tasks that involve semantic coding is a new and promising strategy for research on consciousness.

Another relatively new method for the study of consciousness is the combination of structural MRI and fMRI. This method, unlike PET, enables researchers to monitor cerebral activity without the need to inject isotopes and with much greater spatial resolution than PET. The first fMRI studies of loss of consciousness showed a disappearance of activity in cortical areas with the retention of foci of activity in the depths of the brain. Slow-wave sleep, which is associated with slow oscillations of electrical potential and shutdown of consciousness, is also characterized by a shift of activity to deep brain structures, whereas paradoxical sleep, characterized by rapid eye movements, is associated with the same pattern of electrical activity in the cerebral cortex as in the waking brain.

An important kind of symbolic processing is the encoding of numbers. A word such as "color" has a sensory basis and is represented by corresponding traces in long-term memory. Thus, semantic differences between color terms can be represented as the absolute values of vector differences where excitation vectors represent combinations of excitation of long-term memory neurons that are activated top-down by neurons at the semantic level. But what is the sensory basis for the concept "number of objects"?

To answer this question, Nieder and Miller (2004) recorded the responses of individual neurons in the lateral parietal cortex of monkeys as they presented different numbers of circles, between one and five. The circles varied in size, intensity, and position on a computer monitor. Some neurons responsive to the visual stimuli were selectively responsive to the number of objects regardless of size and position. Each detector neuron showed a maximal number of spikes to a specific number of objects—that is, individual neurons produced a maximal response upon presentation of one, two, three, four, or five objects in the visual field. Thus, neurons "computed" the number of objects. Presumably the computing mechanism for number of objects is based on the same principle as that for detectors of line orientation, motion direction, and color: the number of objects is transformed into the selective excitation of a specific *number detector*.

A possible mechanism for the encoding of object number involves neurons with concentric receptive fields of various sizes. The appearance of a point in the concentric receptive field of appropriate size activates the neuron. In this model neurons with concentric receptive fields converge onto a predetector of object number whose activation level is subtracted from a noisy neuron to determine the excitation vector of the object number predetector. The detectors of object number have specific vectors representing the combined weights of their synaptic contacts with predetectors of objects of different sizes and positions. Thus, the detectors respond selectively to the number of objects regardless of size and position.

The symbol for a given number is associated in human memory with a specific number detector. This makes possible bottom-up generation of the symbol (i.e., naming or writing the symbol through appropriate command neurons). Serial presentation of numbers as stimuli activates corresponding traces in long-term memory. The difference between numerical symbols is measured as the difference between absolute values of the excitation vectors of long-term memory that they evoke. The semantic space of numerical symbols is two-dimensional—that is, it is represented by a semicircle on a plane and correlates closely with the perceptual space of object number when objects are displayed on a monitor screen.

Recognizing the principle of object number coding at perceptual and semantic levels enables one to specify more precisely the principle underlying coding differences in perceptual and semantic values at the verbal level. Previously, it was suggested that the activity of an ON/OFF-neuron, which summates the differences, is integrated with the activity of a noisy neuron to produce an excitation vector of predetector differences. This vector is fed to a family of detectors, each of which is selectively tuned to a certain difference value. These detectors are associated with numerical symbols, and, if a difference is established, excitation of a given detector evokes activation of a command neuron, which in turn leads to the naming or writing of the corresponding number.

Thus, the count of the number of objects in the visual field and the scores for perceptual or semantic difference values are realized through similar mechanisms (viz., the association of a numerical symbol with the excitation of a detector that measures the number of objects or the magnitude of the difference). This mechanism is essentially analogous to the measurement of intensity, which occurs first in the intensity detectors and then in the verbal responses. Numerical symbols represent a special case of symbols originating in the count of objects in the visual field.

5.4. EMOTIONS

As mentioned earlier, damage to area V4 of extrastriate visual cortex leads to a loss of color sensation. A patient with a lesion in that area sees only black–white scenes, with the contours of objects and achromatic contrasts remaining unimpaired. Such perception resembles the screen images of a black-and-white television set. It is important to note that damage to the color module of the brain does not affect other modules: the modules for such functions as perception of moving objects, stereoscopic vision, and face recognition remain intact. In terms of the specificity principle of consciousness neurons, the perception of color can be regarded as superimposed on the black-and-white image as the result of activation of a subset of consciousness neurons devoted to the perception of color. From this perspective the black-and-white screen associated with activation of the system of achromatic consciousness neurons operates independently of the system of chromatic consciousness neurons.

This model can be extended to the *emotional coloring* of perceptions. Whereas in color perception the color module composed of color consciousness neurons is located in area V4, a module of consciousness neurons involved in emotional evaluation is located in the amygdala. Emotionally neutral stimuli, like black-and-white colors in color vision, do not activate emotionally selective consciousness neurons, and the percept does not have an emotional component. Only if a stimulus activates those neurons is it emotionally colored. Neurons in the amygdala, it should be noted, are largely associated with the negative emotions of fear and anger. They can be activated not only by the unconditional response mechanism, but also as a result of association of neutral stimuli with events that elicit negative emotions. Thus, a given object acquires emotional coloring as a result of activation of an additional system of consciousness neurons related to the emotions. Bilateral destruction of the amygdala leads to the loss of such emotional coloring just as damage to area V4 results in achromatopsia, the loss of color sensations.

The term *anthropomorphism* means the automatic attribution of human characteristics to a nonhuman object—for example, the attribution of malice to a god, an animal, or a broken computer. Such negative anthropomorphizing turns out to be associated with amygdalar function, which attaches negative emotional coloring not only to social contacts but also to inanimate objects. A patient with bilateral lesions of the amygdala is not able to recognize emotional facial expressions and also does not anthropomorphize. At the same time, based on earlier acquired long-term memory of emotional experiences, he is able to respond correctly to questions about social aspects of behavior. Thus, social evaluations can derive from either of two functional systems: automatic emotional responses involving the amygdala and information derived from long-term memory. With damage to the amygdala automatic evaluation of emotional content is not possible even though verbal evaluation remains intact.

The noradrenergic system of the brain is involved in the fixation of emotionally colored events in episodic memory. The amygdala in turn acts on the hippocampus, which facilitates the recognition of emotionally significant events. Beta-receptor blockade of noradrenergic effects on the amygdala by propranolol prevents the facilitation of recognition of emotionally colored events and words. Presumably this is because the propranolol blockade prevents activation of the amygdala, which in turn prevents its action on the hippocampus.

Positive emotional coloring is associated with activation of the basal ganglia and related basal forebrain and limbic structures. Positive emotional tone can be assisted through meditation or mental training, which can involve the focus of consciousness on a specific function, such as breathing in object-oriented meditation or a generalized blissful state in non–object-oriented meditation. The latter is associated with the cessation of conscious object-oriented concentration. The entire content of consciousness is occupied by a general sense of harmony regardless of whether focus on a concrete object is involved.

These two forms of meditation are associated with different patterns of EEG activity. Object-oriented meditation is accompanied by an increase in theta and alpha rhythms (4 to 7 Hz and 8 to 12 Hz respectively). Non–object-oriented meditation is associated with enhanced, higher-frequency gamma rhythms in the range 24 to 42 Hz. The frequency of oscillation increases with the number of meditation sessions and total time spent in the training. Increased gamma activity is accompanied by distant phase synchronization of oscillations—that is, the waveforms of EEG at widely distributed brain sites are not only similar in frequency but also synchronous. The increase in gamma activity (i.e., the amplitude of oscillation in the gamma frequency range) depends on two factors: the number of elements involved and the degree to which their signals coincide.

Increased gamma activity can reflect qualitative changes in consciousness. To the extent that the role of meditation consists in extension of a blissful effect into the conscious state of daily life, one might expect the background EEG of individuals who practice non–object-oriented meditation to show a more pronounced gamma rhythm compared to those practicing object-oriented meditation. In any case, mood and attention can be regulated and trained.

5.5. SUBJECTIVE MOSAICS

The focal color analyzer transforms the excitation vector of color predetectors representing a section of the visual field into selective activation of one of the color-specific detectors in visual cortex. A group of color-specific detectors, which are connected with a local ensemble of color predetectors, constitutes a local screen of color perception. Other sections of the visual field are represented in other focal color analyzers that operate independently. People can, however, perceive and differentiate between mosaics of color. This suggests that at a certain level the activities of focal color analyzers are integrated with focal spatial features to form color-spatial gestalts.

To explain the emergence of the color-spatial gestalts, let us return to the mechanism underlying the subjective representation of points in external space. This mechanism involves an ensemble of predetector neurons that encode the location of a point, its displacement, its direction, and its proximity to the starting fixation point. The activation of these four spatial predetectors can be represented by excitation vectors of equal length for all points in physical space. Each spatial excitation vector has its own corresponding spatially selective detector, and all of the detectors together are represented on a surface in a four-dimensional hypersphere.

The outputs of focal color-selective detectors and focal spatially selective detectors are integrated at the next level, where color-spatial detectors receive inputs from the four types of color predetectors and four types of spatial predetectors. As a result, each color-spatial detector becomes tuned specifically for a certain color at a certain place in external space. One can think of the detectors receiving eight independent inputs as distributed in an eight-dimensional space. A given combination of color-spatial detectors forms a color mosaic. The next cognitive level apparently involves the classification of different types of mosaic, including predetectors of different types of color mosaics connected with selective gestalt detectors of those types. Thus, the appearance of a color stimulus in different parts of the visual field activates specific configurations of color-spatial detectors, the signal from which arrives at the predetectors of color mosaics and selectively excites a particular gestalt detector, specifying the category of the color mosaic. The dimensionality of the color mosaic space is determined by the limited number of predetectors that enter into their specification, not by the dimensionality of the color-spatial detectors.

Another example of the mosaic structure of consciousness is seen in the perception of lines, which starts with the excitation of line orientation detectors in visual cortex. These detectors receive excitatory input from two predetectors that are activated predominantly by vertical and horizontal lines. Different parts of the visual field are represented by focal orientation analyzers with their predetectors and detectors of orientation. The analyzers operate independently and cannot themselves mediate the formation of visual configurations. That is done by a layer of complex detectors of location and orientation, which receive inputs from four predetectors of location and two predetectors of orientation. These spatial-orientation detectors are conceived to be represented in a six-dimensional space. Their combinations constitute mosaics representing lines of different orientation in different parts of the visual field. These configurations are classified by a limited number of predetectors. The specification of individual configurations is achieved at the level of gestalt detectors, which receive inputs from the limited number of predetectors. The selective excitation of a given gestalt detector specifies a particular type of line configuration. An example of such a mechanism is the perception of human emotional facial expressions (see Section 4.1).

The general principle underlying the perception of color and orientation mosaics consists in the integration of spatial detectors with detectors of color and orientation, respectively. The color-spatial or orientation-spatial detectors provide input to the next level of predetectors, which, in turn, selectively excite the gestalt detectors of different color mosaics or of different line configurations.

6

Varieties of Consciousness

6.1. GLOBAL AND FOCAL CHANGES OF CONSCIOUSNESS

Physical damage to deep structures of the brain, as well as functional disruption of those structures by hypoxia, hypoglycemia, concussion, or any of a variety of drugs, is associated with a global termination of consciousness. The event itself is not perceived and is not registered in memory, images stored in memory are not actualized in awareness, and voluntary actions are absent. A similar termination of consciousness occurs with slow-wave sleep. Specialized *consciousness neurons* are the neural elements whose function is most involved in the global interruption of consciousness when connections with the reticular activating system are disrupted. Neurons that do not belong to the class of consciousness neurons continue to operate and to support vital functions of the organism.

Besides global interruption of consciousness, a focal type of switching off occurs that is related to individual modules involving subsets of consciousness neurons. Such is the case in the achromatopsia associated with damage to color neurons in area V4 of visual cortex. In that condition the consciousness neurons of other modules remain operational. The module of consciousness neurons for recognition of faces is independent of the color recognition module. If it is damaged, recognition of familiar faces is impaired, but other cognitive operations do not suffer. The thalamic reticular system mediates the shifts in attention that strengthen or weaken specific cognitive modules of consciousness neurons.

An important characteristic of focal changes in consciousness is that they are apparently not recognized introspectively as missing when they fall out of consciousness; their locale is filled in by the contents of neighboring parts. Their absence can only be established by special investigation.

The simplest example of focal absence of consciousness is the *blind spot* in the area of the retina occupied by the optic nerve. A pinpoint light stimulus focused on the circular area occupied by the nerve is not detected by the subject. The blind spot can be measured experimentally by means of a retinal perimeter device, which allows focusing such a stimulus at different sites in the retina. The subject does not see light focused there, yet the part of the visual field occupied by that area of the retina is not perceived as empty. Microscopic study of the blind spot in histological sections reveals a total absence of rods and cones. So the blind spot exists histologically in the retina, but it is filled in perceptually, apparently at the cortical level. Similarly, a *scotoma*, a blank spot in the visual field produced by a lesion in the primary visual cortex, is filled in by signals from neighboring areas.

The fillings of the blind spot and of a scotoma by signals from adjacent areas of the visual field are similar. Perceptually, the blind spot is filled in with the visual pattern of the surrounding area. The mechanism of this phenomenon has been studied in monkeys (Komatsu and Murakami 1994). An animal was trained to distinguish between two stimuli, a disk a little larger than the blind spot and an annulus, a disk of the same diameter with a hole in the center. When the animal's direction of view was fixed such that the image of the annulus fell on the blind spot, the animal was unable to distinguish it from the circle projected to an area of the retina outside the blind spot. Because perceptually the center of the annulus was filled in, its outer border was perceived as no different from the circle, and the animal was unable to distinguish the two. Subsequent studies of neuronal activity showed that the blind spot is represented in visual cortex and receives signals, not directly, but indirectly from neighboring parts of the retina.

One must make a distinction between structural and functional scotomas. K. Lashley (1933) described the filling of a *functional scotoma* that occurred during a migraine headache. The scotoma was located near the fovea of the retina, and when in the course of conversation the subject looked to the right of the investigator's face, his face disappeared. This occurred even though the investigator's shoulders and necktie remained clearly visible. In place of the face the subject saw a continuation of stripes from the surrounding wallpaper. A *structural scotoma* is associated with physical damage to the visual cortex. A patient with a lesion in the occipital cortex of one hemisphere who was tested by retinal perimetry did not perceive pinpoint light stimuli in the corresponding half of the visual field. Under normal conditions he was unaware of this impairment. He did not perceive the scotoma as an empty area, because the scotoma was filled by surrounding elements. Thus, he perceived figures that fell partially in the area of the scotoma as whole.

The visual filling effect is universal in the sense that it also is found under normal conditions. It is reasonable to suggest that this effect, so clearly evident in the blind spot and scotomas, also occurs as an overlay against certain backgrounds, not so much as a filling but as an addition (Kanizsa 1974). In both cases signals from neighboring areas are superimposed on a local area of consciousness. Such an extended interpretation of the filling effect is most clearly applicable in the case of illusory contours. White circles with rectangular cutouts displayed against a black background create a darkening effect along the directions of the cutouts. The same filling effect is seen here as darkening along the boundaries of the lines, which leads to perception of a figure as different in shade from the black background on which the white circles with cutouts appear. [*For a complementary illusion with black on white see Fig. 7.1. (Eds.)*] Just as with the blind spot, this effect is connected with the recruitment of additional neurons activated in adjacent areas of the field of vision.

The appearance of scotomas with damage to primary visual cortex, area 17 (V1), indicates that this area is necessary for the perception of localized visual stimuli. But is this area of visual cortex sufficient for their conscious perception? Posing the question in this form returns us to the issue of the mechanism of consciousness: Does perceptual awareness require the involvement of special neuronal structures lying beyond the borders of the primary projection areas of the cerebral cortex? Or is it sufficient to change their functional state—for example, by activating a generator of gamma waves? Another answer to this question is possible: that perceptual awareness requires nonspecific activation of specialized neuronal structures. This answer corresponds essentially to a concept proposed by Moruzzi (1954) with regard to the mechanism of loss of consciousness in slow-wave sleep. His notion was that only neurons that participate in conscious perception are disabled.

Visual deprivation experiments have clarified the issue of the adequacy of activity in the primary projection areas for perceptual awareness. An animal deprived of visual input for a year early in development is practically blind. This is true even though detectors in visual cortex retain a high level of reactivity. A subsequent year of visual experience does not fully establish visual function. Stereopsis is impaired, so the animal does not perceive distant objects and has difficulty in walking and climbing. The neurons that fail to respond to color stimuli after long-term visual deprivation are located not in visual cortex but in area 7 of parietal cortex. If normally 70 percent of neurons in this area respond to visual stimuli, with early deprivation only 1 to 2 percent respond.

Neurons of area 7 can be classified into three groups in terms of responsivity to visual and tactile stimulation: those that respond only to visual stimulation, only to tactile stimulation, or to both types of stimulation. The responses of cells to visual stimuli appear only under waking conditions and are absent under anesthesia. One can only study the receptive fields of visual neurons in parietal cortex in the conscious animal, whereas it is possible to study neurons in visual cortex under anesthesia. This indicates the critical role of nonspecific factors in the responsivity of parietal neurons. The fact that nonspecific input is essential for their activation suggests that their responsivity is associated with consciousness.

Characterization of the receptive fields of neurons in area 7 indicates that they can be divided into two categories: focal, representing an angular area of 3 to 4 degrees in the foveal area of the retina, and extensive, capturing a whole quadrant or even half, usually contralateral, of the visual field. Neurons in visual cortex are "attached" to the retina in the sense that they change their relation to external space when the eyes move. Thus, investigators study their orientation with constant fixation of the line of sight. This is achieved by special training of the animal to maintain a fixed gaze or by curare blockade of neural control of the external ocular muscles. The extensive receptive fields of neurons in the parietal cortex relative to the retina, however, are referenced to a location in external space. When the eye is allowed to move freely, the neuronal response depends upon the location of the stimulus in external space, not on the locus of its projection on the retina. The parietal cortex provides a constant screen on which external space is represented regardless of the direction of gaze. This corresponds to the *spatial constancy* of visual perception. We do not perceive a shift in scene when we move our head and eyes, even though its projection on the retina depends on the position of the eye.

The mechanism of such a constant screen can be explained by the fact that all points in a hemifield of the retina, which are represented in visual cortex, are potentially connected with all spatial constancy neurons. But the connectivity of a specific area of visual cortex with a specific neuron depends upon signals of eye position. One can show the role of eye movements in perceptual constancy using apparatus that projects an image to the same areas of the retina and visual cortex regardless of eye position. With movement of the eyes the stimulus appears to be displaced in the visual field, because the area occupied by the image in area 17 of visual cortex is transmitted to the constancy neurons in area 7 of parietal cortex appropriate to the eye movement.

The parietal cortex contains neurons specifically related to different types of eye movement: pursuit, fixation, and saccadic movements. Saccadic neurons begin firing 0 to 100 msec before the onset of the saccade and thus are related to the command neurons for eye movements. Fixation neurons fire while the stimulus image falls on the fovea, either because the stimulus is unmoving or during visual pursuit. Pursuit neurons are active only during intervals when the eye follows a moving stimulus. The activity of fixation and pursuit neurons is interrupted during saccades. One can conclude that the integration of perception and eye movements takes place in the parietal cortex. With damage to area 7 of the parietal cortex, visual stimuli in the contralateral portion of the visual field are not perceived, a condition referred to as *contralateral visual neglect*. The patient is not aware of the perceptual defect. In contrast to a scotoma, which is related to a retinotopic location, contralateral visual neglect is related to the constant screen representation of coordinates in external space.

Contralateral neglect manifests itself in the drawing of pictures. The patient drawing a clock face reproduces only the half of the image occupying the ipsilateral part of his visual field, ignoring the other half, which is located in the contralateral part of the field. Similar loss of half of images is seen in other situations. The field of consciousness is apparently limited to the ipsilateral field of vision. Contralateral neglect leads to disruption of movements in the direction of objects represented in that part of the visual field.

One can relate the loss of part of the field of awareness to local disruption of more complex processes. Thus, in the prosopagnosia that occurs with focal damage to temporal cortex, there is a loss of the ability to recognize faces while the perception of inanimate objects remains intact. The principle of focal loss is also applicable to the selective disruption of semantic structures, as when a person who speaks several languages loses one language system while others remain totally intact. But the degree of localization of loss of awareness can extend to loss of individual consciousness neurons that is not immediately apparent.

With advanced age conscious function becomes progressively less effective due to a decrease in the density of consciousness neurons. This kind of process is characteristic of Alzheimer's disease, where structural MRI reveals a reduction in the volume of gray matter, particularly in the hippocampus and other parts of the temporal lobes, the frontal and parietal lobes. One can relate the loss of individual consciousness neurons to changes in long-term memory. Such neurons develop from stem cells, which differentiate and individually integrate themselves into a net of surrounding neurons, acquiring contacts on their dendrites from the axons of specific neurons and establishing their own axonal contacts on the dendrites of cells dedicated to specific purposes. The development of consciousness neurons from stem cells under the influence of new combinations of activation by detectors increases the volume of long-term memory (Sokolov and Nezlina 2003a,b).

The localization of changes in consciousness, the turning on and off of awareness, may extend down to the level of individual consciousness neurons. This could explain the temporary forgetting of events, faces, and names. The destruction of consciousness neurons subserving long-term memory leads to irreversible reduction of memory if the neurons are not replaced by new ones. The effectiveness of long-term memory is determined in the mature organism by a balance between two processes: apoptosis, the programmed death of neurons, and neurogenesis, the development of neurons from stem cells.

6.2. SPECIAL STATES OF NEURONS IN GLOBAL AND FOCAL LOSS OF CONSCIOUSNESS

The vector coding of stimuli suggests that a stimulus acts on an ensemble of receptors, which react in different ways because they possess different response characteristics. With the loss of one type of receptors, the excitation vector changes radically and the representation of the stimulus at subsequent levels of analysis is modified. Consider color vision for example. The local color analyzer is represented by three types of receptor, R, B, and G, whose pigments have overlapping response characteristics to light frequency. Correspondingly, their illumination is transformed into a receptor excitation vector that has three components. In certain types of *colorblindness* where one of the three pigments is not expressed, the receptor excitation vector has only two components, which limits color discrimination. This situation applies as well to neuronal ensembles, where the loss of even a single element also leads to limitation of cognitive operations associated with the ensemble. Such a loss of ensemble elements can be either irreversible, as in genetic disorders of color vision, or functional in nature.

The most important cause of functional loss of neurons is local disruption of blood supply to the brain leading to the inability of individual neurons to generate action potentials. The generation of sodium and calcium action potentials depends upon entry into the neuron of the corresponding ions and the development of a depolarization shift in membrane potential. The membrane potential is maintained at an optimal level by a sodium–potassium pump, which transports sodium ions out of the cell and potassium ions in. The operation of the pump requires the expenditure of energy, which is supplied by adenosine triphosphate (ATP) and mediated by the enzyme ATP-ase, and which transfers the sodium and potassium ions across the neuronal membrane against chemical and electrical gradients. The ATP is converted to adenosine diphosphate (ADP), releasing energy in the form of phosphate bonds. The energy supply is regenerated by the conversion of ADP back to ATP in a special cellular organelle, the mitochondrion. Glucose and oxygen are the ultimate sources of energy. They are transported by a network of capillaries that deliver blood to neural tissue. The supply of ATP is limited, so an interruption of the flow of glucose and oxygen leads to functional disruption of the sodium–potassium pump, failure to maintain membrane potentials at optimal levels, and even death of neurons.

The nerve cell, however, has a protective mechanism to avoid loss of its valuable informational function. When a deficit of energy resources occurs, the neuron is able to convert to a *special state* of inactivation of the sodium and potassium channels on which the membrane potential depends. In this state the influx of sodium and the efflux of potassium are limited and energy expenditure of the sodium–potassium pump is correspondingly reduced. Turning off the ionic mechanism of spike generation reduces energy expenditure sufficiently to maintain the membrane potential at a level vital to the cell for an extended period of time. With the cessation of action potentials, however, the cell drops out of the chain of information transmission (Sharova et al. 2006).

The inactivation of potential-dependent sodium channels, which blocks depolarization, has a great impact on the generation of action potentials. The effect of inactivation can be seen in the refractory period (i.e., the period immediately following a spike when the neuron is unable to generate a second action potential). Normally such inactivation is very short. Its prolongation is related to the conformation of the protein that forms the channel, as a result of which the part of the molecule that acts as sensor of the electrical field is blocked and the channel does not open in response to depolarization of the membrane. The sodium channel's return to electrical sensitivity occurs gradually. The greater the number of channels returning to full electrical sensitivity, the greater is the amplitude of the action potential. Thus, the amplitude of microspikes (i.e., action potentials of less than normal amplitude) reflects the number of sodium channels returning to electrical sensitivity.

At higher stages of information processing, the special state leads to loss of consciousness in the form of fainting. With the reestablishment of blood flow, the special state gives way to normal functioning of the potential-dependent channels, the informational function of the neuron is renewed, and consciousness returns. If, however, the interruption of blood flow to the brain continues beyond a certain time and the energy resources necessary to maintain the negative membrane potential are lacking, the neuron begins to undergo irreversible changes, which can lead to its destruction. In that case, even if it is possible to reestablish blood supply to the brain and to preserve the life of the organism, the loss of neurons that support higher cognitive functions leads to irreversible loss of those functions.

The mechanism by which neurons can escape this special state apparently is at work in the gradual reestablishment of function after a concussion, brain trauma, stroke, or the excision of a brain tumor. Physical force applied to the brain converts some neurons of the activating system and of higher levels into the special state in which the informational function is lost and the individual enters a state of coma. The gradual emergence from coma can be explained by recovery beginning with neurons involved at the lowest levels of information processing reestablishing the corresponding mental processes. A model for such a course of events is seen in the response to physical damage of a neuron when it is implanted with a microelectrode. One observes a cessation of spike generation with maintenance of a stable, normal resting potential. Gradually spike activity returns, first in the form of abortive microspikes of reduced amplitude, then as spikes of normal amplitude. A reversible special state can also be induced by an electrical stimulus. All such states are characterized by an interruption of information processing while vital functions remain intact.

The special state plays a role in transitory focal and global changes in consciousness. The maintenance of vital functions, however, requires uninterrupted neuronal activity. Thus, the special conditions are presumed to be characteristic of neurons involved in higher functions that are not directly involved in the maintenance of life. They can play an adaptive role in coma, for example, because shutting them down temporarily allows more economic distribution of resources to neurons directly involved in life-support activities.

Both consciousness neurons and neurons whose activity is not associated with consciousness are susceptible to the special state. While the special state in consciousness neurons is associated with total or partial loss of consciousness, in neurons not directly associated with consciousness impairment may be restricted to other functions.

6.3. FILLING-IN AND ASSIMILATION

One form of change in the content of consciousness, which originates internally at the level of perception, is contrast as a universal mechanism for distinguishing figures from background. Contrast is distributed over complex stimuli. The study of perceptual contrast includes the feature of salience, in which a particular figure, in distinction from others in the background, "catches one's eye." Understanding the mechanism of this perceptual phenomenon provides an entrée to understanding contrast perception at the semantic level. Before proceeding to an analysis of semantic transformations, it is necessary to consider a phenomenon opposite that of contrast: assimilation.

At the perceptual level assimilation represents a general shift in the brightness or color tone of the background under the influence of local areas that differ from it in brightness or color. The background takes on a hint of the coloration of the embedded areas. Thus, assimilation is the precise opposite of contrast, where the background is altered in the direction opposite that of the brightness or color of the embedded areas; if a green disk is presented on a white background, the area around the disk takes on a reddish tone. In assimilation a group of focal green areas leads to light greening of the surrounding white. The degree of assimilation is determined by the number of local areas: the more areas, the more intense the assimilation effect. If one imagines the whole visual field as a screen, one can say that the visual system integrates the inclusions to determine the brightness and color of the background. Especially interesting is the darkening of the background under the influence of black dots.

With regard to assimilation one must consider the concept of the *whole visual field*, or *ganzfeld*, which is that, in addition to local receptive fields, there exist neurons with gigantic visual fields encompassing the entire field of vision. The concept of the whole visual field is based on recordings from neurons at upper levels of the visual hierarchy indicating that the size of the visual field increases progressively to as great as 50 degrees in diameter. Thus, neurons that selectively respond to a face retain their selectivity for the face regardless of where in the visual field it is located (Rolls 2000).

Confirmation that gigantic visual fields exist comes from experiments involving stabilization of images on the retina. With prolonged stabilization of an image on the retina detailed features of the image fade, but without darkening of the field as a whole. Notably, colored images also fade without the background's becoming dark. This suggests that in the visual system the mechanism underlying perception of the whole visual field continues to function even when stabilization of an image on the retina prevents the perception of individual details. Assimilation means that inclusions in the whole field, in addition to their local effects, have the general effect of changing it in the direction of their own characteristics.

How does one unite the focal perceptions of details and their influence on the field of vision as a whole into an internally consistent model? One can postulate, as mentioned above, that the entire field of vision is represented by a neuron with a vast receptive field. Local stimuli falling on this gigantic receptive field are not perceived as separate objects but contribute to a feature of the entire field. Local stimuli are perceived by neurons at lower levels that have focal receptive fields. The total perception is determined by the parallel functioning of consciousness neurons with receptive fields of different sizes. Neurons with focal receptive fields respond to details of the image, and neurons with gigantic receptive fields, by assimilation, determine the background. Thus, assimilation may be thought of as the spreading of characteristics of local stimuli to the entire field of vision, even to areas not stimulated directly.

Here again one must return to consideration of the blind spot. G. von Bekesy (1967), who was well known primarily for his studies of audition, became interested in vision, particularly in the blind spot. He noted that a bright light focused on the blind spot produces a unique effect: the subject does not see the point of light itself but, instead, the entire eye seems illuminated. The same effect occurs with stimulation of the blind spot by focal color stimuli. According to von Bekesy such general illumination is always present but is inhibited by local stimuli. The inhibitory contribution can be demonstrated by directing focal light stimuli simultaneously to the blind spots of the left and right eyes. In this case a person sees a bright spot surrounded by a diffuse light. This can be explained by central inhibition, which creates a single focal percept from two diffuse effects.

Illumination that spreads across the whole field of vision in response to focal light stimulation of the blind spot indicates that the neurons representing the portion of the visual field that it occupies receive signals from neighboring zones. They do not produce focal sensations but, acting on neurons with a comprehensive receptive field, are perceived as general illumination of the visual field. One can hypothesize that assimilation and filling-in of the blind spot and scotoma are all mediated by the same neuronal mechanism.

To explain the essential similarity of these phenomena, let us examine a modification of the retinal model in which it is proposed that each part of the retina is represented by a column of neurons with successively larger concentric receptive fields. The receptive fields have excitatory centers and inhibitory surrounds. Each neuron in the column thereby is tuned to a light stimulus of a particular size. The response of the neuron is determined by the size of the stimulus. If the stimulus is smaller than the excitatory center, the response is weaker. If the stimulus is larger than the excitatory center, the response is inhibited by the inhibitory periphery. Thus, all neurons in the column with excitatory centers that are smaller or larger than the stimulus produce a weaker response. The maximal response occurs in the neuron whose receptive field is optimal for the stimulus. The inhibition of neurons occurs in ascending order from neurons with smaller receptive fields to neurons with larger receptive fields and thus magnifies the selectivity of the optimal response. Furthermore, all neurons with focal receptive fields are interconnected by excitatory connections to the neuron with the comprehensive receptive field. Thus, any local stimulation adds to that of the optimal neuron, stimulating it to some degree and creating the sense of general background illumination. A similar organization applies to columns of neurons with inhibitory centers and excitatory surrounds, which respond to local darkening. Local darkening is associated with generalized darkening of the background. Local responses do not occur in the blind spot or a scotoma, but the background is illuminated or darkened with adjacent areas. A modification of this model consists in the introduction of a neuron with a comprehensive receptive field on which neurons with local receptive fields converge. Another possibility is the introduction of inhibition organized top-down to sharpen local tuning.

Thus, apart from local excitation, focal stimulation contributes to more general excitation through the activity of neurons with comprehensive receptive fields. Areas adjacent to the blind spot and to scotomas fill them in. Under normal conditions this mechanism provides for assimilation (i.e., changes in the background under the influence of local stimuli). Generalizing from the above, one can conclude that the assimilation phenomenon is based on a mechanism similar if not identical to the mechanism of filling in the blind spot and scotomas.

6.4. CONTRAST

A characteristic feature of consciousness is that its content can be transformed by interaction among the elements that contribute to it. The transformation takes place at a subconscious level and its mechanisms are not recognized directly. The product of these mechanisms can be revealed indirectly by special experiments. One clear example of such a change in the content of consciousness is, again, the filling-in of the blind spot and scotomas by stimulation of neighboring parts of the visual field. The filling-in mechanism itself does not enter consciousness. Another example is the phenomenon of illusory contours, which appear as the result of remote effects of local inhomogeneities in the visual field. An illusory contour, one that we do not see directly, enters consciousness, but the mechanism remains subconscious.

In considering subconscious phenomena one must take into account a complex consequence of signal processing. The result at each level of stimulus processing is not sensed; awareness has access only to the final result. Thus, we are not aware of the processes that take place in the columns or the interactions of opponent neurons for color, which are perceived only in the ultimate form of a specific colored image. This accounts for the ineffectiveness of introspection as a means of understanding the contribution of each stage to the ultimate result, which alone is accessible to consciousness.

The fact that a series of intermediate steps in the processing of information is not accessible to consciousness is evidence that consciousness arises in specific neuronal elements that also receive nonspecific, complementary activation. One can attribute to the subconscious all transformations of information that contribute to the content of consciousness but that are inaccessible to it. In a narrow sense the subconscious is a part of long-term memory. At any given moment, only a portion of memory traces are present as objects of awareness in the form of working memory.

Now we shall consider the subconscious in a broader sense. Closely related to the appearance of illusory contours is the contrast perception of a border at the boundary between two parts of the visual field that differ in brightness. The perception of an edge results from an intensification of the difference in brightness. As with an illusory contour we see the edge directly without awareness of the underlying mechanism. The contrast mechanism emerged at an early stage of evolution. Eccentric cells of the compound eye of the horseshoe crab mutually inhibit each other by means of collaterals, the effect known as *lateral inhibition*. As a result the boundary between areas of different brightness is intensified. This occurs because the more brightly illuminated ommatidia exert more intense inhibition than less brightly illuminated ommatidia. The latter in turn exert weaker inhibition on the ommatidia that are more brightly illuminated. A similar mechanism exists in area 17 of human visual cortex where it determines the brightness contrast at the border between two areas of different brightness. If one arranges rectangles in order of ascending brightness, one can show the Mach bands effect: the edge of the darker rectangle appears even darker, while the edge of the adjacent, lighter rectangle appears even lighter. When only one of the rectangles is in the field of vision, this effect disappears.

Contrast occurs, however, not only at boundaries but also at a distance, and in this case is not entirely attributable to lateral inhibition. The contrast transformation of signals involves neurons that "measure" the difference between dark and light fields. The difference signal from these neurons is computed with a particular coefficient as the sum of the signals from the darker and lighter areas. As a result the brightness difference between the areas is accentuated: the dark area appears even darker and the light area even lighter. With attenuation of the contrast mechanism, discrimination sensitivity decreases and the differentiation between even prominent objects becomes more difficult.

The difference is computed separately in the brightness and darkness channels. Thus, in certain impairments of vision the apparent contrast may be different for the light and dark components. With attenuation of the dark channel the perception of dark objects on a light background is impaired more than the perception of light objects against a dark background. This is reflected particularly in the reaction time, which becomes greater for the detection of dark objects than of light objects.

In summary, one can say that conscious perception is supported by a series of mechanisms that mediate the filling-in of scotomas, the appearance of illusory contours, and apparent contrast at a subconscious level.

The contrast mechanism is, however, of more universal significance. It extends to color, motion, stereopsis, and more complex phenomena both at perceptual and semantic levels. At the perceptual level the contrast between images is manifest in the "catches one's eye" phenomenon. If the visual field is occupied predominantly by lines of equal length, thickness, and slope, a line of different slope stands out, or perceptually catches one's eye. If several such lines are concentrated in a particular part of the visual field, they form a perceptually distinguishable field. If the distinctive lines lie along a particular trajectory, the trajectory becomes perceptually salient. Finally, if the lines distinguished by slope form a closed area, then the area is perceived as a figure.

A large homogeneous field composed of lines of a given slope elicits random eye movements. Individual lines of a different slope elicit movements of the eye toward them, which is associated with the attraction of attention to those contrasting elements. The duration of fixation is greater the more complex the pattern. A similar effect occurs with colored dots distinguishable from their background; they also unite into a figure and stand out, or catch one's eye.

A more complex effect, which is close to semantic contrasts, is the salience of Latin letters scattered randomly among a set of letters from the Russian alphabet. Strictly speaking, semantic contrast occurs when, in a sequence of words of the same general meaning, there appears a word from a different subject area. Such a word also catches the eye, but this effect depends on a difference at the semantic level. The mechanism of semantic contrast is similar to that of perceptual contrast except that it involves not gnostic units but semantic neurons.

The universal mechanism of contrast lies in the automatic calculation of differences with the addition of the difference to a limited set of elements salient to the background. This is particularly significant. If the difference is added to a smaller number of salient elements, then, depending on the balance between the numbers of test elements and background elements, one can expect a degree of uncertainty. Either set of elements can appear as figure, the other as ground. Here we come to the issue of ambiguous images. It is reasonable to propose that ambiguous images arise because the difference signal between figure and ground, a measure of contrast, alternately sums with the figure and with the ground. If so, extending the area of background should eliminate the ambiguity in favor of the figure.

With the collection of elementary signs into patterns there arise *local gestalts*, randomly emergent against the background. If one presents two lines with a slope of 45 degrees and two with a slope of 135 degrees they form local patterns, because each line in a pair constitutes an "illusory" continuation of the other. The center of each configuration is perceived as lighter than background. With this comes a change in perceived organization (i.e., in the gestalt), even though the physical stimulation is the same.

It is necessary to distinguish between global and local gestalts. A global gestalt relates to the entire visual field, whereas a local gestalt involves multiple patterns in the visual field. The change from one gestalt to another with no change in sensory input indicates that the perceptual content of consciousness depends greatly on previous experience. The percept can change depending on the portion of past experience it "attracts," although the input stimulus remains as before.

6.5. MASKING

In his seminal article "Masking as a Technical Specialty," B. M. Teplov (2006) formulated the concept of the profound psychological significance of masking. He singled out *selective masking* as the most important form. Selective masking has two functions: to "color out" objects and to reexpress them as exact copies. He emphasized that the task of "protective coloring" is fulfilled not by painting colors onto the object but by selecting points of color and arranging them on the object. This "field decoration" differs in task from representative art in that it requires the production of a copy, sometimes planar, of the object itself.

Teplov illustrated the principle of selective masking in an unpublished manuscript, "The Psychological Bases of Pointillism." He considered the mechanism of spatial blending of colors. He did not address directly the issue of visual masking, but the concepts formulated there serve as the basis for highly practical applications including visual masking. Comparing in a balanced manner "painted surface" and "surface represented by a selection of color points," Teplov made an important observation: an object consisting of spatially distributed points of varying color elements assumes a generalized color. As an example Teplov cited the creative work of French Neoimpressionists who used the technique of applying multiple points of pure colors, *pointillism*. From a certain distance one perceives homogeneously colored areas in the picture and the whole picture assumes a certain "generalized" color. Mosaic art represents another example of pointillistic coloration. The appearance of a common color gives the impression of transparency: the observer sees the image as though through a transparent barrier. Teplov concluded that from a psychological point of view, spatial blending plays a certain role in the perception of pointillistic coloration. The appearance of a common color for individual areas and for the picture as a whole is a result of assimilation. Assimilation is related to neurons at a high level of visual processing that have giant receptive fields and that summate local excitations to create an average color tone.

Teplov further drew attention to a comparison of temporal and spatial blending of colors. The mixing of pigments leads to a reduction in brightness, whereas the spatial mixing of colors results in enhanced brightness. Viewed from a specific distance pointillistic colors either blend or appear distinct, creating a vibrating effect. Another characteristic of pointillistic coloration is the glittering effect, which is similar to vibration but is determined by differences in brightness between local areas.

Finally, as noted above, pointillistic coloration creates an impression of transparency, which is based on the appearance of a common color. The common color problem continues to attract the attention of psychologists even today. The phenomenon is related to that of color assimilation. Local points of a given color distributed on a homogeneously colored field contribute a hint of their own color to that field. The assimilation effect is opposite that of contrast, where a local area of color on a homogeneous field acquires a color opposite that of the background.

Recent studies of assimilation at the neuronal level indicate a connection between it and the filling-in effect. This appears most clearly with the filling-in of the retinal blind spot by signals from neighboring parts of the visual field such that the spot is not subjectively apparent and only the delivery of stimulation directly to the spot reveals its existence. The filling effect involves horizontal connections within the cerebral cortex (Spillmann 1999; Spillmann et al. 2000).

Assimilation involves the spatial blending of colors; even before total blending, the colors of neighboring areas appear more similar to each other. One might postulate that the critical distance for spatial blending of colors is uniquely defined by an angular measure. The blending associated with line elements, however, depends on several factors. The greater the width of the lines and their difference in brightness, as well as the brightness of the blending colors, the greater is the critical distance for the observer to perceive blending.

One observes a difference between the blending of the chromatic and achromatic components of colors. Even after the blending of chromatic components is complete, differences in brightness are noticeable and create the glitter effect. The blending of chromatic colors does not depend on the degree of color difference. Thus, the spatial blending of colors depends more on brightness than on the background color. The apparent brightness in the blending zone is more significant than the physical brightness.

Recent data on the neuronal mechanisms of color vision have made a new contribution to understanding the spatial blending of colors and to the general problem of visual masking. It has been shown that the perceptions of color, shape, motion, and space are mediated by the parallel functioning of modules that form a ventral "what" system and a dorsal "where" system in the posterior cortical areas of the brain. The modules themselves are organized hierarchically. An important feature of the hierarchical organization is enlargement of the receptive field of neurons at higher levels, which enables particular ones of them to respond selectively to complex stimuli occupying the entire field of vision. Neurons at the cognitive level are modulated by the activating systems of the brain and by hippocampal neurons responsive to novelty (Vinogradova 1975).

The portion of the retina occupied by one local color analyzer forms its *perceptive field* (Spillmann 1999). If the term *receptive field* refers to the portion of the receptive surface from which it is possible to elicit the reaction of an individual neuron, then *perceptive field* relates to an ensemble of neurons that participate in the perception. Two stimuli acting simultaneously within the boundaries of a single perceptive field summate to create a new excitation vector and a qualitatively new percept. In the local analyzer, the summated effect of two color stimuli is determined as the sum of their excitation vectors. With a change in stimulus at the input, the excitation vector changes and a different color detector is activated. Thus, a burst from the maximally activated detector codes, or specifies, the input stimulus.

A direct implication of the proposed color coding scheme relates to the temporal and spatial blending of colors. Two color stimuli following one after the other with a short interval generate a single excitation vector as a result of temporal blending of the colors. Similarly, two spatially separated fields of different color fall on a portion of a local perceptive field and summate vectorially to create a new color.

What determines the critical interval for temporal blending of colors? As mentioned above, neuronal studies at the level of the retina show that, in addition to tonic bipolar cells, there exist phasic ON- and OFF-neurons that generate spike volleys with increasing (ON) or decreasing (OFF) excitation of tonic neurons. The discharges of ON- and OFF-neurons summate in ON/OFF-neurons that measure the magnitude of the color difference between the blending color stimuli. As long as discharges of the ON/OFF-neurons reach the detector to specify the color, blending of the colors is not possible. With shortening of the stimuli, the discharge of ON/OFF-neurons disappears and there is a temporal blending of the colors.

The critical distance at which spatial blending of colors occurs depends on *edge neurons*, which measure the brightness of a color gradient and thereby specify a certain portion of the visual field. Filling, which involves distant horizontal connections between color detectors, occurs within its bounds. As a result of spatial color blending, such a limited area is perceived as a homogeneously colored field. Border neurons, described as *edge-polarity neurons* by Ehrenstein and colleagues (2003), are involved in distinguishing figure from ground; they react only to the brightness gradient in the direction of figure to ground.

With masking it is necessary to destroy the boundary that distinguishes figure from ground and to create virtually a different boundary, which produces the impression of a new object. Here the illusory contours of Kanizsa (1974) are of particular interest. Three black circles with triangular cutouts on a white background give the illusion of a white triangle brighter than the background (Fig. 7.1). Neurophysiological studies have shown that in area V2 of monkey visual cortex, there exist neurons that react to the imaginary contour. When the directions of the cutouts are changed, the imaginary triangle disappears, as does the reaction of the subjective contour neuron. Such *contour neurons* contribute to the filling of figures with a homogeneous color that contrasts with the color of the circles responsible for the illusion (Ehrenstein et al. 2003). Contour neurons, by defining the figure and distinguishing it from background, participate in the perception of ambiguous and hidden images. The subjective discrimination of figure from ground is seen in the *pop-out* phenomenon, where the figure suddenly becomes salient. Destroying the boundary of a figure or creating new contours, including illusory contours, can make it difficult to perceive an object. On the other hand, emphasizing the boundaries of a figure contributes to its unmasking.

In conclusion, one can say that the psychology of vision involves some mechanisms that contribute to masking and others that prevent it. Thus, the destruction of the original contour and reduction of contrast between figure and ground contributes to masking, which leads to an increase in the time necessary to identify the object. An imaginary contour and induced contrast create the illusion of a real object. One of the factors in unmasking is movement of the masked object. This occurs because movement activates a special population of neurons, motion detectors.

6.6. SUPERSENSITIVITY

Considering consciousness as an active process that involves filling, assimilation, and contrast, one must recognize humans' exquisite sensitivity of discrimination, which is especially obvious at higher levels of information processing. This *supersensitivity* represents a unique form of filling, which one can think of literally as an embedding of new neurons derived from undifferentiated stem cells. It is proposed that newly formed neurons take their place among earlier elements of the neuronal network where they contribute to an increase in discriminative capability.

Is it possible to distinguish stimuli whose size is smaller than that of a receptor or of a receptive field? A first glance it would appear that such discrimination is impossible. The actual acuity of vision, however, exceeds that computed on the basis of photoreceptor size. What exactly is the mechanism of such supersensitivity?

The answer is to be sought in the principles that underlie the coding of signals in the nervous system. One is the principle of vector coding, which determines the selective reactions of neurons that make up the detector maps representing the signals. In the simplest case the vector corresponds to a signal represented by two coordinates, which are determined by the excitation levels of two neurons with input to a neuronal ensemble. Different stimuli elicit different patterns of excitation in neurons of the ensemble. Thus, each stimulus is represented by a particular excitation vector, or combination of activated neurons in the ensemble. Two stimuli acting simultaneously on a neuronal ensemble activate each neuron in the ensemble in proportion to the sum of the original excitations. This establishes a new combination of activated neurons, a new excitation vector, the components of which are equal to the sum of the original excitations. In this way the sum of stimuli in the nervous system can give rise to a combination of excitations that differs from its physical characteristics.

The vector principle holds for other kinds of receptors. The mechanoreceptor, which detects pressure applied to the skin, can be viewed as a conical surface whose apex is equidistant from all points on the circumference of its base. This surface consists of molecules of a receptor protein that respond to pressure by the opening of ionic channels to generate a receptor potential. The amplitude of the receptor potential depends on the number of molecules of receptor protein subjected to pressure. The magnitude of the reaction to a mechanical stimulus depends on the site of mechanical stimulation: a stimulus applied at the apex of the mechanoreceptor evokes a maximal reaction, while the same stimulus applied at the base evokes a minimal reaction.

Now let us consider the case of two receptor ensembles that are activated by a single stimulus. A combination of excitations, a *receptor excitation vector*, appears in each of them. Suppose them to be two pressure receptors, the spatial characteristics of which are not mixed relative to one another but totally coincide. Let us conduct a thought experiment with regard to the local stimuli. Since the characteristics of the receptors coincide spatially, depending upon the site of stimulation the only percept will be of a change in intensity at that location on the receptor surface. In all cases the excitation vectors coincide in direction. If the tuning characteristics of the receptors to different pressure values are mixed and partially overlap, then with a change in the site of stimulation, the excitation vectors also change to code the spatial location of the stimulus relative to those receptors in the interval where the tuning characteristics of the receptors overlap. The discrimination of spatial location of the stimulus is improved if the difference between the peaks of the spatial characteristics of the receptors is optimally increased. However, if the tuning characteristics of the receptors do not overlap, intermediate positions of the stimulus are not differentiated and the perception jumps from one position to the other. Thus, the overlap of receptors and vector coding enable discrimination of changes in the position of a stimulus that are smaller than either of the receptors. Each position of the stimulus corresponds to its own receptor excitation vector.

The shape of a mechanoreceptor is represented by its cone, the characteristic response function of which is a two-dimensional function with a normal Gaussian distribution. With a shift by a stimulus of constant intensity relative to the center of the receptor, the receptor's response first intensifies, achieves a maximum, and then is reduced, forming a one-dimensional curve. To code uniquely the position of a stimulus in space requires a minimum of three receptors with optimally overlapping response functions. Under those conditions each position of the stimulus corresponds to a three-dimensional receptor excitation vector. A necessary condition is partial overlap of response functions of the three receptors. A shift in the spatial position of a stimulus gives rise to a three-component excitation vector, the length of which represents the summed intensity of the responses of the receptors and the orientation of which codes the position in space. The overlap of receptor response functions means that they form a basis, the vectors of which are not orthogonal or equal in length. This makes it difficult to perform further operations with the vectors, which are based on linear combinations. The next step is transformation to an orthonormal basis where the vectors are orthogonal to one another and equal in length.

The transformation to an orthonormal basis is achieved in the next layer of neurons, relative to the receptor layer, by the assignment of weights to the synaptic connections between the receptors and the neurons. The usual normalization by division of the component into the length of the radius vector sacrifices one degree of freedom. In neural networks normalization is achieved by transformation to a space of higher dimensionality, in this case to a four-dimensional space, by incorporating a *noisy neuron*. Neural nets do not perform quadratic operations with extraction of the quadratic root; instead they operate by algebraic summation. This means a predominance of city-block metrics (i.e., Minkowski metrics with an index of degree equal to one). In city-block metrics the length of a vector equals the sum of the absolute values of its coordinates. The coefficients of connection of three receptors with four neurons are derived in such a way that the sum of excitations of those neurons remains constant regardless of the stimulus acting on the receptor ensemble. The transformation to Euclidean metrics (i.e., to Minkowski metrics with index of degree equal to two) occurs as a result of neuronal adaptation, which is greater the greater the excitation of the neuron. As a result, every mechanical stimulus is reflected as a point on a spherical surface in four-dimensional space. Each point on the hypersphere is represented by four Cartesian coordinates and three angular coordinates with radius-vectors of constant length. Three independent variables representing the excitation of the receptors are transformed into three independent spherical coordinates. Normalization of the vectors is achieved without the loss of an independent variable. The external, physical three-dimensional space is transformed into a spherical neuronal space with three angular coordinates.

How do different excitation vectors activate focal detectors to account for supersensitivity? Before addressing that issue it is necessary to take one further step: to extend the principle of vector coding to synaptic contacts. According to this principle the weights of individual synapses are considered components of a vector of synaptic contacts or, more simply, a *synaptic weights vector*. The lengths of synaptic weights vectors are equal. Let us analyze the case in which the synaptic weights are not plastic (i.e., do not change with repeated activation). The activity of an individual synapse creates in the postsynaptic neuron an elementary postsynaptic potential equal to the product of the intensity of the presynaptic excitation and its effectiveness (i.e., the weighting of the synapse).

The postsynaptic neuron, summating the elementary potentials, generates a complex postsynaptic potential equal to the sum of the products of the presynaptic excitations and the corresponding synaptic weights. In terms of vector coding, this means that the complex postsynaptic potential equals the sum of the pairwise products component of two vectors, the excitation vector and the synaptic weights vector. A description of the operation of the postsynaptic neuron in these terms involves the concept of a scalar product of two vectors. That number equals the product of the lengths of the vectors times the cosine of the angle between them. But the scalar product can be expressed also as the components of the vectors, and in those terms it equals the sum of the pairwise products of their coordinates. Thus, the response of the postsynaptic neuron equals the scalar product of the excitation vector and its synaptic weights vector.

The representation of the neuronal response in terms of the excitation vector and the synaptic weights vector makes it possible to formulate the conditions for selective sensitivity of the detector to its input signal. Since the length of the input excitation vector and the length of the synaptic weights vector of each detector for a given ensemble are constants, the response of the detector is determined only by the cosine of the angle between those vectors. This means that each detector is selectively tuned to a particular excitation vector, namely that which coincides in direction with its synaptic weights vector. A change of stimulus leads to a change in the excitation vector. As a result the detector maximally activated is the detector whose synaptic weights vector coincides in direction with the new excitation vector.

Returning to the issue of supersensitivity, we note that it involves detectors selectively tuned to particular orientations of excitation vectors that change direction with changes in the position of a stimulus in the area of overlapping receptor response characteristics. It is especially important to note that a particular stimulus does not just activate a single neuron but elicits in an ensemble of detectors a profile of excitation with maximum in a specific detector. The detectors are interconnected by lateral inhibition; they inhibit one another more intensely the closer their locations to one another. As a result a stimulus creates a local maximum surrounded by an inhibitory zone. On the detector map this looks like a Mexican sombrero, with a peak of excitation sunken in a broad inhibitory brim.

Consequently, identification of the location of signals with a precision that exceeds the size of the receptor results from the unification of receptors in an ensemble in which the response characteristics of the receptors partially overlap and the different positions of a stimulus correspond to different receptor excitation vectors. Each such vector selectively activates a particular detector that is supersensitive to it.

Supersensitivity is closely related to perceptual learning, a major feature of which is heightened discriminative sensitivity. Progress in perceptual learning is associated with expansion of areas of the cortex as indicated by the emergence of new neurons in the detector map. The formation of synaptic weights vectors occurs under the influence of presynaptic excitation vectors to form new detectors. The new detectors are able to support discrimination of the stimuli involved in the perceptual learning. With restricted sensory flow, the newly formed detectors may undergo programmed death (i.e., apoptosis).

7

The Neurophysiology of Consciousness

7.1. INTROSPECTIVE AND NEUROCONCEPTUAL MODELS OF CONSCIOUSNESS

Consciousness, which exists at several levels, is best characterized by comparison to unconsciousness. Because the neuronal and molecular mechanisms of consciousness are still poorly known, most progress in the description and classification of different forms of consciousness derives from introspection. However, taking for granted the existence of unconsciousness, introspection cannot penetrate the mechanisms of the unconscious. Conclusions as to its contents are based only on the extent to which it "pops out" and becomes a fragment of consciousness. Adamar (1970), illustrating the existence of the unconscious, gives the example of familiar face recognition. The act of conscious recognition is based on the fact that all of the facial characteristics of a familiar individual exist in a unit at the unconscious level to integrate with the image of the person at the moment of recognition. This implies a contribution of unconscious operations that culminate in a single conscious act, recognition.

Consciousness can be divided into *primary consciousness*, the full form that controls voluntary acts, and a peripheral form analogous to the peripheral retina that surrounds the fovea. In *peripheral consciousness* there is preparation for a subsequent act of consciousness. Thus, during the utterance of a phrase under the control of primary consciousness, the continuation of the statement is already present in peripheral consciousness. In addition to peripheral consciousness there is recognized a *preconscious*, a ready set of fragments for use in either peripheral or primary consciousness.

Even the unconscious, however, can be represented in two parts. The first we call *unconscious proper*. We are unaware of the intermediate stages of information processing behind the screen filled with the highest-level results of synthesis. Thus, we perceive a flash of light when signals reach the visual cortex, whereas the physiological excitation of the receptors and afferent neurons is not perceived. Another part of the unconscious is the *subconscious*, where the combining of long-term memory traces takes place. Preliminary selection of combinations appropriate to the dominant trend produced by active processing at the conscious level takes place there. A governing factor in the preliminary selection of combinations at the subconscious level is their degree of novelty. One can think of this by analogy with the orienting reflex, which occurs in response to a new stimulus. If one considers the subconscious to be a reflection of events in memory, a new combination of traces is equivalent to a change of stimulus. Instead of the combination of neural activation and motor components that is evoked in the form of the orienting reflex by an external stimulus, however, only the activation mechanism operates, and a new combination of memory traces is highlighted at the level of the long-term memory screen (Vinogradova 1975).

Not every new combination is appropriate to the problem being solved. An additional mechanism for the selection of suitable combinations is activation, which emerges from the problem as dominant. Here again we can discern an analogy to the orienting response in terms of an amplification of meaningful stimuli. This is similar to the way in which an artificial dominant induced by polarization of an area of the cortex is intensified by weak unrelated stimuli (Rusinov 1987). Another factor in the selection of combinations that occurs at the subconscious level is an aesthetic component (Puankare 1983). Involvement of such a factor is supported by observations from Gestalt psychology where it has been shown that symmetrical figures stand out and are intensified against a background scene of random elements. Possibly a similar process mediates the formation of combinations at the subconscious level.

One can identify introspectively a number of fundamental operations within the realm of consciousness itself. This is primarily the transition from unconscious transformations to recognition of a stimulus as the stimulus becomes fixed in the subconscious and preconscious. Depending on the dominant trends in consciousness, a recognized stimulus can be retained in primary consciousness, moved to peripheral consciousness, or removed from consciousness altogether. It remains in the preconscious as a possible preparation for conscious function. If a conscious fact lies off the trajectory to problem solution, it is held in the subconscious, freeing the conscious from a surfeit of information but at the same time maintaining a reserve of creative combinations. If difficulty is encountered in solving the problem, some subconscious content enters preconsciousness or peripheral consciousness to provide an operational reserve of creative consciousness.

It is apparent from this model of consciousness that the introspective approach is limited. First, it relates to operations that are inherently unconscious, since even peripheral consciousness and the preconscious as well as the subconscious become objects of introspection only to the extent that their content enters primary consciousness. This limitation forces us to turn to objective neurophysiological studies of consciousness while preserving a crucial role for introspection, because only in combination with introspective data are neural mechanisms of value in understanding the mechanisms of consciousness.

Different parts of the introspective consciousness model have been deciphered to varying degrees at the neuronal level. Most advanced are studies at the unconscious level of automatisms and unconscious sensory encoding. The mechanism whereby the ascending activating system of the brain determines the presence or absence of consciousness has been studied in depth. The subconscious level as represented by long-term memory remains relatively inaccessible. Possible guides to its study are provided by advances in the study of working memory. The mechanism whereby integrated scenes are generated is a fundamental question of conscious functioning that also remains an area of great speculation. Noteworthy in currently proposed models is the general lack of mechanisms for symbolic encoding (i.e., the second signaling system). This is because without understanding how integrated scenes are generated, it is hard to imagine the true mechanisms of symbolic encoding, although recent years have seen striking success in this area. From research led by N. P. Bekhtereva it appears to be associated with symbol-specific, *second signal neurons* (Dan'ko et al. 2005).

The attempt to establish a quantitative measure of consciousness is of particular interest with regard to conceptual models. This is the work of W. A. Tiller, a specialist in the area of solid-state and semiconductor physics (Tiller 1997). Based on the fact that consciousness is primarily a feature of the waking brain, he has introduced a quantitative measure of consciousness as a systems property: the brain's channel capacity for information transmission.

A comprehensive analysis of accumulated data, however, forces us to recognize that consciousness is associated with the activity of specific neurons that differ from other neurons. Attempts have been made to link the mechanism of consciousness to intracellular processes in the nerve cell cytoskeleton. According to that hypothesis the microtubules of neurons constitute an intracellular information system in which signals are transmitted by coherent photons (Hagan et al. 1994; Penrose 1994; Penrose et al. 1997).

Studies of the phenomenology of perception represent an approach to consciousness as an object of introspection independent of objective content and brain mechanisms. A representative of the phenomenological school of perceptual psychology is G. Kanizsa. Using a limited number of visual stimulus elements, he developed a great array of perceptual patterns (Ehrenstein et al. 2003). The most widely known are Kanizsa's *illusory contours* (Kanizsa 1974). An example of the induction of an illusory contour is the illusory square (Fig. 7.1). Four black disks with symmetrical cutouts on a white background form the impression of a white square that is lighter than the surrounding white background. The square seems to rest on four circular bases. The contrast between the induced square and the surrounding white background creates the illusion of a contour. Another feature of the square is that its entire surface appears to be uniformly colored, the filling-in effect.

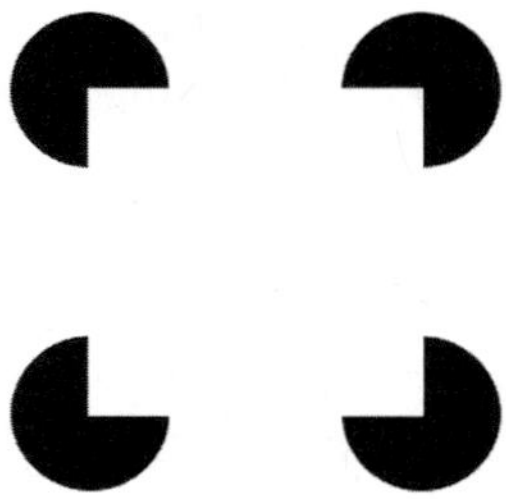

Figure 7.1 Kanizsa square. A white square brighter than the white background appears to rest on four black circles, although in objective reality its brightness is the same as that of the background. (With permission from Grossberg 2004, copyright Lawrence Erlbaum Associates.)

Kanizsa postulated that such perceptual phenomena cannot be explained at the neuronal cell level (Ehrenstein et al. 2003). As early as 1984, however, cells responding to an illusory contour were reported in secondary visual cortex, area 18, which receives signals from primary visual cortex, area 17. Cells in area 17 did not respond to such a contour (Baumgartner et al. 1984). That finding has been confirmed by EP studies in the human (Korshunova 1999).

Progress in the study of neuronal mechanisms of illusory contours has also been achieved in the form of imaginary lines. If two black circles on a white background have opposed rectangular cutouts, a white stripe lighter than the surrounding background appears to join them. The stripe appears to rest on two round black bases, which it partially overlaps. Such an illusory line allows one to conduct experiments similar to experiments with real lines. First, using real lines of optimal length, the size of the receptive field of a neuron in area V2 of visual cortex is determined. When the illusory line was presented to the receptive field of the same neuron, the cell responded to the illusory line even though in actuality no signal was delivered to that area. The interpretation of this finding is that in addition to its basic, local receptive field, the neuron has a global receptive field. The lines defining the rectangles within the black circles are real stripes in the global receptive field and activate it, causing the discharge of the neuron during presentation of the stimulus (Ehrenstein et al. 2003). Thus, this illusory contour can be regarded as resulting from activation of the global receptive field of the neuron by partial line segments.

The uniformity of luminance within the illusory square and the illusory stripe is more difficult to explain. These effects are associated with assimilation, where signals from the illusory contour conveyed by horizontal cortical connections induce an image of the area bounded by it (Ehrenstein et al. 2003). A more detailed description of the interaction between boundary neurons and surface neurons is contained in reports by Grossberg (2004). He develops a theory of complementarity of neuronal operations. A special case of this theory is the complementarity of border detection and the formation of a visually perceived surface area. It is known that three channels of information flow from the retina to the LGB. A magnocellular channel (M pathway) transmits signals that determine the perception of motion; a parvocellular channel (small-cell or P pathway) determines the perception of color and form; and a koniocellular channel (K pathway) is involved in color encoding. Signals from each eye arrive at independent layers of LGB. Inferior layers 1 and 2 represent the M pathway. The upper layers, 3, 4, 5, and 6, belong to the P pathway. The K pathway is represented by the intralaminar layers between the M and P layers. Axons of M, P, and K neurons arriving in primary visual cortex, area V1, project to groups of neurons characterized by high concentrations of cytochrome oxidase, a sign of high metabolic activity. At the histological level, blobs of high metabolic activity alternate with areas of low cytochrome oxidase concentration. Neurons originating in the blobs of area V1 transmit signals to area V2 neurons, which also have a high concentration of cytochrome oxidase. There the M neurons aggregate in wide stripes and the P neurons form narrow stripes. Axons from the wide-stripe neurons project to area V5, the area involved in the perception of motion, and the narrow-stripe neurons project to area V4, the area involved in color perception. The neurons in the parts of V1 that lie between the blobs of high cytochrome oxidase activity project to areas between the stripes of V2.

According to Grossberg, neurons with low metabolic activity encode borders through the following pathway: LGB → areas between the blobs of area V1 → areas between the stripes of V2 → area V4. The coding of surfaces is performed by cells with high metabolic activity through the pathway: LGB → blobs in area V1 → narrow stripes in area V2 → area V4. Thus, the channel leading to identification of borders and the channel mediating perception of filled surfaces form complementary systems. Kanizsa's illusory square (Fig. 7.1) represents the conscious correlate of activity in such complementary systems. The borders are induced by the cutout areas of the black disks. Through the surface-filling channel, local brightness contrast occurs in the areas of induced borders. The filling of the square can be thought of as a diffusion process that starts from the borders and covers the whole area of the square (Grossberg 2004). This process involves horizontal cortical connections similar to the collaterals of long axons that are responsible for filling the blind spot and scotomas.

7.2. REENTRY

The term *reentry* was introduced by J. Edelman (1987, 2003) to explain the transformation of sensory activation into conscious perception (see Fig. 4.1). The essence of this concept, which was proposed earlier by A. M. Ivanitskiy and colleagues (1984), is that excitation of a cortical projection area proceeds to cortical association areas, and thence to the hippocampus, to the hypothalamus, and back to the cortical projection area. As a result, sensory information is enriched by integration with memory content and acquires the quality of conscious perception. Reentry is not a means of error calculation. Its function is strictly enrichment of the sensory flow with the accumulated experience of the individual. Passage of the signals through the reentry circuit is associated with an increase in the latency of conscious perception and allows retention of the recognized image in working memory due to activation of neurons in the prefrontal cortex.

The function of image retention mediated by neurons in prefrontal cortex is revealed in delayed-response experiments. In the delayed-response paradigm a subject is presented with two stimuli separated by a 15-second interval. He should respond to the second stimulus only if he perceives it as identical to the first. Retention of the first stimulus trace is associated with continuous spike discharges of certain neurons in prefrontal cortex throughout the delay interval. Activation of another closed circuit, Papez's circuit in the limbic system, has been proposed as a mechanism for the emotional coloring of events (Papez 1937). Reverberation in a thalamocortical circuit plays an important role in maintaining the state of active wakefulness.

Pyramidal neurons in the cortex, with axons that descend into the depths of the brain, together with afferent neurons constitute the structural basis for multiple parallel reverberating systems. A striking feature of the layered cerebral cortex is that the number of axons at the output is five times greater than at the input. A corticofugal system projects to the thalamus, striatum, midbrain, pons, and spinal cord. One should also include the corticocortical projections. A portion of the descending fibers is involved in motor control, including movements of the sensory organs themselves. Another portion projects to the cortical afferents that feed the cortical areas from which the descending fibers originate. The clearest example of overlap in the topography of ascending and descending systems is seen in the thalamocortical and corticothalamic systems. The pyramidal cells that give rise to descending pathways to specific thalamic nuclei are located in layer VI. Pyramidal cells in layer V project to motor nuclei in the tectum. All axons exiting the cortex are excitatory. Their primary mediator is glutamate. The corticothalamic projections provide the reentry link in the thalamo–cortico–thalamic circuits.

One example of reentry is a corticothalamic feedback projection (Jasper 1949), which has been studied in detail by R. R. Llinas (1998). The resonant frequency of the circuit between cortical pyramidal cells and neurons of the specific thalamus is in the gamma range of EEG rhythms (≥35 Hz). This intensifies the response of cortical detectors, increasing their selectivity with respect to the stimulus by augmenting activation that comes from nonspecific thalamic nuclei. Nonspecific input shifts the membrane potential of thalamic neurons in the direction of depolarization, and there emerges the high-frequency gamma rhythm that underlies resonance enhancement of the sensory signal. Nonspecific activation evoked by the stimulus in neurons of the thalamic reticular nuclei is necessary for generation of the gamma rhythm. Thus, the onset of gamma oscillations coincides with the onset of the depolarizing shift, which is determined by resetting of the alpha wave (8 to 12 Hz). The external signal is digitized by the frequency of the alpha rhythm. Within a single time slice there occurs one conscious perception. Two stimuli falling in one time slice merge into a single percept, or, if the two components are of different intensities, the more intensive stimulus masks the weaker.

The descending corticofugal system, however, addressed to the thalamic afferents, has an even more general function as the substrate of reentry. The stimulus can again activate the thalamic afferents, establishing a cyclical mechanism for strengthening the afferent flow. The principle of excitatory reentry can extend to a longer chaining of events: sensory cortex → association cortex → hippocampus → sensory cortex. According to Ivanitskiy, the re-excitation of sensory cortex by signals from the hippocampal system is the mechanism underlying consciousness (Ivanitskiy 2005; Ivanitskiy et al. 1984). Edelman (2003) also emphasizes the role of reentry in consciousness. The involvement of the hippocampus in cyclical excitation allows comparison of the input signal with the contents of memory. And a similar reentry model emphasizing the cyclical mechanism of consciousness has been proposed by V. Y. Sergin (1998).

One should not lose sight of the contribution of nonspecific activation to reentry as the primary mechanism mediating consciousness. Such activation is a parallel form of cortical activation, which is delayed relative to the specific excitation. A further mechanism of re-excitation has been revealed in studies of working memory, the content of which is transmitted to the primary cortical projections, strengthening the input signals represented in working memory.

Combining the major reentry circuits into a general scheme, one sees that cortical projection neurons receive sensory flow from the thalamus. That flow is enhanced by descending excitation at the gamma-oscillation frequency. The onset and maintenance of gamma oscillation is supplemented by nonspecific activation. The sensory stream reaches working memory neurons in prefrontal cortex. Working memory contains preparatory "blanks" for the expected signals in the form of self-supporting excitation of neurons in prefrontal cortex. Reentry from those neurons to neurons in sensory cortex intensifies the activity of neurons whose excitation coincides with that of the neurons in working memory. Thus, the first cascade of intensification mediated by the nonspecific system identifies significant stimuli, and the second amplifying cascade mediated by descending pathways from the prefrontal cortex accentuates the signals most probable in the given situation. In this model of consciousness several processes are organically combined: nonspecific activation, gamma-rhythm generation, and two basic reentry circuits, one involving the thalamus and one the prefrontal cortex. Nonspecific activation is a necessary condition for the functioning of this consciousness mechanism. That is why switching off the nonspecific activating system leads to global loss of consciousness. Local fallouts of consciousness occur as the result of local breakdowns in connections between the nonspecific and specific systems.

There are several reentry mechanisms. One is the circuit of excitation between specific sensory cortical areas and the prefrontal area. Studies of the frequency-specific gamma rhythm in the range of 30 to 75 Hz using equivalent current dipole localization have shown that during active attention an acoustic stimulus induces activation first in the prefrontal cortex. The excitatory focus moves to auditory cortex and then returns to the prefrontal region. The estimated locations of the generator of the frequency-selective gamma rhythm and of the positions of equivalent dipoles were projected onto a map of the subject's brain obtained by MRI. It was found that such a cycle typically occurs four times during the 100 ms after termination of the acoustic stimulus (Danilova 2006).

What is the function of this gamma-activity cycle? It is reasonable to assume that the signal from prefrontal cortex to auditory cortex provides sensory facilitation. The appearance of activation first in prefrontal cortex and then in the auditory area is probably explained by the fact that the sound stimuli were presented at constant intervals, which creates conditions for the development of sensitization in the prefrontal cortex. Frontal cortex is where the *expectancy wave*, or contingent negative variation, was first recorded (Walter et al. 1964). The expectancy wave is observed at a constant interval between an alerting, conditional stimulus and the imperative stimulus for a delayed response (Walter 1963).

Participation of the orbital prefrontal cortex in facilitating recognition of visual stimuli has been shown in experiments carried out in the laboratory of E. Halgren (Bar et al. 2006). Studies involving a combination of magnetic encephalography (MEG), which provides recordings with high temporal resolution, and fMRI, which provides high spatial resolution, have shown that a visual stimulus first activates the primary visual cortex. Low spatial frequencies in a visual image excite only the orbitofrontal cortex. From orbitofrontal cortex the signal passes to the fusiform area of the temporal lobe. The fusiform area is responsible for the perception of objects and receives direct input from primary visual cortex via the ventral visuocortical pathway. The function of the orbital cortex is to facilitate recognition (Fig. 7.2). Its clearest role in perception has to do with difficulties in the process of recognition. It is important to note that activation of the orbital cortex occurs before the fusiform area receives signals from the primary visual cortex. Presumably, this anticipatory excitation of the orbital cortex is achieved via the rapidly conducting dorsal magnocellular pathway.

It is reasonable to propose that reentry activates consciousness neurons that can only be switched on by a combination of direct excitation and re-excitation.

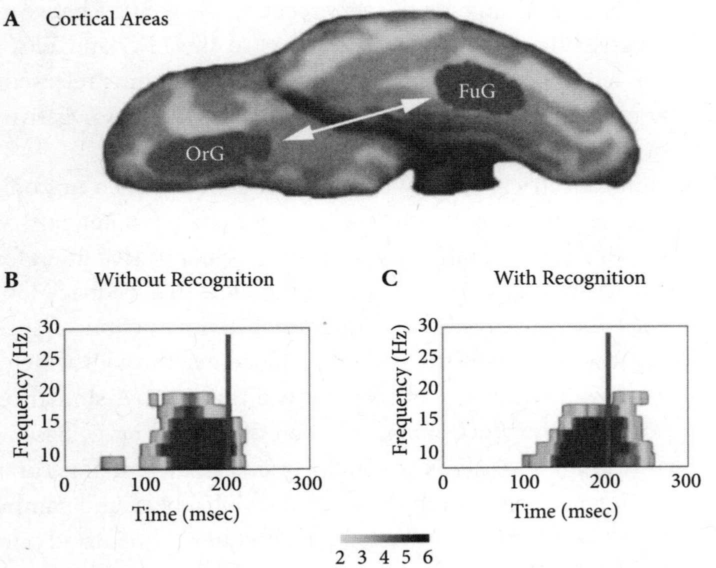

Figure 7.2 A visually perceived object elicits phase-locked electrical activity in the orbital gyri (OrG) and the fusiform gyrus (FuG). (**A**) Representative locations of OrG and FuG on ventral surface of hemisphere; (**B**) phase-lock statistics for trials in which objects were not recognized; (**C**) phase-lock statistics for trials in which objects were recognized. If the object is recognized, the phase-lock continues 40 msec longer than if it is not recognized. (With permission, modified from Bar et al. 2006, copyright National Academy of Sciences, U.S.A.)

Thus, the concepts of consciousness neurons and of reentry circuits in which they are embedded are quite consistent.

7.3. CONSCIOUSNESS AND RHYTHMIC BRAIN ACTIVITY

The reentry concept relates to the mechanism of rhythmic brain activity, particularly as expressed in background EEG and EPs. Studies of EPs in response to sudden stimulus changes have shown that there exist neurons in the cortex that measure the difference between stimuli with regard to a number of features. The number of spikes in the difference discharge of such a neuron is greater the greater the difference between the stimuli. One can assume that these *difference neurons* are also activated by reentry.

It has also been shown that the number of spikes in a difference discharge correlates positively with the amplitude of the accompanying EP. This suggests that the background EEG is formed by series of EPs that occur with each reentry. Thus, the background EEG reflects cycles of excitation in neuronal circuits that generate difference discharges with every reentry. The relation between the difference discharges of neurons, negative peaks in the EEG and EPs, is determined by the fact that during spike discharges potassium is released into the intercellular medium. The depolarization of glial cells creates negative peaks in the waves of the background EEG.

The rhythmic electrical activity of the brain is determined not only by circulating impulses but also by endogenous pacemaker potentials, which in combination with a certain repetition rate of postsynaptic potentials form a *resonant filter*. Thalamocortical connections contribute to a feedback loop, which plays a special role in this filtering function. The interaction of specific and nonspecific pathways makes the thalamus the center through which individual cortical areas can influence other areas (Llinas 1998). A similar resonance interpretation of brain functioning has been developed by E. Basar and colleagues (Basar 1998). Basar looks upon the brain as a system of natural resonators representing oscillators in the delta, theta, alpha, beta, and gamma bands. These oscillators provide the mechanism for a frequency-mediated information system. Frequency-specific information coding is performed by endogenous oscillators.

An analogous example is the mechanism governing the cardiac rhythm. When sympathetic and parasympathetic influences are blocked, the frequency is determined primarily by the frequency of pacemaker oscillations in cells of the sinoatrial node. Normally the pacemaker frequency is modulated by parasympathetic afferents that mediate respiratory arrhythmia and sympathetic afferents that mediate the effect of oscillations in blood pressure, as well as by temperature and metabolic oscillations. The combined effects of these oscillators regulate cardiac rhythmicity and can be isolated by spectral analysis. Factor analysis of cardiac rhythm spectra reveals three oscillators distributed in the frequency domain. The contributions of the oscillators can be represented as excitation vectors associated with different functional states (Danilova 1998).

The EEG can also be dominated by different frequencies. Oscillations in the range of 18 to 35 Hz (beta band) and 40 to 120 Hz (gamma band) appear in the human EEG in response to contrast stimuli. A part of the gamma oscillation is linked in phase to the external stimulus. The gamma rhythm is subject to modulation by system-specific neurotransmitters. Thus, gamma oscillation is activated by increases in Ca^{2+} conductance under the control of NMDA receptors. This effect is enhanced by cholinergic input from cortical and subcortical sources. Intensification of gamma oscillations also occurs in the hippocampus in response to GABA-receptor antagonists. The universality of gamma oscillations suggests the existence of a parallel frequency-modulating coding system (Loizzo and Sannita 1998).

The involvement of gamma oscillations in cognitive processes is clearly demonstrated in the case of somatosensory hallucinations. Strange somatosensory sensations that begin in the neck and temple of a patient and then spread through the body to the abdomen and the limbs have been found to be associated with changes in the EEG. Frequency analysis of the EEG showed gamma oscillations in the 35- to 70-Hz range, with amplitudes reaching 40 to 200 mV during the hallucinations. The oscillations were particularly pronounced in the right central frontal and parietal regions. The stability of the focus of activation made it possible to localize the equivalent dipole of gamma oscillations and to map it onto an MRI of the patient's brain. It was located in areas of primary and secondary somatosensory cortex. The dipole locus in the right hemisphere corresponded to somatosensory hallucinations on the left side of the body. Thus, the intensification of gamma oscillations in a local area of cortex can transform subliminal somatosensory excitation into a supraliminal, conscious somatosensory hallucination.

Oscillations in the frequency range of 8 to 12 Hz are classified as occipital (alpha rhythm of the visual cortex), motor (mu rhythm), and temporal (tau rhythm), depending on the cortical location from which they are recorded. An additional rhythm recorded by MEG and designated sigma rhythm has been reported from secondary somatosensory cortex. Unlike the mu rhythm, which is suppressed during the performance of a movement, the sigma rhythm is suppressed during tactile stimulation. With rhythmic somatosensory stimulation at the same frequency as the endogenous rhythm, 8 to 9 Hz, the response is intensified, just as with rhythmic visual stimulation. Even an individual stimulus evokes a series of oscillations. Within each cortical area one can detect more restricted localization of alpha-like rhythms. This is particularly evident with respect to the mu rhythm, which is most suppressed in that part of the motor cortex where the performed movement is represented.

In considering rhythmic activation of the brain, one should not overlook the role of specialized nerve cells in the encoding of information. Such cells include detector neurons that are selectively tuned to specific stimulus features and gnostic units that are selectively responsive to certain stimulus complexes, gestalts. These selectively responsive cells form neuronal maps on which stimuli are represented by neurons in specific locations. The selective responses of detectors and gnostic units depend in turn on monotonic predetector neurons.

Recall that in the study of color vision it was found that stimuli of different spectral composition are represented in the nervous system by combinations of activated predetector neurons, which are formally modeled as excitation vectors. Subjective color differences are defined by the distances between the terminations of the vectors that represent the colors. The same kind of vector encoding is found in perceptual processing of emotional facial expressions and vocal intonation.

How does one combine the principle of vector coding with frequency-specific signal amplification? One must consider the frequency-specific responses of each individual predetector neuron. It is possible that the selective tuning of detectors increases to the extent that the frequency of synaptic activation matches the frequency of endogenous pacemaker activity of a given detector. In other words, the specificity of sensation depends on the coincidence of the predetector excitation vector with the synaptic weights vector of the detector, and its intensity depends on the amplitude of high-frequency tuning of the neuronal channel, which in turn is determined by resonance between the frequency of synaptic activity and the frequency of the endogenous pacemaker. So, returning to the somatosensory hallucination in which the EEG was characterized by a high-amplitude gamma rhythm, it is necessary to emphasize that its specificity is determined by the anatomic location and strength of the gamma rhythm (i.e., by the amplitude of the gamma rhythm in a given focal area of the cerebral cortex).

With the transition from gamma frequencies to the alpha-like frequencies of calm wakefulness, the dominance of local processes is reduced in favor of scanning the sensory cortex in "survey" mode. The depolarizing phase of alpha-like fluctuations creates sequential pre-excitations of cortical neurons providing conditions for conscious functioning. The alpha-like rhythm fulfills the function of sequentially scanning the scene with the focus of attention. When a new element appears on the scene, the scanning is interrupted in a narrower or wider area, as evidenced by a local or more generalized suppression of alpha-like oscillations. The area of focal suppression is determined by specific features of the stimulus. The degree of generalized suppression depends on the novelty, intensity, and biological significance of the stimulus.

An original theory of the relation of rhythmic brain activity to the state of consciousness has been set forth by T. and M. Sewards (Sewards and Sewards 1999). The essence of their proposal is that consciousness is associated with both alpha and gamma oscillations. The rhythms are correlated, but the alpha rhythm derives from a parvocellular system and the gamma rhythm from a magnocellular system. The frequency of gamma rhythms in neurons representing a part of the visual scene is three times higher than the alpha-rhythm frequency. The authors consider a sensory event of consciousness to be a percept in the form of a visual scene. The triggering of a conscious percept requires integration of data from individual detector maps (e.g., of motion, color, and shape). One can assume that this unification is achieved by synchronizing the activities of the neurons that detect different aspects of visual stimulation. The gamma rhythm is most evident in responses to moving stimuli. The Sewards suggest that moving objects, which are detected by the magnocellular system, evoke the gamma rhythm there. The parvocellular system, which detects static objects, gives rise to alpha activity. The gamma and alpha rhythms show a phasic correlation. It is suggested that gamma synchronization occurs over short distances and that alpha synchronization occurs over large distances. The authors argue that moving objects evoke phasic synchronization in both the gamma and alpha bands, whereas static objects evoke synchronization only in the alpha range. Therefore, perception of a static scene is associated with alpha oscillations.

These statements are valid when the eyes are immobile. When the eyes move, however, both the alpha and the gamma rhythms appear. The role of synchronization is to create as a conscious event a single percept from the simultaneous activities of neurons located in different parts of the cortex. In considering the involvement of gamma and alpha rhythms in the acts of consciousness, it is important to recognize that the rhythms themselves do not contain information, but by phase synchronization they increase the effectiveness of stimulus processing.

How does phasic synchronization come about? At least two mechanisms are known: by means of synaptic connections between neurons and by means of endogenous oscillators that are triggered by an incoming stimulus and synchronized in phase. Under normal conditions the result of synchronization is intensification of the response at a given frequency. The synchronized neurons constitute a *functional ensemble* representing a part of a scene.

Let us consider the relationship of rhythmic activity to neuronal specificity by comparing frequency coding and detector coding. We begin with *frequency coding* as represented in the work of E. Basar (1998). The relationship between mental processes and the electrical activity of the brain is addressed by Basar within the framework of synergetics, a multidisciplinary approach that unites the study of coherent processes in lasers, cooperative processes in neuronal networks, transformations of gestalts and cognitive structures, as well as such social phenomena as the formation of public opinion. Briefly, the proposed solution to the problem of neural codes is that they are oscillations of different frequencies. The frequencies are analogous to letters of the alphabet. Arising sequentially in time, they combine to form a "word" that serves as the password for selective activation of neuronal structures. The principle of frequency coding is particularly clear in the consideration of gnostic units, which Basar attributes to *resonating frequencies* when, in response to a certain sequence of different frequencies, not one gnostic neuron but a combination of neuronal ensembles scattered through the brain are united into a single cognitive process.

The study of neuronal mechanisms mediating the analysis of external stimuli within the framework of detector theory is reasonably advanced at this point; however, questions remain as to the neuronal mechanisms of perceptual synthesis. Konorski's (1967) introduction of the concept of gnostic units was based on the discovery of neurons selectively responsive to certain facial expressions of emotion. The mechanism whereby the elementary attributes of stimuli are integrated to create a conscious percept remains unexplored. The study of frequency coding offers a promising approach to that issue. The concepts of gnostic units and frequency codes are not inherently contradictory. Frequency coding is a possible mediating factor in the selective excitation of gnostic units.

How might one integrate the findings from studies of rhythmic activity with the neuronal detector model? One needs to take into account the endogenous activity of neurons in the form of pacemaker potentials, which in effect makes the neurons operate within certain frequency bands. Detector maps are determined by the detector units that receive inputs from the receptors processed through predetector neurons. A combination of predetector excitations creates an excitation vector that, acting on all detectors of the detector map, creates an excitation profile with maximum at one of the detectors. Thus, a vector code is converted into a spatial code that represents the stimulus by the position of maximal excitation on the detector map. The frequency of the pacemaker potential determines the effectiveness of selective excitation among the detectors.

7.4. THE GAMMA RHYTHM AND CONSCIOUSNESS

The gamma rhythm plays an essential role in cognitive processing (Dumenko 2002). One way to explore this connection is by analysis of the EEG during complex cognitive activity. For example, perceptual complexity can be induced through the use of Kanizsa's illusory contours (Kanizsa 1974; see Fig. 7.1).

Functional MRI studies have shown that the perception of stimuli with illusory contours involves special areas of the visual cortex. Illusory contours in a stimulus also make a particular contribution to the form of visual EPs, suggesting that the perceptual response involves specific groups of neurons (Korshunova 1999). EEGs recorded during the perception of Kanizsa figures with illusory contours exhibit gamma oscillations in the frequency range of 70 to 80 Hz, which are localized to the occipital region. Kanizsa figures without illusory contours also evoke gamma oscillations, but in the frequency range of 35 to 40 Hz under electrodes located in the range of N1-P2 over cortex either side of the longitudinal fissure.

The illusory contour paradigm is of great interest because it suggests the involvement of additional neuronal channels in percept formation. The extra channels are activated not by the direct sensory effects of objects in the field of vision, but indirectly by signals coming from other parts of the image. An interesting feature of this process is that in a roundabout way channels are activated that are similar to those activated directly. Thus, four black circles with horizontally and vertically oriented rectangular cutouts on a white background create the illusion of a square whose outline is determined by the orientation of the cutouts and that is whiter than the background. The mechanism of this illusion is apparently that the predetectors of orientation of the cutout areas activate unidirectional detectors even though the real stimuli that would excite them are absent. Activation of those detectors creates a new, square gestalt that is whiter than the surrounding background.

Another variant of complex cognitive processing involved contrast stimuli. The stimuli were patterns of vertical or horizontal light and dark stripes in which the intensity of adjacent dark and light stripes was modulated sinusoidally. Presentation of such stimuli resulted in two bursts of gamma oscillation coinciding with EP waves P100 and P300. The P100 wave occurred with gamma oscillations that were synchronous with the stimulation frequency predominantly in the occipital area; the P300 wave coincided with a central gamma rhythm that was not in phase with the stimulus. Thus, gamma oscillations in phase with the stimulus occur in the primary projection areas and oscillations out of phase with the stimulus appear in the association areas. This is presumably because gamma oscillations in the association areas are not driven directly by the stimulus but indirectly and with various delays. Thus, gamma oscillations occur in connection with the primary visual perception and also with a later stage of cognitive processing.

What is the mechanism whereby gamma oscillations enhance the perception of stimuli? Since gamma oscillations are associated with high-frequency spike discharges followed by increased efficacy of synaptic transmission, the most probable mechanism is posttetanic potentiation. Thus, neuronal pathways in which gamma oscillations occur show increased responsivity. The higher the frequency of gamma oscillations, the greater is the posttetanic potentiation and the more intense the excitation induced in the postsynaptic neuron. This mechanism of enhancement of synaptic transmission has been investigated by T. A. Palikhova (Sokolov and Palikhova 1999).

Palikhova studied synapses of sensory neurons on command neurons in the mollusk. After a series of action potentials evoked in the sensory neuron by intracellular electrical stimulation, the amplitude of the elementary excitatory postsynaptic potential (EPSP) evoked by a single action potential in the command neuron increased in amplitude. A feature of posttetanic potentiation is that during a high-frequency train of action potentials, suppression of postsynaptic potentials occurs. The amplification effect emerges only after a period of time. Thus, the most effective way to induce posttetanic potentiation is to trigger spikes in trains with optimal intervals between trains. Of interest in this regard are the inherent neural modulating mechanisms that produce the rhythmic bursts of spikes alternating with periods of inactivity that are optimal for posttetanic potentiation. The slow oscillations in cell potential that modulate spike activity in the brain provide a mechanism for the posttetanic potentiating effect.

This mechanism, which is associated with the gamma rhythm, may be involved in active attention. Predicting the future position of a target stimulus facilitates its detection and reduces the time required for the sensorimotor reaction. In experimental settings an instruction given to the subject on the one hand leads to general nonspecific activation and on the other creates a selective resonance between the cortical representation of the target position in working memory and the corresponding channel of nonspecific activation. When the target appears in the expected location, resonant enhancement of gamma oscillations occurs with additional activation of neurons in that area of the visual field. In other words, estimation of the future target position in space enhances the activity of local detectors, which is experienced subjectively as a voluntary act of attention.

This mechanism is dependent upon the retinotopic organization of neurons in the visual cortex. The same principle, however, can be extended to any of the detector maps, for example, with the coding of intensity in a local portion of the visual analyzer. A stimulus of a given intensity evokes maximal excitation in a particular region of the intensity detector map in the same way that stimulation of a certain area of the retina evokes maximal excitation at a particular location in the retinotopic map. Now, if the subject is given an instruction to respond to stimuli of a given intensity, the gamma-resonance mechanism increases excitation of the intensity detector that corresponds to the intensity designated in the instruction. When stimuli of other intensities are presented, the amplification mechanism is not invoked and the response time increases. The analogy between the retinotopic map and maps of detectors selective for other features enables one to consider involvement of the gamma rhythm in the accentuation of any stimulus feature that becomes the object of attention.

Neural functions that have emerged in studies of the brain's analysis of spatial features of stimuli also apply to the analysis of temporal parameters. In a delayed response task that requires subjects to respond with a hand movement to a stimulus that is preceded at a standard time interval by an alerting signal, an expectancy wave appears in the EEG due to a depolarization shift that peaks when the imperative stimulus to respond appears. In this case, verbal instruction is replaced by a conditional response to time. The expectancy wave is referred to as contingent negative variation (Walter 1963). Again the amplification of activity is associated with the generation of gamma oscillations in detectors, but in this case they are detectors of temporal interval. The activation is greater the shorter the interval between the alerting stimulus and the imperative stimulus that is recognized by a given time detector.

This brings us to a more general question: What is the neural correlate of *anticipation*? Responding with a hand movement to a stimulus that is presented at fixed intervals involves only one type of anticipation. Anticipation is also manifest in changes in the perception of a particular stimulus depending on the stimulus that precedes it. One can draw an analogy between anticipation and the perception of Kanizsa's illusory contours. If in the case of illusory contours activation of additional detectors occurs on the basis of the spatial configuration of image elements, the modification of perception in anticipation can be represented as the result of activation of new elements by time detectors. Both involve change in a percept mediated indirectly by the activation of different detectors. One might expect that, as in the case of illusory contours, perceptual anticipation is associated with gamma oscillation.

The study of postsynaptic potentiation in identified synapses between sensory and command neurons of the mollusk indicates that it affects only local elementary postsynaptic potentials regardless of the processes occurring at other synapses. A high-frequency presynaptic burst of spikes initially depresses the elementary EPSP, but after a period of time it produces an increase in the amplitude of EPSPs to levels significantly higher than the initial amplitude. The plasticity of synapses is also selective, which is consistent with the concept that the detector maps on which certain features of a stimulus are represented can acquire certain relief maps of increased activity under the influence of local high-frequency stimulation. If subsequently a stimulus is introduced that matches one of the loci of a map, the stimulus will be accentuated and distinguished from the entire set of stimuli that do not belong to the zone of increased reactivity.

The "relief map of increased reactivity" principle can be illustrated by the example of the retinotopic map. Local high-frequency stimulation of the retina leads to reduction of the latent period for target detection in that location. The same principle can be extended to detector maps, which develop on the basis of vector coding of stimulus features identified by predetectors. The encoding of intensity of a visual stimulus considered earlier serves as an example. In this case we have not a map but a "strip" of intensity detectors as though cut from the map of color-brightness coding. Nevertheless it can help to illustrate the principle. High-frequency stimulation at a given intensity creates a locus of increased reactivity in the corresponding strip of detectors. If a stimulus is then applied whose intensity coincides with the locus of increased detector reactivity, its perception is facilitated. In conclusion, we can say that local posttetanic potentiation is intimately entwined with the detector principle of information encoding in neuronal maps. When the excitation of a certain detector generates the neuronal code of a given stimulus parameter, local posttetanic potentiation of that detector determines the level of awareness of the percept of the parameter.

In considering the mechanism of posttetanic potentiation, we did not take into account the influence of action potentials that may arise in the postsynaptic neuron preceding or following the EPSP. Depending on the sequence of these events, if an action potential in the postsynaptic cell follows the EPSP, the amplitude of the EPSP is increased; if an action potential precedes the EPSP, the latter is decreased. Such multidirectional interaction is governed by the number of calcium ions entering the postsynaptic neuron. In an EPSP the entry of calcium is limited to the head of the dendritic spine. An action potential induces calcium entry into all spines, entry of the same magnitude in both the spine head and the dendrite itself. The amount of calcium in the spine head is the same in either case.

The entry of calcium, however, occurs through different channels. The EPSP provides a calcium current by the stimulation of N-methyl-D-aspartate receptors (NMDARs), a type of glutamate receptor, whereas the action potential opens potential-dependent calcium channels. These processes have been observed microscopically by illuminating a cortical slice with light of wavelength 840 nm and measuring the fluorescence signal emitted by calcium-sensitive chemicals. The similarity of the fast front of the optical signal representing the influx of calcium with an EPSP and with an action potential indicates that both processes take place in the spine. The total amount of calcium entry is determined by the order in which the EPSP and the action potential occur. An action potential evoked by intracellular depolarization spreads as a global signal from the soma to the dendrites, where it affects calcium flux in the spine where the EPSP arose. If an action potential follows the EPSP the entry of calcium is increased, and if an action potential precedes the EPSP it is decreased.

The mechanism whereby calcium entry is reduced when an action potential precedes the EPSP can be explained by the inhibition of NMDAR channels due to the rapid increase in intracellular calcium concentration induced by the action potential. While glutamate produces prolonged activation of NMDARs, the receptors do not conduct a calcium current because they are blocked by extracellular magnesium. Increased calcium entry induced by an action potential following an EPSP removes the magnesium blockade, allowing the entry of calcium through the NMDAR channels. Thus, the NMDAR mechanism of calcium entry into neuronal spines of the cerebral cortex is sensitive to the short interval between the EPSP and the postsynaptic action potential. It should be added that the study of identified synapses in the mollusk has demonstrated that, as in the case of posttetanic potentiation, the greatest effect is achieved by multiple presynaptic action potentials in quick succession. It is possible that, as in the case of cortical neurons, such bursts are associated with increased entry of calcium into the postsynaptic cell.

Basar (1998), studying the electrical activity of snail ganglia with surface electrodes, showed that the spectrum of background activity included delta, theta, and alpha components, as well as the high-frequency gamma rhythm. The presence of the gamma rhythm in the central nervous systems of organisms at vastly different levels of evolutionary development led him to conclude that it is the most important factor in the processing of information by the nervous system. This conclusion does not necessarily establish an association between the gamma rhythm and the mechanisms of consciousness. The evolution of consciousness is apparently associated with the emergence of specific neuronal structures, which allow one not only to record and store images of the surrounding world, but also to transform them by the processes of imagination and scientific creativity.

The relation of the gamma rhythm to cognitive processes has been addressed in electrographic studies of meditation. As mentioned in Section 5.4, meditation or mental training consists in the concentration of consciousness on empathic awareness in relation to a specific function such as breathing (object meditation) or to a generalized emotional state (non-object meditation). These two forms of meditation are reflected differently in the EEG. While object meditation leads to an intensification of theta and alpha rhythms, non-object meditation is associated with increased EEG rhythms in the range of 24 to 42 Hz (Hassett 1978). The oscillation frequency increases with the number of meditation sessions and the total time spent in training.

The growth of gamma activity is accompanied by phase synchronization between widely distributed cortical areas. The development and amplitude of oscillation depend on two factors, the number of elements involved and the precision of their phasic characteristics. Increases in gamma activity may reflect qualitative changes in consciousness. Since the role of meditation is to influence one's mental state in everyday life, one might expect that the background EEG of people who practice non-object meditation would differ in comparison with those who practice object meditation by exhibiting a more pronounced gamma rhythm. Thus, attention as well as emotional states such as mood may be regulated and trained with involvement of the gamma rhythm.

Another phenomenon of interest is the role of working memory in creating a picture of the surrounding world. The neurons of working memory, which are located in prefrontal cortex, are notable for the selectivity of their receptive fields for a combination of spatial and image components. Signals from the "what" and "where" systems converge on those cells. Their activity does not stop with termination of the stimulus but lasts for up to ten seconds as a neuronal trace of the incoming signal. The mechanism of the trace is based on comparison of alerting and imperative stimuli that arrive at different moments in time.

A further aspect of the gamma rhythm is its participation in voluntary movements implemented under conscious control. The EEG of human motor cortex is characterized by a mu rhythm, or rolandic rhythm. At rest this rhythm coincides in frequency with the alpha rhythm that, during motor acts, is replaced by higher-frequency oscillations in the range of beta and gamma rhythms. Similar shifts occur during an imagined limb movement. When a subject imagines the movement, the electromyogram (EMG) of the involved limb exhibits the same or a similar oscillation frequency. The coincidence of frequencies at first suggests that the gamma rhythm in cortex may be an artifact of spread of the myogenic signal to cortical electrodes. Cross-correlational studies between MEG and EMG have shown, however, that the cortical MEG wave leads the wave of the muscular EMG (Hari and Salenius 1999). The fact that the cortical signals in the range of 20 or 40 Hz lead the discharges of muscle units indicates that the activity of cortical neurons modulates activity in the spinal motor neurons. This link between cortical and muscle activity indicates a readiness of motor neurons in the spinal cord and muscle units to recognize and implement commands for voluntary movements.

The gamma rhythm is also involved, apparently, in the estimation of differences between stimuli. This idea is based on the following observations. A study of the neurons in rabbit visual cortex that measure the difference between color stimuli presented in rapid succession showed that the neurons generated bursts of spikes in the range of 40 to 90 ms after the stimulus changes (Polyanskiy et al. 2005). The greater the color difference between the stimuli, the greater was the number of spikes in the difference discharge—up to 130 spikes per second for maximal differences. The number of spikes in the difference discharge correlated positively with the amplitude of the negative peak, N84, of the EP. The closeness of the spike frequency to the gamma frequency suggested that the gamma rhythm is involved in the genesis of electrical activity during the evaluation of stimulus differences.

To test this hypothesis, averaged EPs recorded from human subjects as a light of a given intensity was replaced by another were subjected to selective filtering at 1-Hz intervals. The selected narrowband signal was then used to determine the location of the equivalent current dipole. It was expected that with increasing difference between stimuli, the frequency of the signal giving the most reliable dipole localization would increase. That turned out not to be true. No systematic increase in frequency of the gamma rhythm was detected with increases in the difference between stimuli. However, the total number of dipole sources at different frequencies (from 30 to 70 Hz) increased systematically with increases in stimulus difference. The number of dipole sources also correlated positively with the amplitude of the EP in response to the stimulus changes. It is reasonable to assume that spikes were generated at random intervals within a burst and that their total number in the range of 40 to 90 ms after the stimulus change corresponded to the total number of dipole sources (Danilova et al. 2002).

7.5. SEMANTIC EPs

Consciousness includes two basic operations: identification of stimuli and measurement of differences between them. When one stimulus changes to another with no intervening time interval, an EP consisting of a series of negative and positive waves appears in the human brain. With nonverbal stimuli the amplitude of the EP is directly proportional to the magnitude of the perceived difference. The greater the amplitude, the greater is the perceptual difference between the successive stimuli. If the stimuli are the same, no EP appears and the subject sees no difference. An example of a perceptual EP in the human is the negative peak with latency of 87 msec (N87) that occurs in response to sudden replacement of one color stimulus by another.

If in the same experimental protocol two different verbal stimuli are used instead of nonverbal stimuli, a complex EP appears with a latency of 180 ms (N180). It consists of two superposed components, one perceptual and the other semantic, which can be separated by mathematical analysis. For example, in the EP response to replacement of one color name by another, the perceptual component reflects the change of the word's "envelope," which is primarily due to the different number of letters in the color name; the greater the semantic difference between the color names, the greater is the semantic component.

The elicitation of a semantic EP can be explained by analogy to the elicitation of perceptual EPs. But here the difference between the color terms is computed as the difference between the color memory traces activated during the change from one word to the other. The similarity of perceptual and semantic EPs suggests that the neurons of long-term color memory also activate phasic subtraction neurons whose discharges determine the amplitude of the semantic EP. The greater the difference in the composition of verbally activated neurons in long-term color memory, the higher is the number of action potentials generated in phasic subtraction neurons and the greater is the amplitude of the semantic EP. The coincidence of the perceptual and semantic trajectories of color stimuli is explained by the fact that the traces in long-term color memory are themselves formed under the influence of color perceptual processes, so the cognitive color space is a replica of the perceptual color space.

To explain how the envelope of a word is filled with semantic content, one must postulate an associative process between color memory traces and the traces that retain the envelope in memory. The connections are reciprocal. Bottom-up, when a color memory trace is activated, the trace of the color name is turned on. Top-down, when the memory trace of the symbol representing the color is activated, the corresponding color memory trace is turned on. If one color name is replaced by another, one complex of long-term color memory neurons is replaced by another. The change in complexes activates phasic neurons that compute the difference between the traces. The greater the difference between the color memory traces activated by the color symbols, the greater is the amplitude of the semantic EP. If two names activate the same memory trace, the semantic component of the EP is absent, even though the perceptual component, which reflects the difference between the envelopes of the names, is preserved.

This model for generating semantic EPs was tested by Izmailov and colleagues (2003). Three-letter pseudowords, in the form of nonsense consonant–vowel–consonant combinations, were presented to subjects one at a time on a computer monitor. Evoked responses to replacement of one word by another were recorded. A matrix was created that contained the amplitudes of the EPs to all possible transition pairs of words, and the matrix was subjected to multivariate analysis. Since the number of letters in the words was identical, the word length, which is the primary factor affecting the envelope variable, did not emerge as a significant determinant of EP amplitude. While the word space defined by the analysis was almost random, it was possible to identify a small contribution of vowels to the amplitude of the EP. A training procedure followed in which the different three-letter pseudowords were associated with different colors until the subjects were able to respond to presentation of the colors with the corresponding color names. The final phase of the study was to construct the semantic color space. Having controlled for the effect of word length, a two-dimensional, semantic space emerged—that is, coordinates on two dimensions were adequate to define the positions of the pseudonames of the colors on a circle. Comparison of this space with the perceptual color space indicated that they shared common axes: red–green and blue–yellow. This suggested that the color memory traces are ordered according to the hue characteristics of the corresponding perceived colors.

Perceptual and semantic EPs share a common mechanism: the replacement of one excitation vector by another. They differ in that a perceptual EP occurs when one excitation vector representing the actual object is replaced by a vector representing another object, whereas a semantic EP is generated by a similar change of vectors representing memory traces. The latter are activated by associative connections of verbal or other symbols with relevant memory traces. The overlapping of the mechanisms mediating perceptual and semantic EPs is illustrated by the fact that when one word is replaced by another, the perceptual component of the EP to the change in the envelope of the word is superimposed on the semantic component of the EP with which it coincides in time and form. Multivariate analysis of the potentials enables one to distinguish between the perceptual space representing the envelopes of words and the semantic space where the words are located according to their meanings.

The combined envelope and semantic potentials in response to changes in simple words peak with a latency of 180 msec. With more complex comparisons involving groups of words rather than single words, later semantic potentials emerge with latencies of 400 msec (N400) and 600 msec (N600). If a group of words belonging to one category is replaced by words from another semantic category, the N400 or N600 peak occurs, depending on their length. The amplitudes of N400 and N600 are determined by the magnitude of the difference between the semantic groups. If, instead of words from semantically contrasting groups, words of the same category replace one another, the N400 or N600 peak does not appear. This suggests that the longer latency peaks represent measures of the difference between semantic categories (Kutas and Federmeier 2000; Kutas and Iragui 1998).

The generation of N400 and N600 peaks can be understood as follows. The presentation of a series of semantically related words leads to a summation of the associated memory traces. The transition to another group of semantically related words produces another summary memory trace. The difference between these traces determines the amplitude of the late semantic potential as a measure of categorical difference. Thus, the analysis of word sequences distinguishes semantic complexes and establishes the magnitude of difference between them. Phasic subtraction neurons are presumably involved in the mechanism of late semantic potentials. The number of action potentials generated by them is a measure of categorical difference. The relationship of the number of spikes occurring in phasic subtraction neurons to the amplitude of the negative peak of the semantic EP is based on the same mechanisms that determine the appearance of any EP.

Usually the EP has been considered to represent a summation of postsynaptic potentials. In the retina, however, it was found that the summary response potential, namely wave b, results from the activation of Mueller glial cells (Nicholls et al. 2001). Spike discharges in retinal neurons lead to release of potassium ions that depolarize glial cells, creating a wave of negativity. R. Galambos arrived at a similar concept regarding the mechanism of EPs in cerebral cortex; in his view they result from the depolarization of astrocytes by potassium released into the intercellular medium by action potentials of nearby neurons (Galambos and Juhasz 1997).

The perceptual EP to replacement of one stimulus by another is a measure of perceived difference. The early semantic peak reflects the semantic difference between words, while the late semantic peak is a measure of categorical difference. How can one explain the observation that when subjects assign a number between zero and ten to differences between words representing colors, the amplitudes of perceptual and semantic EPs correlate highly with the subjective perceptual and semantic differences represented in their verbal estimates? The answer lies in the mechanism underlying the perceptual EP to a change in color.

When one color replaces another, phasic subtraction neurons in the retina produce bursts of spikes whose frequency is greater the more one color differs from the other. This phasic difference discharge is processed by the nervous system to produce a specific verbal response, the name of a number. To understand how the discharge of phasic subtraction neurons generates a specific response by the articulatory apparatus, we turn again to the neuronal mechanism of light-intensity encoding. Two kinds of neuron are involved in the encoding of light intensity: brightness neurons responsive to brightness and darkness neurons that are spontaneously active in the dark and silent in the light. The excitation of the brightness neuron is subtracted from the excitation of the darkness neuron, so that the sum of their excitations for all values of light intensity remains constant. The length of the vector formed by the contributions of brightness and darkness neurons remains constant (in Euclidian metrics) because of an adaptation mechanism. The vector that encodes light intensity reaches a map of selective intensity detectors that have different sets of synaptic weights. As a result, only that intensity detector whose combined synaptic weights vector coincides with the incoming excitation vector is excited.

With training, individual detectors become associated with individual command neurons for verbal responses. Thus, a given intensity of light is attached to the appropriate verbal, numerical evaluation.

This mechanism of transition from light intensity to its numerical evaluation is similar to the mechanism of numerical evaluation of other perceptual differences. A phasic difference discharge is subtracted from the excitation of a background-active neuron to produce a two-component excitation vector, which acts on a population of difference detectors and activates one of them. Each detector of difference magnitude is connected with its own command neuron, and the detected difference thus triggers the appropriate articulation. The amplitudes of perceptual and semantic potentials in response to words are determined by difference discharges that act through selective detectors to trigger the activity of the command neurons appropriate to the numerical values of the differences. Neurons that detect the numerical values of excitations are important elements of this model. Cells of this kind that are particularly selective for number of objects have been identified in the temporal cortex of monkeys (Nicholls et al. 2001).

7.6. CONSCIOUSNESS NEURONS

As previously noted, J. Eccles introduced the term "psychon" to denote individual psychic phenomena including highly localized sensations. He related an individual psychon to an anatomic unit, a bundle of dendrites on pyramidal neurons in the neocortex of mammals. In his view consciousness was attributed to those individual "dendrons." I. S. Beritashvili (Beritov 1961), explaining the mechanism of image memory in higher vertebrates, linked consciousness to stellate cells in neocortex. Combining these concepts suggests that consciousness is distributed over a set of neocortical neurons, and that an individual neuron corresponds to a subjective phenomenon specific to itself.

Not all neurons of the neocortex generate psychons when activated. Only a subset of neurons have that ability, a subset that can be referred to as *consciousness neurons*. Other nerve cells involved in the processing of information necessary to activate a consciousness neuron are not directly involved in the generation of mental phenomena. One is unaware of their activities, which constitute the sphere of the unconscious. From this perspective consciousness is distributed over a set of consciousness neurons. The destruction of any one of them leads to loss only of the psychon that is directly associated with it without affecting other aspects of awareness. Higher levels of consciousness such as self-consciousness are represented by individual consciousness neurons, damage to which leads to reduction of those levels of awareness without affecting the underlying mechanisms.

The concept of consciousness distributed over a set of specialized neurons allows a new perspective on the progressive dementia of Alzheimer's disease. There the death of individual neurons, which is not apparent in the initial stages, steadily leads to a narrowing of the sphere of consciousness. Normally long-term memory neurons are formed from undifferentiated stem cells under the influence of novelty signals from hippocampal neurons. The death of hippocampal neurons hampers this process and narrows the sphere of consciousness. The connection between hippocampal damage and anterograde amnesia, the inability to fix and recognize events that occur after damage to the hippocampus, is confirmed clinically by numerous cases in which memory traces of events that take place after surgery or bilateral hippocampal injury are absent, while memory traces from events that occurred before the surgery or trauma are preserved. A vivid illustration of the role of the hippocampus in the formation of long-term memory traces is the effect of bilateral removal of this structure from the brain of the much-studied patient H. M. (Scoville and Milner 1957). After the operation, which was performed to treat intractable epilepsy, H. M.'s memory for episodes in his life prior to surgery was fully preserved, but he no longer retained in memory events that occurred after the surgery. He remembered clearly the names of political figures and artists from the presurgical period but could not name public figures who achieved renown in the years after his operation. The retention of memories of events that preceded the operation indicates that the hippocampus itself does not serve as the repository of memories; it only mediates the recording of long-term traces, which takes place in the cerebral cortex.

As mentioned earlier, this interpretation is consistent with the concept introduced by A. R. Luria (1973) of two types of memory: modality-nonspecific and modality-specific. *Modality-nonspecific memory* involves the hippocampus, which must be intact for any form of long-term memory to be possible. *Modality-specific*, or categorical, long-term memory involves temporal association cortex as well. The concept that the formation of long-term memory in temporal cortex involves the hippocampus is based on the emergence of retrograde amnesia after damage limited to the temporal lobes. Thus, while extirpation of the hippocampus leads to anterograde amnesia with no sign of retrograde amnesia, a lesion restricted to temporal cortex leads to retrograde amnesia—that is, to the loss of memory traces acquired before the lesion was sustained. The notion that neurons in the temporal cortex represent individual units of information storage would explain, by the fallout of modality-specific neurons, the gradual impairment of recognition of previously familiar objects observed in Alzheimer's disease. Different forms of recognition impairment may dominate depending on the type of neurons lost (e.g., impaired recognition of familiar faces, prosopagnosia, or of familiar surroundings). The loss of selectivity is particularly clear with prosopagnosia, in which the inability to identify a person may occur with full ability to recognize household objects intact and, moreover, with preservation of the ability to identify emotional facial expressions. Such selective impairment is obviously based on different locations for neurons responsible for face identification and neurons that detect emotional expressions.

Thus, long-term memory can be thought of as a field of scattered neurons, each of which is associated with a certain event. With training and the accumulation of experience, new neurons are added to the field from the reserve of undifferentiated stem cells. These cells divide such that one daughter cell remains a stem cell and can divide again while the other becomes the precursor to a neuron or glial cell. A neuronal precursor migrates to a certain part of the cortex or hippocampus, differentiating as it goes. In the final stage of differentiation the migrant forms axon collaterals that establish synapses on target cells and receives terminals of axons from other cells, which form synaptic contacts on its dendrites and soma. If a dead neuron is replaced, the migrant reproduces its synapses and thus integrates into the neuronal network. The formation of a new long-term memory neuron is associated with the establishment of new synapses, the weights of which reproduce the combination of presynaptic excitations created by a new stimulus. As a result, the newly formed neuron becomes selectively tuned to a given stimulus. With repetition of the stimulus the neuron responds more intensely than other long-term memory cells whose synaptic weights are coordinated with other combinations of presynaptic effects created earlier in response to other stimuli. The formation of synapses on long-term memory neurons is conditional on the novelty of a stimulus, which activates *novelty neurons* in the hippocampus to produce trophic factors. Those factors stabilize synaptic contacts and ensure their stability during the recording of a long-term memory trace of the stimulus object or event.

The most important function of consciousness lies in the planning of actions. The execution of an action is preceded by the formation of an intention. Consciousness neurons related to subjective experiences can be divided into *cognitive neurons*, whose activity is connected with the perception of signals from the external and internal environments, and *intention neurons*, which are excited even before the beginning of a voluntary action and are associated with a sense of intention to commit the act. Thus, among the variety of consciousness neurons, besides those associated with the perception of stimulus qualities, there is a special group of neurons responsible for the experience of intention that are referred to as intention neurons. Their activation generates both a subjective intention and a physiological process in the form of neurotransmitter release, which activates a command neuron.

One feature of intention neurons is that they are activated in response to a combination of a specific memory trace of an object and preparation for action toward the object, which has not yet appeared. These neurons are selective for combinations of conceptualization leading to a program of action. Intention neurons belong to the domain of working memory, encoding the connections between objects and actions. Thus, they cannot be classified strictly as either afferent or efferent neurons.

Intention neurons are also called *mirror neurons* (Rizzolatti and Craighero 1998). Mirror neurons were discovered in monkeys as they produced gestures imitating the movements of another animal. Neurons were found that were selectively activated in association with a specific combination of imminent action in relation to a particular object. Thus, movement of the upper limb in the direction of a cylinder was associated with activation of one mirror neuron. But with anticipated movement of the same limb toward a cube, another mirror neuron was activated. Depending on the intensity of activation of intention neurons, the intention either attenuates, remaining a trace in memory, or is executed by the triggering of movements through command neurons. Factors that can lead to activation of intention neurons include their own pacemaker potentials as well as traces in long-term memory selected at their activation level. Execution of the movement itself occurs through connections to premotor and motor neurons. Thus, if one thinks of the intention neuron as at the top of an executive pyramid, command, premotor, and motor neurons constitute the extended base of the pyramid that determines the response.

Hierarchical pyramids also operate in semantic structures. A characteristic of semantic neurons is their ability to be activated not only by an external stimulus, but also by a link between an image associated with activation of long-term memory neurons and a meaning associated with activation of a semantic neuron. In addition to phoneme detectors, neurons are formed during development that are selectively responsive to syllables, words, and combinations of words (Creutzfeldt 1993). Mirror neurons of articulation apparently are formed when the motor pattern is matched with acoustic signals from the speaker himself. Self-correction of speech is based on comparison of the fed-back acoustic signal with its trace in long-term memory. The error signal is generated by phasic ON/OFF-neurons that compute the magnitude of difference between the memory trace and the sound. The difference signal governs restructuring of the mirror neurons to achieve convergence of the acoustic signal with the memory trace. The semantic content of the verbal signal is determined by a set of long-term memory neurons, which are activated top-down by a semantic neuron on the memory screen.

Research on the activities of intention neurons suggests that they are specific to various behavioral acts. But they are also specialized in relation to the objects toward which the acts are directed. Consequently, the appearance of a certain object at a given location in the visual field activates an intention neuron specific with regard to the location of the object and its particular characteristics. For example, a knife located at a certain place on a table and a fork located in the same place will activate different intention neurons. What is the advantage of specialization of intention neurons to particular objects? Such neurons not only determine the orientation of a movement in space but also pre-organize a certain combination of finger positions for grasping the object.

Intention neurons participate in the process of reading aloud. By combining object specificity with word sequence specificity, they pre-organize the articulatory organs to speak words as they appear in text. The fact that intention neurons can either activate or not activate the behavioral act allows for flexibility of behavioral control. The behavioral act itself is triggered by the activation of a specific command neuron. This activation may occur as a result of input from an intention neuron in combination with inputs representing other features of the situation. The participation of an intention neuron in a behavioral act gives it "voluntary coloration." The behavioral act may also be driven by direct excitation of a command neuron, in which case it is associated with the feeling of its being an involuntary, forced motor act. Activation of a command neuron by a dominant circuit and its collateral excitations is associated with a feeling of an unmotivated involuntary response. Such a mechanism is consistent with Ukhtomskiy's (1966) concept of the dominant as confirmed experimentally by the induction of a specific motor response to a specific external stimulus by polarization of motor cortex (Rusinov 1987).

The activity of intention neurons is the basis for the *readiness potential*, a slow negative potential in the EEG that precedes a voluntary movement by 0.5 to 2.0 sec. It is recorded from both hemispheres of the brain but appears more clearly in the contralateral cortex. The amplitude of the readiness potential correlates closely with the number of neurons in premotor, supplementary cortex (Brodmann's area 6) involved in the preparation for a movement. The readiness potential drops sharply with onset of the movement (Porter and Lewis 1975). Activity begins to be recorded from neurons in premotor cortex 500 msec before onset of the movement. By the moment the movement begins, the number of premotor neurons involved decreases. Cells in area 6 not only send axons to but also receive axonal input from primary motor cortex, Brodmann's area 4. Cells in motor cortex respond to specific sensory signals as well, but sensory input before the onset of movement is more evident in neurons of premotor cortex, Brodmann's area 6. This indicates clearly that sensory signals play a role in cortical preparations for movement.

The relationship between the number of neurons activated in premotor cortex and the amplitude of the readiness potential is interpretable from the standpoint of glial theory. The greater the density of spikes, the greater is the release of potassium ions and the greater is the depolarization of glial cells. Thus, the amplitude of the readiness potential reflects the mobilization of the neurons in premotor cortex. Those neurons, however, do not control the onset of movement. That depends on the motor neurons of primary motor cortex. The activation of neurons that precedes the movement is associated with the subjective experience of intention to implement an action. Therefore, the readiness potential occurs in a variety of tasks, including movements of the limbs, the eyes, and the organs of speech.

The excitation of consciousness neurons is associated with certain perceptions. Investigators have found opportunities to study this phenomenon in the course of neurophysiological evaluations of patients with epilepsy. They have isolated individual neurons in temporal cortex that respond with a burst of spikes to the image of a ball but do not respond to the image of a human face. The question they addressed was whether the same neuron would be activated selectively by the mental image of a ball or a human face. Records of neuronal activity as the patient pictured in his imagination a ball or face showed the same selectivity as neuronal responses observed during perception of the external images. A given neuron was activated only during the imagination of an object whose direct perception activated it. The spike activity of the neuron ceased with the transition from imagination of the object to imagination of an unrelated object. Thus, a cognitive neuron can be activated either bottom-up in response to the real stimulus or top-down in response to verbal instructions to imagine the previously perceived object.

One mechanism of top-down activation of cognitive neurons may involve working-memory neurons of prefrontal cortex. It is possible that they not only activate neurons in temporal association cortex but also have an inhibitory effect on neurons that represent adjacent areas of the visual field. This inhibition helps distinguish the perception of a real object from its mental representation by depriving the imaginary image of spatial reference. The fact that the same neuron in temporal cortex may be selectively activated either during perception of the object or during its mental representation indicates the close relationship between perception and imagination. More importantly, the fact that the selective neuron of perception coincides with the neuron selectively activated during imagination of the object makes more understandable the mental construction of objects, which can then be implemented in reality. Preliminary work of the imagination is aimed at selecting the most closely coinciding consciousness neurons. Test of the adequacy of the imagined construct is achieved by building and perceiving the object conceptualized. The activation of neurons of the imaginary object must coincide with the activation of neurons in perception, evoking a sense of creative satisfaction. More generally, the fact that the neurons of perception and of imagination are the same explains the mechanism of productive creativity.

7.7. NEUROCOMPUTATION ON DENDRITES

Karl Pribram (1997) has emphasized that a functional description of the central nervous system in terms of action potentials is not sufficient. The control of action potentials lies at a deeper level: in the network of multiple presynaptic axon terminals that contact postsynaptic sites on dendrites of the target cell. Local interactions there determine the fate of action potentials in the postsynaptic neuron. The neuron has a set of microsynaptic modules that work independently. While ordinarily the action potential is considered to be determined by the summation of excitatory and inhibitory postsynaptic potentials at the axon hillock, the concept of *micromodules* postulates localized synaptic operations that interact within the dendritic membrane of the postsynaptic neuron.

Such micromodules have been demonstrated experimentally in the dendrites of hippocampal neurons in tissue culture (Liu 2004). The basic micromodule is a pair of excitatory and inhibitory synapses. If adjacent presynaptic terminals deliver excitatory (glutamate) and inhibitory (GABA) transmitters, the inhibitory postsynaptic potential sums with the excitatory potential to cancel the excitatory response, in essence performing a *veto operation*. If only an excitatory or an inhibitory transmitter arrives within a time window of 20 msec, the output of the micromodule is excitation or inhibition. If both arrive simultaneously, however, the micromodule does not respond. Based on these observations, Liu postulates that micromodules operate by a ternary (−1, 0, 1) coding system. The possibility of ignoring incoming information distinguishes the neuron from a computer, which operates on a binary system (1, 0). Liu believes that a transition to the ternary system in a future generation of computers may bring solutions to currently intractable problems. It should be said that N. P. Brusentsov, in 1959, designed and successfully implemented an electronic data-processing machine, the *Setun*, that offered several advantages over binary-coded computers (Brusentsov 1994).

In considering computational operations performed by neuronal dendrites, it should be noted that excitatory and inhibitory synapses are evenly distributed over the surfaces of dendritic branches where they express at different times excitation, inhibition, or, if the two are superimposed, the veto operation. Thus, a "word" forms on the dendrite that consists of a combination of ternary coded units: −1s, 0s, and +1s. Other dendrites function similarly. The summation signal from such micromodules contributes to generation of the somatic action potential.

Separation of the functions of dendritic modules from those of the neuronal soma suggests that a given consciousness neuron may be associated with different states of consciousness depending on one or another combination of micromodules with different patterns of spike activity—in other words, it may "produce" different states of consciousness. Extending the micromodular principle to neurons of long-term memory, several combinations of dendritic modules may be written on a given neuron, the combinations being activated sequentially by different stimuli depending on changes in the pattern of presynaptic signals. The subjective content is determined not by the pattern of spike discharge at the output of the neuron, but by a specific set of activated modules. The proposed multivalency of memory neurons expands the range of possible events that can be recorded in memory.

The hypothesis that individual stimuli can be encoded by the formation of synapses on specific dendritic branches implies that the recording of new stimuli is associated with continuous dendritic growth. The formation of new neurons is not required. Such an increase in dendritic mass without increase in the number of neurons has been observed in bees (Horridge 2009). The brain of the bee, the mushroom body, increases in volume due to the growth of dendrites, while the number of nerve cells remains constant. The increase in dendritic mass is proportional to the expansion of the territory explored by the bee in its search for nectar.

The formation of dendrites involves the action of acetylcholine on muscarinic receptors. Presumably, as in vertebrates, acetylcholine release occurs in response to new stimuli. Evidence that the growth of dendrites is linked with muscarinic receptors has been obtained by application of the cholinergic agonist, pilocarpine, to the mushroom body. Such application leads to dendritic growth comparable to that seen as a bee familiarizes itself with the environment. By the same token, applying a cholinergic antagonist, atropine or scopolamine, to the mushroom body impairs memory and search behavior. The molecular mechanism of synapse formation on the newly formed dendrites of mushroom body neurons involves calcium- and calmodulin-dependent adenylyl cyclase, protein kinase A, and cAMP response element-binding factor (CREB). The participation of acetylcholine in the "training" of mushroom body neurons is supported by the fact that the neurons synthesize acetylcholinesterase, an enzyme that breaks down acetylcholine.

Impaired acetylcholine synthesis in the human leads to the kind of memory loss seen in Alzheimer's disease. Muscarinic cholinergic receptors belong to a group of transmembrane receptors that are associated with G proteins. These proteins trigger the expression of genes involved in the synthesis of structural proteins during the formation of pre- and postsynaptic structures. The role of muscarinic receptors in the growth of neuropil in the mushroom body of the bee is similar to the action of acetylcholine at muscarinic receptors in neurons of mammalian auditory cortex. It has been shown that muscarinic receptors are involved in the tuning of frequency-specific detectors of auditory cortex to the frequency of conditioned acoustic stimuli (Weinberger 2004). An example of micromodule participation in computing operations on the dendrites is found in the visual perception of moving stimuli. A stationary object that simultaneously activates both excitatory and inhibitory synapses does not affect the retinal neurons that perceive motion. If the object moves at a rate such that the excitatory and inhibitory inputs do not coincide in time, the excitatory inputs are no longer blocked by inhibition, and a sequence of local excitations occurs on the dendrite leading to the generation of spikes in the somatic membrane. Selective activation with regard to the rate of motion of the object is determined by the time within which the inhibitory input blocks the neighboring excitatory synapse. Selectivity with regard to direction of motion is determined by the orientation of dendrites. Maximal response is obtained when the direction of an object's motion coincides with the orientation of the dendritic branches. This mechanism may mediate the perception of speed and direction of motion.

In more general terms, considering the representation of external signals on detector maps, the orientation of dendrites of neurons at higher levels in the hierarchy may mediate perception of the type of shift in the focus of excitation. A gradual intensification or attenuation of a stimulus evoking sequential activation of the intensity detectors can selectively activate those dendrites of higher-level neurons that coincide with the direction of intensity change. Thus, micromodules on the neuronal dendrite and the orientation of dendritic branches can determine the selectivity of neuronal responses both at the sensory and at a more abstract cognitive level.

Introspective data indicate that a person remembers complex visual scenes and is capable of reproducing them from memory. What is the neuronal mechanism of such image memory? First let us consider the perception of complex images in the color mosaics example. Colors are represented within the spatially selective color analyzer by four-dimensional color detectors. Spatially distinct color analyzers form a four-dimensional subjective representation of external, three-dimensional space. *Complex color-spatial detectors* receive inputs from four color predetectors and four spatial predetectors. Thus, the complex color-spatial detectors form a spherical surface in eight-dimensional space on which spatially distinct color combinations, *color mosaics,* are displayed. These combinations of excitations of complex color-spatial detectors enter the memory screen and form synapses on the next, as yet not fully differentiated neuron. The synapses are weighted to match the excitations of the corresponding complex detectors. This neuron becomes a gnostic unit selectively tuned to a certain color mosaic. Long-term maintenance of the synapses formed on the gnostic neuron is accomplished by synthesis of the receptor protein in postsynaptic densities. Activation of such a gnostic unit by local electrical microstimulation elicits the subjective image of the earlier color mosaic. With repeated experience of the mosaic, the object comes to be recognized as familiar.

The gnostic unit just described responds only to a single color mosaic; other mosaics are represented by other gnostic units that are selectively tuned to them. Recordings of spike activity from gnostic units shows that there exist *categorical neurons*, which respond to a number of similar color mosaics. What is the mechanism of such categorization? Presumably it is based on the coding of mosaics in individual dendrites. The function of a gnostic unit is based on the convergence of a set of color-spatial detectors on its dendrites. Some combination of activated detectors is recorded in the synaptic weights of a gnostic unit whereby the unit becomes selectively tuned to that combination and does not recognize other mosaics. It is proposed that a categorical gnostic unit receives a full set of inputs from color-spatial detectors on each dendrite. An individual dendrite fixes a particular combination of excitations from the color-selective detectors and then ceases to respond to other combinations of signals. Thus, an individual dendrite becomes the physical equivalent of a gnostic unit.

The termination of recording of a color mosaic on a dendrite pre-excites the next dendrite, on which the next color mosaic is recorded. This scheme allows the recording of many color mosaics on one memory neuron. Moreover, dendritic activation evokes growth of new dendrites, extending the amount of information recorded on the individual neuron. Dendrites that have recorded information do not record more. But all receive signals from the color-spatial detectors, and only coincidence of the pattern of incoming excitation coincides with the recorded synaptic pattern activating the dendrite, which constitutes identification of the signal. In the proposed scheme subjective experience is associated with activation of a specific detector corresponding to information encoded on individual dendrites.

Introspective data suggest that a person remembers sequences of events and can reproduce their order from memory. In addition, tagging the time of a past event allows one to retrieve the event from memory. The proposed scheme of information encoding on dendrites provides a mechanism for recording sequences of events, where the time-stamp is the dendrite on which the event is recorded. Only subjectively experienced events are recorded, which is why events that occur during slow-wave sleep are not retained in memory. On the other hand, dreams that occur during paradoxical sleep may create an impression of long duration, which is determined by the number of dendrites involved. The sequential recording of events in brain structures was demonstrated in studies by the neurosurgeon W. Penfield, who showed that prolonged electrical stimulation of temporal cortex elicited memories of one life episode after another corresponding in sequence to the person's life experience.

Long-term retention of traces in memory requires continuous maintenance of the effectiveness of synapses formed in the course of experience. They are first formed as the result of postsynaptic potentiation due to the coincidence in time of transmitter-mediated activation and a novelty signal from the hippocampus. The synaptic potentiation is subsequently replaced by receptor protein synthesis in the postsynaptic membrane, a mechanism involving DNA. Since the products of synthesis are addressed to synapses in different locations on the dendrite, one would expect that certain parts of the dendritic membrane are labeled by a specific protein. This protein transports mRNA of the receptor protein from the nucleus to the specific synapses labeled by the protein. Synthesis of the receptor protein occurs by translation on the mRNA molecule in the vicinity of the specifically labeled synapse. This process is carried out continuously throughout the entire life of the organism, enabling the recognition of familiar objects and memorizing new ones.

The concept of dendritic micromodules allows a new approach to the mechanism of encoding verbal information. Patients undergoing cerebrocortical exploration to identify epileptic foci were presented with individual words in a quiet auditory setting (Creutzfeldt 1993). Recordings from individual neurons in the right temporal cortex revealed high selectivity for the *acoustic envelope* of the word. One neuron responded to only one of 20 different words: "corkscrew." The neuronal response consisted of two bursts of spikes separated by an interval in which spike activity was absent. One burst pattern corresponded to the word "cork," the other to the word "screw." The consonant "s" did not evoke a response. This neuron showed the identical pattern of spike discharges when the task was to repeat the same word. To explain such a response one might propose that each word in the complex is encoded on a separate dendrite. The sequence of recording of the words is determined by neurons that detect time interval. A specific sequence of sounds activates the corresponding dendrites in order. According to this model, the neuron will not respond if the order of the sounds in words is rearranged. This corresponds to the unintelligibility of speech played backwards.

The participation of neurons selectively responsive to different time intervals allows one to distinguish different sequences of acoustic signals. Time detectors have been investigated in detail in bats (Ma and Suga 2001). By ultrasonic irradiation of complex objects, such as trees and bushes, the bat receives a sequence of echoes at different time intervals. The temporal sequence of the echoes allows the bat to assess the distance of external objects.

The coincidence of formants in a given time window determines the specificity of a biologically significant sound signal (Geissler and Ehret 2002). Chaffinch nestlings listening to the songs of an adult male adopt its melody and reproduce it. The chaffinch song consists of several syllables 100 msec in duration separated by intervals of 25 msec. Each syllable is represented by a set of formants of constant or descending frequency.

How is this information recorded in memory neurons, and how is the record converted into a sequence of sounds for reproduction? First consider the recording of an individual syllable. Each syllable generated from a set of formants is represented by an excitation vector, the components of which are individual formant detectors, or detectors of formant frequency modulations. Such auditory detectors are analogous to motion detectors in the visual system. Each syllable is converted into a vector of synaptic weights on an individual syllable detector. The next syllable, separated from the first by an empty time interval, activates the next syllable detector and forms the next vector of synaptic connections. The entire melody is fixed as a sequence of syllables on a memory neuron, which is connected to two command neurons. One command neuron generates formants of a constant frequency; the other generates formants of descending frequency. Under the influence of internal factors, such as testosterone, the dendrites of a memory neuron may be activated, creating excitation in a certain command neuron that reaches the motor neurons responsible for reproducing the sequence of syllables recorded in the memory neuron. The length of syllables is determined by time detectors as they are recorded. When the syllables are reproduced, their durations are determined by the activation times of the corresponding dendrites of the memory neuron, which determines the discharge of command neurons to generate formants of different frequencies.

Syllables can be generated both by formants of constant frequency and by formants whose frequency decreases with time. Accordingly, the formants activate two types of detector: formant detectors of constant frequency and formant detectors of descending frequency. The latter detectors are, again, similar to motion direction detectors in the visual system. While in the visual system a stimulus moves in a straight line in visual space, however, a constantly descending frequency formant crosses sequentially the different frequency components of the acoustic spectrum. The formant detectors converge on higher-level neurons, syllable detectors, which are similar to the gnostic units of the visual system. Detectors of constant frequency formants form synapses on the gnostic unit of a syllable with constant frequency formants. Detectors of descending frequency formants form synapses on the appropriate gnostic unit of another syllable. Gnostic units with different sets of synapses become selectively tuned to different syllables, and they are connected to command neurons for different sets of motor neurons. Tonic motor neurons generate constant frequency formants. Command neurons associated with phasic motor neurons determine the formants associated with variable frequency. Thus, the excitation of a gnostic unit activates the corresponding command neuron, leading to reproduction of the corresponding syllable.

One can distinguish two ways of activating the gnostic unit of a syllable. The first is by presentation of the syllable to which the gnostic unit is tuned, which in turn leads to its reproduction. This is the basis for imitation. The other is by endogenous activation of the gnostic unit. An example of the latter is the singing mechanism triggered in songbirds by a seasonal increase in testosterone level. Recorded in the memory of the chick, the syllable provides a sample for learning to produce the song itself. If the reproduced syllable does not match the sample in memory, there occurs a difference signal equal to the difference between two vectors: the synaptic weights vector on the gnostic unit and the excitation vector of acoustic feedback from the sound produced. This vector difference is subtracted from the synaptic weights that connect the command neuron to the motoneurons that generate the sound. The learning process of tuning the motoneuron's activation pattern terminates when the synaptic weights vector of the gnostic unit comes to equal the excitation vector generated during reproduction of the sound.

From the recording and reproduction of an individual syllable, let us proceed to the recording of a melody as a sequence of syllables. This recording happens at the next higher level, where an individual memory neuron stores the trace of the sequence of syllables. Each syllable is recorded on a single dendrite of the memory neuron. The first syllable is recorded on the first dendrite; the second is recorded on the next activated dendrite; and so forth. The order of syllables is recorded in the sequence of activated dendrites. The neuron that stores the melody trace is connected with the command neurons for all of the syllables. When the memory neuron is activated by testosterone, the dendrites are activated sequentially. This leads in turn to the activation of the syllable command neurons in the same sequence, resulting in reproduction of the melody. It should be added that time detectors, which code syllable duration, are involved in the recording of the syllable. In other words, the memory neuron that stores the trace of the melody controls the sequence of syllables during reproduction.

While favoring the consciousness neuron hypothesis, we cannot ignore a different conceptualization of the issue in which consciousness is considered to result from systemic neuronal interactions based on their rhythmic activity. Comparisons of the role of intracellular mechanisms of individual neurons versus the role of their systemic organization will be important in future studies of consciousness (Alexandrov and Sams 2005).

7.8. THE INTRACELLULAR MECHANISM OF CONSCIOUSNESS

Having accepted the concept of specific consciousness neurons and the accumulated evidence for a relationship between individual neurons and the perception not only of basic features but also of complex objects, we find ourselves facing a new question: What is the mechanism of consciousness within the individual neuron? We must assume that a unique set of genes is expressed in consciousness neurons and that their products constitute the intracellular mechanism of consciousness. This line of reasoning led S. Hameroff and colleagues (1993) to propose a quantum mechanism of consciousness. Those authors suggested that the individual microtubules that form the cytoskeleton of cells, including neurons of the neocortex, constitute fiberoptic channels for the lossless distribution of laser radiation generated by the difference in electron energy levels of two types of tubulin molecule, the protein from which microtubules are built.

The idea of a quantum information-processing mechanism in the cytoplasm of neurons was developed further with the concept of a grid of microtubules—that is, parallel tubules cross-connected by bridges of a specific microtubule-associated protein (MAP). Individual microtubules are connected with local postsynaptic sites through which information enters the network of microtubules to form an analog of the nervous system within the individual neuron. The function of the neuronal cytoskeleton is usually considered to provide a means of active transport of macromolecules within the cell. The novel additional function envisioned in the quantum model of the cytoskeleton is a quantum mechanical information function.

Hameroff's hypothesis of microtubules as fiberoptic channels of laser radiation has been supported by another group of researchers (Hagan et al. 1994; Jibu et al. 1994). They have proposed a mechanism of laser radiation in which the original energy pumping is replaced by the summation of water molecule charges along the microtubule. Working from a theory of Dicke (1954), the authors conclude that the total charge along the microtubule is capable of converting the random transitions of electrons from one energy level to another to achieve an ordered process that generates coherent radiation. According to this hypothesis, microtubules function like pulsed lasers, but unlike conventional lasers they do not require preliminary pumping. Pumping is replaced by the ordering of water molecules according to their energy levels. This is achieved by the exchange of energy between water molecules and quantized values of electromagnetic radiation, heat quanta. As a result, an ordered sequence of water molecules of high energy level appears on a certain section of the microtubule. These molecules move collectively to a lower energy level, emitting a pulse of coherent photons. This mode of emission functions similarly to a laser that uses light pumping to transfer molecules to a higher energy level. The frequency of the pulse mode of generating coherent photons, *superradiance*, is about 40 Hz, a frequency widely represented in the nervous system. The coherent radiation passing along a microtubule is susceptible to corruption in the form of a quantum process called *self-induced transparency*. This process can be thought of as the formation of a new section of water molecules ahead of the front of radiation that are converted to a higher energy level and that generate new coherent photons. The switching on and off of the mechanism that generates coherent photons is conceived to be mediated by the reticular activating systems of the brain stem and thalamus, which are responsible for the maintenance of global and focal consciousness respectively.

Microtubules are present in all nerve cells as supporters of macromolecular transport and ion flux. In this model, however, consciousness neurons possess an additional mechanism for generating coherent photons. That is why they are the primary neurons disabled by anesthetics, hypoglycemia, and oxygen deficiency. The proposed intracellular mechanism that distinguishes consciousness neurons from neurons not associated with consciousness involves the generation of coherent photons in the microtubules of individual neurons, which are propagated along microtubules without corruption of coherence. In addition, the transmission of coherent photons through the microtubule makes it transparent, turning it into an ideal fiberoptic channel.

The attractiveness of the quantum hypothesis of consciousness is primarily that it is subject to experimental verification by the arsenal of methods of modern physics. One needs first to associate individual neurons with specific states of consciousness and then to connect consciousness with the localized generation of coherent photons. The applicability of quantum interpretations to biological processes is not in doubt. A quantum process governs the absorption of light quanta by photoreceptors. Thus, it is logical to assume that a quantum mechanism might mediate the generation of coherent photons to form a final product in the chain of neuronal transformations that gives rise to subjective experience.

This theory, however, contains an internal contradiction. The cytoskeleton, which consists of microtubules interconnected by MAPs, is found in all cells from paramecia to neurons of the brain. This forces one to either of two alternative courses of consideration: either to accept consciousness to be a common property of all cells or to pursue a search for specific intracellular mechanisms that only consciousness neurons possess. In the latter case one cannot rely on a common quantum mechanism of information processing in the neuronal cytoskeleton to differentiate between consciousness and nonconsciousness cells. It is necessary to identify distinctive qualities of the quantum processes of consciousness neurons.

Research in this direction should take into account such features of consciousness neurons as their dependence on the activating and synchronizing systems of the brain. Shutting off the brain stem activating system leads to a global loss of consciousness. This implies a dependence of all consciousness neurons on a flow of activating influence from the brain stem. Such a comprehensive switching off of consciousness neurons implies a mechanism governed by a single source, the turning off of which leads to simultaneous inactivation of all consciousness neurons. Such a source is the activating system of the brain, which supports the activity of consciousness neurons through monoaminergic and cholinergic pathways. The concept of localization of consciousness is not inconsistent with its global shutdown.

Study of the activation mechanism can help to identify the distinctive features of consciousness neurons. A natural model in which to study the loss of consciousness associated with disabling the brain activating system is the transitions between waking, slow-wave sleep, and dreaming. Consciousness can be restored from slow-wave sleep in either of two ways: through awakening or through the transition to paradoxical sleep in which cortical activation is accompanied by inhibition of voluntary action. In paradoxical sleep, consciousness is manifested in the form of dreams with an intensity of experience that can compete with perceptions in the waking state. Distinctive features of dreams are their involuntariness and randomness. Here we encounter an interaction of consciousness neurons that goes beyond the hierarchical relationships considered above. The difference between consciousness in the waking state and consciousness in dreams relates to different states of intention neurons. Inhibition of these neurons in paradoxical sleep renders impossible both voluntary actions and voluntary control over dreaming. Thus, in paradoxical sleep the intentional component of the unified consciousness mechanism of the waking state is paralyzed.

Let us return to the issue of neuronal multivalency. A thorough study of a neuron in temporal cortex that was selectively responsive to a portrait of President Clinton and not to portraits of other individuals known to the subject indicated that the neuron responded not only to the one portrait but to a variety of portraits of the same president (Kreiman et al. 2002). What is the mechanism underlying the invariance of such a neuron's responses? E. T. Rolls (2000) explains the invariance of individual neuronal responses to different views of the same person in terms of distributed memory. An alternative hypothesis is that one gnostic unit can store a large number of visual patterns that are selectively activated depending on the pattern of stimulation at the input. What mechanism might mediate the formation of multiple traces in a single neuron? The concept of synaptic mechanisms mediating the process runs into difficulty with identical spike discharges in response to all variants of a person's portrait. We would propose that each constellation of activated synapses associated with a particular image corresponds to a specific state of the neuron. So, what is the mechanism whereby a single neuron produces the same response to diverse images?

The answer to this question lies in a search for intracellular structures that form a neuronal-like network within the individual neuron. The most likely candidates for that role are the microtubules of the cytoskeleton. The synaptic pattern that forms on a gnostic unit in response to a stimulus is converted into a certain pattern of microtubules and MAP. The conscious perception of a certain object occurs only when a corresponding set of tubules and MAP bundles is activated. The activation of microtubules is associated with coherent radiation due to different electron energy levels involved in the interaction between water molecules and the tubulin molecules that form the wall of microtubules. This specific quantum mechanical radiation may be the intraneuronal mechanism of consciousness. The recording of images within an individual neuron presumably consists in the formation of specific patterns of microtubules and MAP as a result of synaptically evoked, localized transformation of tubulin and MAP molecules. These transformations represent the mechanism of long-term memory leading to coherent radiation in the tubular system upon subsequent activation of the stimulus fixed in memory.

The role of genetic factors in the development of consciousness is illustrated by FoxP2, the gene associated with speech and language, which is located on human chromosome 7. The lack of a functional variant of FoxP2 is associated with impairment of the sensorimotor feedback necessary for learning articulatory movements and recording the memory traces thereof. The expression of genes belonging to the Fox family is controlled by transcription factors. Human FoxP2 differs from the FoxP2 of all other species. Mutation of the prehominid gene FoxP2 is thought to have occurred about two hundred thousand years ago, superseding other variants in evolution of the gene. This event slightly preceded the onset of symbolic communication.

Although a direct connection between mutations of FoxP2 and language development has not been established, this gene is expressed early in the development of brain areas specifically associated with speech. Individuals with mutations of this gene show a lack of activation of Broca's area as they perform linguistic tasks. Variants of the gene that differ from human FoxP2 are found in other mammals and birds. Particularly strong expression of these variants is found in male songbirds in the nuclei of cells of the neuronal network that mediates singing. Heightened expression occurs during the training of young birds as well as during periods when the singing pattern of adult birds is unstable, which suggests a relationship of the gene to the formation of memory traces. One should keep in mind that the expression of FoxP2 in human evolution contributed to a language environment, which in turn stimulated the further development of human language.

Presumably FoxP2 is expressed in neurogenesis during the differentiation of specialized nerve cell precursors. Increased neurogenesis is observed in songbirds during periods when their singing programs are destabilized. The destabilization can be explained in terms of apoptosis of previously formed *song neurons* and the neurogenesis by their replacement with new neurons that acquire new melodies more effectively. This relearning mechanism further presupposes that a temporal *melody image* is stored in the neuron. Reproduction of the melody involves activation of the temporal sequence by a sequence of pacemaker waves that trigger bursts of spikes at peaks of depolarization.

How does an individual neuron store synaptically the sequence of sensory input signals received in the course of learning? Presumably the sequence of synaptic activations leads to creation of a spatial structure within the cell, elements of which correspond to specific moments in time. The temporal pattern is transformed into a spatial pattern in which each element corresponds to a temporal delay. The spatial pattern is read out as a series of pacemaker waves that reproduces the order in which the signals were recorded.

By what mechanisms does the neuron transform a sequence of synaptic events into a spatial structure that preserves information about the temporal sequence? Hameroff's model suggests that this involves microtubules of the cytoskeleton. The spatial organization of microtubules and MAP-2 stably retains the sequence of events. By generating waves of gamma rhythm with each coherent optical radiation, the neuron repeatedly reproduces the recorded melody.

How does the vector coding of stimuli on individual dendrites relate to the role of cytoskeletal microtubules in the mechanism of consciousness? Presumably the activation of a specific dendrite by a stimulus input leads to the generation of coherent photons in the microtubules of that dendrite. The selective switching on of a specific set of microtubules and the emergence of coherent photons there determines a specific state of consciousness. If a stimulus activates another dendrite, the generation of coherent photons occurs in another set of microtubules and another subjective image appears. Thus, the selective excitation of a specific dendrite on a categorical neuron corresponds to the set of microtubules in which coherent photons arise and each set of activated microtubules responds with its specific state of consciousness. This means that the same response of one categorical neuron can originate from different areas of the microtubule network.

Thus, the coding of information on individual dendrites makes each of them an independent *gnostic module* whose input synaptic mechanisms are similar to the synaptic mechanisms of individual *gnostic units*. The gnostic modules represented by individual dendrites are associated with specific sets of microtubules through the synapses activated by a given stimulus. The coherent photons arising in a given set of microtubules determine the emergence of a specific act of consciousness.

Conclusion: The Spherical Model of Consciousness

The greatest mystery facing science remains the nature of the association between the processes occurring in neuronal networks and their manifestation as subjective experiences and behavioral acts. An approach to understanding this correlation is the proposed model of a hypersphere in *n*-dimensional Euclidean space that integrates subjective, neuronal, and behavioral processes. The Cartesian coordinates of the model represent excitations of neurons in an ensemble that performs vector encoding of input stimuli. The angles between vectors in *n*-dimensional Euclidean space represent the subjective aspects of cognitive processes. Individual points on the surface of the hypersphere correspond to detector neurons that are selectively tuned to specific excitation vectors to represent input stimuli in the form of subjective phenomena (Fomin et al. 1979).

The spherical model extends to behavioral acts. In this case the hypersphere represents intention neurons, which are associated with subjective experiences of intentions to perform voluntary acts. The transformation of intentions into actions involves command neurons, which transmit excitation to modules of premotor neurons. Thus, stimuli are displayed on a cognitive hypersphere and an intentional hypersphere represents the totality of experienced intentions.

The process of associative learning is represented in the model by modification of plastic synapses, as conceptualized by Hebb, on command neurons. The combination of presynaptic effects evoked by a conditional stimulus and subsequent reinforcement alters the weights of synaptic connections on the command neuron such that they come to equal the corresponding presynaptic effects. Thus, the synaptic weights vector representing the synaptic connections of the command neuron becomes equal to the excitation vector, and the command neuron becomes selectively tuned to the conditional stimulus.

The vector coding of objective and subjective information provides an understanding of the mechanism by which a person evaluates differences between stimuli. When each stimulus is represented by its excitation vector, the difference between the stimuli is the absolute value of the vector difference (i.e., the chord distance between the ends of the two vectors). Calculation of the difference on each dimension is computed by specific neurons that respond only to the change of excitation in corresponding channels. Neurons at the next level, summing the differences in the individual channels, compute the difference between the signals from those ensembles.

The emergence of conscious experience, a cognitive process or an intention, depends on the additional activation of an area of the hypersphere associated with involuntary or voluntary attention. The recognized object is highlighted by the spotlight of attention provided by supplementary, nonspecific activation. Involuntary attention is elicited by novel stimuli (i.e., by stimulation different from the preceding sensory flow). A novelty signal arises as the result of mismatch between the existing neural model of the stimulus and current input. In spherical model terms, the formation of the neural model of a stimulus involves *negative learning* in specific hippocampal neurons with heavily weighted synaptic connections. With repetition of a standard stimulus, the synaptic connections of such a *novelty neuron* are weakened in proportion to the presynaptic effects of the standard stimulus. The synaptic weights vector of the novelty neuron becomes opposite to the excitation vector generated by the standard stimulus. Since the novelty signal is equal to the absolute difference between those vectors, the response of the novelty neuron is greater the greater the difference between the neural model of the stimulus represented by the synaptic weights vector of the plastic connections and the excitation vector of the new stimulus. Thus, a novelty neuron is a neuron that computes a vector difference, but not between the vectors of current stimuli. It computes the difference between a vector representing the trace of the standard stimulus and the excitation vector of the new stimulus. The magnitude of this difference coincides with the magnitude of the difference between the corresponding stimuli, the standard and the new.

Voluntary attention is linked with the intention mechanism. It involves the anticipation of signals and the implementation of appropriate actions. Automatisms are not accompanied by voluntary attention and remain in the sphere of unconscious processes. In the most general terms, one can say that consciousness is based on neurons of the hypersphere whose excitation is supplemented by nonspecific activation. Events mediated by neurons on the hypersphere without nonspecific activation remain unconscious.

The spherical structure of cognitive space has been confirmed in experimental studies at the psychophysical, behavioral, and neuronal levels. The results of psychophysical experiments on humans are consistent with those from behavioral and neurophysiological studies in animals. Multidimensional scaling of the matrices of subjective differences between stimuli reported by humans reveal a spherical structure—namely, a hypersphere in n-dimensional space. The amplitude of EPs in response to the replacement of one stimulus by another coincide with the magnitude of the subjective difference between the two stimuli. Analyses of the probability matrices of conditional responses in animal experiments also indicate that signals are encoded by excitation vectors of constant length. The magnitude of cerebral activation, in the form of alpha-rhythm suppression as an index of involuntary attention, coincide with the absolute difference between the excitation vectors of standard and new stimuli. Voluntary attention is associated with enhanced cortical activation in response to a signal stimulus accompanied by anticipatory activation of the premotor area.

Studies of color vision have shown that the perceptual color space of a person with normal trichromatic vision is a hypersphere in four-dimensional space. The Cartesian coordinates of points representing colors on the hypersphere correspond to the responses of the four types of neurons involved in color coding: red–green, blue–yellow, brightness, and darkness types. Three angles of the color hypersphere correspond to the subjective color characteristics: color tone, brightness, and saturation. Color stimuli are coded by excitation vectors of constant length in four-dimensional space.

Neurophysiologically, the EP to change of a stimulus from one color to another matches the magnitude of the subjective difference. Behavioral experiments conducted on monkeys have shown that the differences in probabilities of instrumental conditional responses to color stimuli reveal a four-dimensional color space matching that obtained in psychophysical experiments with humans. The four Cartesian coordinates of monkey color space correspond to the activities of red–green, blue–yellow, brightness, and darkness neurons in the lateral geniculate nucleus of the thalamus. The three angles of the monkey's color hypersphere match the color tone, brightness, and saturation of colors in human color space. The fact that one can obtain coordinates in color space from the probabilities of conditional responses suggests that in the formation of the conditional responses, the synaptic weights vector of the command neuron comes to match the excitation vector evoked by the conditional stimulus. The EPs evoked by color changes also match the differences between conditional response probabilities.

To establish the role of color-encoding neurons in the proposed model, parallel behavioral and neurophysiological studies have been conducted in fish. Behavioral experiments conducted on carp have shown that the differences in probabilities of responses conditioned to color stimuli reveal a four-dimensional color space, which matches that obtained in psychophysical experiments with humans and behavioral experiments with monkeys (Latanov et al. 1997). The behavioral experiments were complemented by intracellular recordings from bipolar cells of isolated retina exposed to monochromatic light of different intensities. Again, four types of color-coding bipolar cells were identified: red–green, blue–yellow, brightness, and darkness types. The sum of squares of excitation evoked in the neurons by different color stimuli was constant, indicating that the spherical structure of color space already exists in the visual pathway at the peripheral level of retinal bipolar cells.

The response characteristics of the bipolar cells to color stimuli correlate closely with the Cartesian coordinates of color space obtained by analyzing the probabilities of conditional responses to color stimuli. The three spherical coordinates of the color space of the fish were close to the color tone, brightness, and saturation coordinates in the human. Thus, comparison of the color spaces obtained in psychophysical, behavioral, and neurophysiological experiments supports a four-dimensional spherical model that integrates color perception, learning of response to color, and the neuronal coding of color.

Studies of emotional space based on the perception of emotion in human facial expressions have shown that it is similar in structure to the color space. In this case the space is a hypersphere in four-dimensional space in which the Cartesian coordinates represent levels of excitation of hypothetical neurons that identify different combinations of slope of the eyebrows and angles of the mouth; the spherical coordinates, the three angles of the hypersphere, correspond to emotional tone, emotional intensity, and emotional saturation. The mechanism of stereoscopic vision also fits a hypersphere in four-dimensional space.

The role of vector coding in the performance of behavioral acts has been demonstrated in studies of emotional facial expressions as motor acts—that is, as forms of gesture, each of which is determined by a four-dimensional driving vector. Direct evidence for vector coding in the performance of motor acts follows from the study of eye movements, where the control vector is based on four types of premotor neurons that excite different combinations of motor neurons to control degree of convergence and shifts in the direction of gaze. Conscious cognitive processes and voluntary acts are accompanied by nonspecific but selectively directed activation of relevant neuronal groups represented on the cognitive and intentional hypersphere.

The proposed spherical model, which integrates subjective, behavioral, and neuronal mechanisms, presupposes vector coding in the functioning of neuronal networks. This principle is manifest already at the receptor level, where the stimulus, activating an ensemble of receptors, creates a receptor excitation vector. Because receptor characteristics overlap, however, they are interdependent and therefore not orthogonal. In addition, if a qualitative feature of the stimulus is represented by the orientation of an excitation vector, the intensity of the stimulus is represented by its length. Thus, the qualitative characteristics of the stimulus and its intensity are encoded separately. Since the frequency response characteristics of the photoreceptors are not orthogonal, the range of directions of a vector is limited depending on the degree of overlap. At the same time, overlap of receptor characteristics is essential for encoding a set of stimuli by various combinations of receptor excitation. If the characteristics of receptors did not overlap, an individual stimulus would excite only one receptor rather than exciting a combination of receptors. Finally, the length of receptor excitation vectors equals the sum of the absolute values of their excitations. Representation of vector length as the sum of absolute coordinate values is referred to as *city-block metrics* by analogy to the distance covered when, to get from one corner of a block occupied by buildings to the opposite corner, one must follow streets up one side and across the other. Formally, the city-block metric is a special case of the more general Minkowski metric in which the length of a vector is computed as the root of the arithmetic sums of coordinate differences in degrees from one to infinity.

Besides the transformation in neural computation from city-block to Euclidean metrics, one needs to recognize the transformation by orthogonalization that is achieved in the next layer of nerve cells. These neurons are connected to the receptors by synaptic connections that vary in sign and strength such as to make their response functions orthogonal. Again, the qualitative characteristics and the intensity of the stimulus are encoded by the orientation and the length of the vector respectively. Further transformations of signals in the nervous system involve the calculation of vector scalar products, which requires coding of signal intensity also by the orientation of the excitation vector. At the next level the excitation vector is normalized by transformation to a space of greater dimensionality. This is done by means of a spontaneously active neuron from whose excitation level the excitations of the initial neurons are subtracted. Thus, the sum of excitations of all neurons in an ensemble remains constant. Such normalization in the city-block metric is replaced by the Euclidean metric through limitation of the maximal values of excitation by neuronal adaptation. Excitation vectors of constant length act in parallel on detector neurons to produce a population excitation vector with maximal excitation in one of the detectors. With a change in the input signal, intersection of the population excitation vector with the spherical surface shifts as maximal excitation shifts from one detector to another. Subjective recognition of the input signal involves an additional activation mechanism that arises involuntarily in response to novel stimulation or purposefully if the mechanism of voluntary attention is engaged. Coincidence of excitation of a detector at a specific location on the hypersphere with nonspecific activation creates the effect of recognition.

The physical set of detector neurons is determined genetically, but their tuning to particular stimuli requires specific activation from the external environment postnatally. The specific activation must be accompanied by nonspecific activation from the reticular system of the brain. A similar combination of specific and nonspecific activating processes underlies the formation of gnostic units, which are the basis for declarative memory in the mature organism. The immense reservoir of declarative memory constitutes an archive from which, as required by certain circumstances, working memory is derived. It provides the content of consciousness in the absence of stimulation or with voluntary ignoring of stimulation during cognitive or imaging operations.

Cognitive operations are achieved by symbolic encoding that is based on the imagery of long-term memory and that enables operations involving complexes that are represented by different portions of long-term memory. Symbolic encoding, Pavlov's second signaling system, operates in close collaboration with the imagery of long-term memory. Symbols that are represented by the same sets of long-term memory neurons are synonyms, and semantic differences reflect differences between the complexes of long-term memory neurons that are excited by the symbols. Disruption of the links between symbols and the sections of long-term memory they represent leads to two types of defect: inability to name an object even though the word is known and inability to imagine, describe, or depict an object from its name.

An important operation of consciousness is to compare stimuli and situations, evaluating their differences and similarities. Comparative operations are executed by a special system of neurons that subtract the excitation vectors of the compared objects from one another; the subjective difference between the objects reflects the absolute difference between the excitation vectors. The comparative operation involving excitation vectors is closely related to decision making. The principle of vector encoding extends to emotional processing. The making of a decision and the resultant behavior depend on the mechanism of extrapolation and the expectation of positive or negative outcome. Voluntary behavior is determined by neuronal mechanisms that represent intentions. The dominance of certain intentions indicates the probable direction of behavior.

The spherical model of cognitive processes provides a universal description of perceptual imagery, memory traces, and semantic phenomena. It is based on the concept that the association of several predetector pairs creates an ensemble of predetectors of higher dimensionality represented by a hypersphere in a space whose dimensionality is determined by the number of predetectors in the ensemble. Thus, the association of two predetectors, which encode the intensity of light, with two predetectors of chromaticity forms a color ensemble of predetectors represented by a color hypersphere in four-dimensional space. Similarly, two predetectors that encode line orientation combined with two predetectors that encode direction of movement form a new predetector ensemble corresponding to a hypersphere in four-dimensional space where each detector represents a particular combination of two characteristics: the orientation of a line and the direction of its motion. Color mosaics are encoded in the spherical model by a combination of four color predetectors and four predetectors of spatial features to form an ensemble of eight predetectors, which are represented by a hypersphere in eight-dimensional space. Each color mosaic is represented by a particular detector on the hypersphere.

A general outcome of such a model of predetector ensembles building on one another is the accommodation of increases in the dimensions of cognitive space while maintaining the spherical structure of increasingly complex cognitive processes. In this model a neuronal converter lies between the physical stimulus and its subjective image. Therefore, any psychophysical approach that attempts to establish a direct connection between the physical properties of the object and its subjective image without decoding the neuronal converter is doomed to failure. By the same token, decoding the neuronal converter that transforms signals from the physical object into the neural network activity that generates the subjective image enables one to establish direct correspondence between the subjective image and the particular pattern of activity of the network that corresponds to that image. Only by knowing the structure of the neuronal converter for a given class of physical objects can one predict the subjective image induced by an object of that class. Thus, the psychophysical paradigm gives way to the psychophysiological paradigm.

The valuable feature of the spherical model that distinguishes it from other models is that it integrates psychophysical and neuronal processes. This opens the prospect of neurobiological research into the mechanisms of consciousness.

REFERENCES

Adamar Zh. (1970) *Research on the psychology of the creative process in mathematics.* [In Russian: "Issledovanie psikhologiy protsessa izobreteniya v oblasti matematiki."] Moskva: Sovetskoe Radio.

Alexandrov Yu.I. and Sams M. (2005) Emotion and consciousness: ends of a continuum. Cognitive Brain Research, 25 (2): 387–405.

Alving B.O. (1968) Spontaneous activity in isolated somata of aplysia pacemaker neurons. Journal of General Physiology, 51: 29–45.

Bar M., Kassam K.S., Ghuman A.S., et al. (2006) Top-down facilitation of visual recognition. Proceedings of the National Academy of Sciences USA, 103 (2): 449–454.

Basar E. (1998) *Brain function and oscillations.* Vol. 1–2. Berlin: Springer-Verlag.

Baumgartner G., von der Heydt R., and Peterhans E. (1984) Anomalous contours: a tool in studying the neurophysiology of vision. Experimental Brain Research, Suppl. 9: 413–419.

Bekesy G. von (1967) *Sensory inhibition.* Princeton, NJ: Princeton University Press.

Beritov I.S. (1961) *Neural mechanisms of behavior in higher vertebrates.* [In Russian: "Nervnye mekhanizmy povedeniya vysshikh pozvonochnykh zhivotnykh."] Moskva: Izdatel'stvo AN SSSR.

Bermeitinger C., Frings D., Wentura. N400 effects for category exemplars primed by category labels. Scientific Report, PsyDok, April 2010: 1–10. http://psydok.sulb.uni-saarland.de/volltexte/2010/2604/pdf/BermeitingerFringsWentura2010.pdf (accessed 19 November, 2012)

Brusentsov N.P. (1994) *Introduction to computer science. [*In Russian: "Nachala informatiki."] Moskva: Fond "Novoe tysyacheletie."

Chernorizov A.M. (1999) *Neuronal mechanisms of color vision.* [In Russian: "Neyronnye mekhanizmy tsvetovogo zreniya."] Avtoreferat doctorskoi dissertatsii. Moskva: MGU.

Chernorizov A.M., Dergam A., and Bandres J. (2008) A tribute to Yevgeniy Nikolaevich Sokolov (1920–2008). Spanish Journal of Psychology, 11 (2): 345–348.

Chernorizov A.M. and Sokolov E.N. (2001) Vector encoding of color in bipolar cells of carp retina. [In Russian: "Vektornoe kodirovanie tsveta v sloe bipolyarnykh kletok setchatki karpa."] Vestnik MGU. Seriya 14. Psikhologiya, 1: 12–35.

Chernorizov A.M. and Sokolov E.N. (2010) Mechanisms of achromatic vision in invertebrates and vertebrates: A comparative study. Spanish Journal of Psychology, 13 (1): 18–29.

Creutzfeldt O.D.(1993) *Cortex cerebri: performance, structural and functional organization of the cortex.* Göttingen: Springer-Verlag.

Crick F. and Koch C. (2002) The problem of consciousness. Scientific American, special edition, 12 (1): 11–17.

Danilova N.N. (1998) *Psychophysiology.* [In Russian: "Psikhofisiologiya."] Moskva: Aspekt Press.

Danilova N.N. (2006) Role of high-frequency EEG rhythms in the maintenance of mental processes. [In Russian: "Rol' vysokochastotnykh ritmov elektricheskoy aktivnosti mozga v obespechenii psikhicheskikh protsessov."] Psikhologiya. Zhurnal Vysshey Shkoly Ekonomiki, 3 (2): 62–72.

Danilova N.N., Bykova N.B., Anisimov N.V., et al. (2002) Evoked and induced gamma-rhythm in sensory encoding. [In Russian: "Vyzvannyy i indutsirovannyy gamma-ritm v sensornom kodirovanii."] *Meditsinskaya Fizika* (pod red. V.I. Trukhina i dr.). Moskva: Izd-vo Mosk. Un-ta, str. 97–107.

Dan'ko S.G., Bekhtereva N.P., Kachalova L.M., et al. (2005) Electroencephalographic correlates of brain states during verbal learning. Fisiologiya Cheloveka, 31 (6): 5–12.

Dicke R.H. (1954) Coherence in spontaneous radiation processes. Physical Review, 93: 99–110.

Dobrokhotova T.A., Grindel' O.M., and Bragina N.N. (1985) Restoration of consciousness after long-term coma in patients with severe brain trauma. [In Russian: "Vosstanovlenie soznaniya posle dlitel'noy komy u bol'nykh s tyazholoy cherepno-mozgovoy travmy."] Zhurnal Nevropatologii i Psikhiatrii im. S.S. Korsakova, 5: 720–726.

Dumenko V.N. (2002) Functional importance of high-frequency components of brain electrical activity in genesis of inner images. [In Russian: "Funktsional'noe znachenie vysokochastotnykh komponentov elektricheskoy aktivnosti golovnogo mozga v protsesse formirovaniya vnutrennikh obrazov"] Zhurnal Vysshey Nervnoy Ceyatel'nosti im I.P. Pavlova, 52 (5): 539–550.

Eccles J.C. (1993) Evolution of complexity of the brain with the emergence of consciousness. pp.1–28 In K.H. Pribram (Ed.), *Rethinking neural networks: quantum fields and biological data.* Hillsdale, NJ: Lawrence Erlbaum Associates Publishers.

Edelman G.M. (1987) *Neural Darwinism: The theory of neuronal group selection.* New York: Basic Books.

Edelman G.M. (2003) Naturalizing consciousness: A theoretical framework. Proceedings of the National Academy of Sciences USA, 100 (9): 5520–5524.

Ehrenstein W.H., Spillmann L., and Sarris V. (2003) Gestalt issues in modern neuroscience. Axiomathes, 13: 433–458.

Everson R.M., Prashanth A.K., Gabbey M., et al. (1998) Representation of spatial frequency and orientation in the visual cortex. Proceedings of the National Academy of Sciences USA, 95: 8334–8388.

Evtikhin D.V., Polyanskii V.B., Alymkulov D.E., and Sokolov E.N. (2008) Coding of luminance and color differences of neurons in the rabbit's visual system. Spanish Journal of Psychology, 11 (2): 349–362.

Fodor J. (1983) *Modularity of mind.* Cambridge, MA: MIT Press.

Fomin S.V., Sokolov E.N., and Vaitkevicius G.G. (1979) *Artificial sensory systems.* [In Russian: "Iskusstvennye organy chuvstv."] Moskva: Nauka.

Galambos R. (1971) The glia-neuronal interaction: some observations. Journal of Psychiatric Research, 8: 219–224.

Galambos R. and Juhasz G. (1997) The contribution of glial cells to spontaneous and evoked potentials. International Journal of Psychophysiology, 26: 229–236.

Geissler H. and Ehret G. (2002) Time-critical integration of formants for perception of communication calls in mice. Proceedings of the National Academy of Sciences USA, 99: 9021–9025.

Grossberg S. (2004) The complementary brain: from brain dynamics to conscious experiences. In C. Kaernbach, E. Schroger, and H. Muller (Eds.), *Psychophysics beyond sensation* (pp. 417–449). Mahwah, NJ: Lawrence Erlbaum Associates.

Hagan S., Jibu M., and Yasue K. (1994) Consciousness and anesthesia: an hypothesis involving biophoton emission in the microtubular cytoskeleton of the brain. In K.H. Pribram (Ed.), *Organs: Brain and self organization* (pp. 154–171). Hillsdale, NJ: Lawrence Erlbaum Associates Publishers.

Hameroff S., Dayhoff J.E., Lahoz-Bettra R., Rasmussen S., Insinna E.M., and Koruga D. (1993) Nanoneurology and the cytoskeleton: quantum signaling and protein conformational dynamics as cognitive substrate. Chapter 10 in K.H. Pribram (Ed.), *Rethinking neural networks: Quantum fields and biological data (pp. 318–376).* Hillsdale, NJ: Lawrence Erlbaum Associates.

Hari R. and Salenius S. (1999) Rhythmical corticomotor communication. Neuroreport, 10: 1–10.

Hassett J. (1978) A primer of psychophysiology. San Francisco: Freeman.

Horridge A. (2009) *What does the honeybee see? And how we do we know?* Australian National University, Canberra ACT 0200, Australia.

Hubel D. (1990) *Eye, brain, vision.* [In Russian: "Glaz, mozg, zrenie."] Moskva: Mir.

Hubel D.H. and Wiesel T.N. (1979) Brain mechanisms of vision. Scientific American. 241: 130–144.

Ivanitskiy A.M. (2005) Consciousness and the brain. [In Russian: "Soznanie i mozg."] Mire Nauki, 11: 3–11.

Ivanitskiy A.M., Strelets V.B., and Korsakov I.A. (1984) *Informational processes and mental activity.* [In Russian: "Informazionnye protsessy i psikhicheskaya deyatel'nost'."] Moskva: Nauka.

Izmailov Ch.A. and Chernorizov A.M. (2005) The language of perception and the brain. [In Russian: "Yazyk vospriyatiya i mozg."] Psikhologiya, Zhurnal Vysshei Shkoly Ekonomiki, 2: 22–52.

Izmailov Ch.A., Korshunova S.G., and Sokolov E.N. (2000) The connection between visual evoked potentials and differences in emotional expressions of schematic faces. [In Russian: "Svyaz' zritel'nykh vyzvannykh potentsialov s razlichiyami mezhdu emotsional'nymi vyrazheniyami skhematicheskikh lits."] Zhurnal Vysshey Nervnoy Deyatel'nosti imeni I.P. Pavlova, 50: 805–818.

Izmailov Ch.A., Korshunova S.G., and Sokolov E.N. (2003a) The evoked potential as a measure of semantic color differences in the human. [In Russian: "Vyzvannyy potentsial kak mera semanticheskikh tsvetovykh razlichiy u cheloveka."] *V knige 'A.R.*

Luriya i Psikhologiya XXI Veka', T.V. Akhutina i Zh.M. Glozman (Eds.), Moskva, MSU, pp. 283–289.

Izmailov Ch.A., Korshunova S.G., and Sokolov E.N. (2003b) A semantic component of evoked potentials in visual discrimination tasks. [In Russian: "Semanticheskiy komponent vyzvannogo potentsiala razlicheniya."] *V knige 'Sovremennye Napravleniya Mezhditsiplinarnykh Issledovaniy'*, Moskva, Izd-vo IP RAN, pp. 295–308.

Izmailov Ch.A., Korshunova S.G., Sokolov E.N., and Chudina Yu.A. (2004) A geometric model of recognition of line orientation based on subjective estimates and visual evoked potentials. [In Russian: "Geometricheskaya model' razlicheniya orientatsii liniy, osnovannaya na sub'ektivnykh otsenkakh i zritel'nykh vyzvannykh potentsialakh."] Zhurnal Vysshey Nervnoy Deyatel'nosti imeni I.P. Pavlova, 54: 237–249.

Izmailov Ch.A. and Sokolov E.N. (1991) Spherical model of color and brightness discrimination. Psychological Sciences, 2: 249–259.

Izmailov Ch. A. and Sokolov E. N. (1992) A semantic space of color names. Psychological Science. 3: 105–111.

Izmailov Ch.A. and Sokolov E.N. (2004) Subjective and objective scaling of large color differences. In C. Kaernbach, E. Schroger, and H. Muller (Eds.), *Psychophysics beyond sensation* (pp. 27–43). Mahwah, NJ: Lawrence Erlbaum Associates.

Izmailov Ch.A., Sokolov E.N., and Korshunova S.G. (2005) Multidimensional scaling of schematically represented faces based on dissimilarity estimates and evoked potentials of difference (EPD) amplitudes. Spanish Journal of Psychology, 8: 119–133.

Jasper H.H. (1949) Diffuse projection systems: the integrative action of the thalamic reticular system. EEG and Clinical Neurophysiology, 1: 405–419.

John E.R. (2002) The neurophysics of consciousness. Brain Research Reviews, 39 (1): 1–28.

Kanizsa G. (1974) Contours without gradients or cognitive contours. Italian Journal of Psychology, 1: 93–113.

Komatsu H. and Murakami I. (1994) Behavioral evidence of filling-in at the blind spot of the monkey. Visual Neuroscience, 11: 1103–1113.

Konorski Yu. (1967) *Integrative activity of the brain.* [In Russian: "Integrativnaya deyatel'nost' mozga."] Moskva: Mir.

Korshunova S.G. (1999) Visual evoked potentials to an illusory contour. [In Russian: "Zritel'nye vyzvannye potentsialy na illuzornyy kontur."] Zhurnal Vysshey Nervnoy Deyatel'nosti imeni I.P. Pavlova, 49: 186–199.

Kreiman G., Fried J., and Koch C. (2002) Single neuron correlates of subjective vision in the human medial temporal lobe. Proceedings of the National Academy of Sciences USA, 99: 8378–8383.

Kutas M. and Federmeier K.D. (2000) Electrophysiology reveals semantic memory use in language comprehension. Trends in Cognitive Science, 4 (12): 463–470.

Kutas M. and Iragui V. (1998) The N400 in a semantic categorization task across 6 decades. Electroencephalography and Clinical Neurophysiology: Evoked Potentials, 108(5): 456–471.

Lashley K.S. (1933) *Brain and intellect.* [In Russian: Leshli K.S., "Mozg i intellect."] Moskva: OGIZ.

Latanov A.V., Leonova A.Yu., Evtikhin D.V., et al. (1997) Comparative neurobiology of color vision in human and animals. [In Russian: "Sravnitel'naya neyrobiologiya tsvetovogo zreniya cheloveka i zhivotnykh."] Zhurnal Vysshey Nervnoy Deyatel'nosti imeni I.P. Pavlova, 47: 308–320.

Ledoux J. (1991) Systems and synapses of emotional memory. In L.R. Squire, N.M. Weinberger, G. Lynch, et al. (Eds.), Memory: *Organization and locus of change* (pp. 205–216). New York: Oxford University Press.

Leonov Yu.P. and Sokolov E.N. (2005) Spherical geometry of color space. [In Russian: "Sphericheskaya geometriya tsvetovogo prostranstva."] Vestnik MGU. Seriya 14. Psikhologiya, 3: 58–75.

Leonov Y.P. and Sokolov E.N. (2008) The representation of colors in spherical space. Color Research and Application, 33: 113–124.

Liu G. (2004) Local structural balance and functional interaction of excitatory and inhibitory synapses in hippocampal dendrites. Nature Neuroscience, 7: 373–379.

Llinas R. (1998) Oscillatory brain activity and cognitive perception. International Journal of Psychophysiology, 30: 1.

Loizzo A. and Sannita W.G. (1998) Neuromodulation of visual oscillatory events. International Journal of Psychophysiology, 30: 7.

Luria A.R. (1970) *Traumatic aphasia, its syndromes, psychology and treatment*. The Hague, Amsterdam: Mouton and Company.

Luria A.R. (1973) *The working brain: an introduction to neuropsychology*. London: Penguin Books Ltd.

Luria A.R. (1982) *Language and cognition*. New York: John Wiley & Sons.

Ma X. and Suga N. (2001) Corticofugal modulation of duration tuned neurons in midbrain auditory nucleus in bats. Proceedings of the National Academy of Sciences USA, 98:14060–14065.

Mangina C.A. and Beuzeron-Mangina J.H. (1996) Direct electrical stimulation of specific human brain structures and bilateral electrodermal activity. International Journal of Psychophysiology, 22: 1–8.

Mangina C.A. and Beuzeron-Mangina J.H. (2004) Brain plasticity following psychophysiological treatment in learning disabled/ADHD preadolescents. International Journal of Psychophysiology, 52: 129–146.

Marinkovic K., Trebon P., Chauvel P., et al. (2000) Localized face processing by the human prefrontal cortex. Cognitive Neuropsychology, 17: 187–199.

Miyashita Y., Sakai K., Higuchi S., et al. (1991) Localization of long-term memory in the primate temporal cortex. In L.R. Squire, N.M. Weinberger, G. Lynch, et al. (Eds.), Memory: *Organization and locus of change* (pp. 239–249). New York: Oxford University Press.

Moruzzi G. (1954) *The physiological properties of the brainstem reticular system. Brain mechanisms and consciousness (pp. 21–48)*. Oxford: Oxford University Press.

Moutoussis K. and Zeki S. (2002) The relationship between cortical activation and perception investigated with invisible stimuli. *Proceedings of the National Academy of Sciences USA*, 99: 9527–9532.

Näätänen R. (1992) *Attention and brain function*. Hillsdale, NJ: Lawrence Erlbaum Associates.

Nicholls J.G., Martin A.R., Wallace B.G., and Fuchs P.A. (2001) *From neuron to brain: A cellular and molecular approach to the function of the nervous system* (4th ed.). Sunderland: Sinauer Associates.

Nieder A. and Miller E.K. (2004) A parietofrontal network for visual numerical information in the monkey. Proceedings of the National Academy of Sciences USA, 101: 7457–7462.

Ojemann G.A. (2003) The neurobiology of language and verbal memory: observations from awake neurosurgery. International Journal of Psychophysiology, 48: 141–146.

Papez J.W. (1937) A proposed mechanism of emotion. Archives of Neurology and Psychiatry (Chicago), 38:725–743.

Pavlov I.P. (1947) *Function of the cerebral hemispheres.* [In Russian: "Lektsii o rabote bol'shikh polushariy golovnogo mozga."] Moskva, Leningrad: AN SSSR.

Penfield W.C. (1958) Centrencephalic integrating system. Brain, 81: 231–234.

Penrose R. (1994) *Shadows of the mind. A search for the missing science of consciousness.* New York, Oxford: Oxford University Press.

Penrose R., Shimoni A., Cartwright N., Hawking S., and Longair M. (1997) *The large, the small and the human mind.* Cambridge: Cambridge University Press.

Pleskaciauskas A., Stabinyte D., Satinskas R., and Vaitkevicius H. (1995) Neurophysiological and psychophysical investigation of the perception of movement direction. Perception, 24 (suppl.): 107.

Polley D.B., Heiser M.A., Blake D.T., et al. (2004) Associative learning shapes the neural code for stimulus magnitude in primary auditory cortex. Proceedings of the National Academy of Sciences USA, 101: 16351–16356.

Polyanskiy V.B., Alymkulov D.É., Evtikhin D.V., and Sokolov E.N. (2008) Assessment of brightness and color differences by neurons in the superior colliculus of the rabbit. Neuroscience and Behavioral Physiology, 38 (9): 971–983.

Polyanskiy V.B., Evtikhin D.V., and Sokolov E.N. (1999) The brightness component of visual evoked potentials to color. [In Russian: "Yarkostnyy komponent zritel'nogo vyzvannogo potentsiala na tsvet."] Zhurnal Vysshey Nervnoy Deyatel'nosti imeni I.P. Pavlova, 6: 1046–1051.

Polyanskiy, V. B., Evtikhin, D. V., and Sokolov, E. N. (2000) Reconstruction of the perceptual spaces of brightness and color on the basis of visual evoked potentials and their comparison with data from behavioral experiments [In Russian: "Rekonstruktsiya pertseptivnogo prostranstva yarkosti i tsveta krolika na osnove zritel'nykh potentsialov i ikh sravnenie s dannymi povedencheskikh opytov"] *Zhurnal Vysshey Nervnoy Deyatel'nosti im I.P.Pavlova, 50:* 843–854.

Polyanskiy V.B., Evtikhin D.V., and Sokolov E.N. (2005) Calculation of color and brightness differences by neurons in rabbit visual cortex. [In Russian: " Vychislenie tsvetovykh i yarkostnykh razlichiy neyronami zritel'noy kory krolika."] Zhurnal Vysshey Nervnoy Deyatel'nosti imeni I.P. Pavlova, 55: 60–70.

Polyanskiy V.B., Evtikhin D.V., Sokolov E.N., and Alymkulov D.E. (2006) Calculation of color and brightness differences by neurons in the lateral geniculate body of rabbits. [In Russian: "Vychislenie tsvetovykh i yarkostnykh razlichiy neyronami lateral'nykh kolenchatykh tel krolika."] Zhurnal Vysshey Nervnoy Deyatel'nosti imeni I.P. Pavlova, 56: 75–85.

Porter R. and Lewis M.M. (1975) Relationships of neuronal discharges in the precentral gyrus of monkeys to the performance of arm movement. Brain Research, 98: 21–36.

Posner M.I. and Raichle M.E. (1994) *Images of mind.* New York: Scientific American Library.

Pribram K.H. (1991) *Brain and perception: Holonomy and structure in figural processing.* Hillsdale, NJ: Lawrence Erlbaum Associates.

Pribram K.H. (Ed.) (1993) *Rethinking neural networks: Quantum fields and biological data.* Proceedings of First Appalachian Conference on Behavioral Neurodynamics at Radford, VA. Hillsdale, NJ: Lawrence Erlbaum Associates.

Pribram K.H. (1997) The deep and surface structure of memory and conscious learning: Toward a 21st century model. In R.L. Solso (Ed.), *Mind and brain sciences in the 21st century* (pp. 127–156). Boston, MA: MIT Press.

Puankare A. (1983) *Science and method.* [In Russian: "Nauka i metod."] Moskva: Nauka.

Rizzolatti G. and Craighero L. (1998) Spatial attention: mechanisms and theories. In M. Sabourin, F. Craik, and M. Robert (Eds.), *Advances in psychological science. Vol. 2: Biological and cognitive aspects (pp. 171–189).* Hove, UK: Psychology Press.

Rolls E.T. (2000) Memory system in the brain. Annual Reviews of Psychology, 51: 599–630.

Rusalova M.N. (1990) Levels of consciousness and levels of activation. [In Russian: "Urovni soznaniya i urovni aktivatsii."] Zhurnal Vysshey Nervnoy Deyatel'nosti imeni I.P. Pavlova, 40 (6): 1097–1104.

Rusinov V.S. (1987) The dominant as a factor in memory trace formation in the central nervous system. [In Russian: "Dominanta kak factor sledoobrasovaniya v tsentral'noy nervnoy sisteme."] In G.A. Vartanyan (Ed.), *V knige Mekhanizmy Pamyati (pp. 197–234).* Leningrad: Nauka.

Satinskas R., Stabinyte D., Pleskaciauskas A., and Vaitkevicius H. (2000) Influence of the relative velocity of two moving stimuli on detection of the movement direction by the neurons of the primary visual cortex of the cat. Biologija, 4: 62–66.

Schrödinger E. (2000) *Mind and matter.* [In Russian: "Razum i materiya."] Moskva, Izhevsk: RKhD.]

Scoville W.B. and Milner B. (1957) Loss of recent memory after bilateral hippocampal lesions. Journal of Neurology, Neurosurgery and Psychiatry, 20: 11–21.

Sergin V.Ya. (1998) Psychophysiological mechanisms of consciousness: hypothesis of self-identification. [In Russian: "Psikhofiziologicheskie mekhanizmy soznaniya: gipoteza samootozhdestvleniya"] Zhurnal Vysshey Nervnoy Deyatel'nosti imeni I.P. Pavlova, 48: 558–571.

Sewards T.V. and Sewards M.A. (1999) Alpha-band oscillations in visual cortex: part of the neural correlate of visual awareness? International Journal of Psychophysiology, 32: 35–45.

Sharova E.V., Amchislavskiy V.G., Potapov A.A., and Angimirov V.A. (2001) EEG effects of therapeutic electrostimulation of the CNS in post-traumatic unconsciousness. [In Russian: "EEG effekty lechebnoy elektrostimulatsii TsNS pri posttravmaticheskom bessonatel'nom sostoyanii."] Fiziologiya Cheloveka, 27: 29–39.

Sharova E.V., Mel'nikov A.V., Novikova M.R., et al. (2006) Electrographic effects of transcranial electrical and electro-magnetic stimulation of the brain. [In Russian: "Elektrograficheskie effekty transkranial'noy elektricheskoy i elektromagnitnoy stimulyatsii golovnogo mozga."] Zhurnal Vysshey Nervnoy Deyatel'nosti imeni I.P. Pavlova, 56: 363–370.

Shvyrkov V.B. (1995) *Introduction to objective psychology: The neuronal basis of mind.* [In Russian: "Vvedenie v ob'ektivnuyu psikhologiyu: neyronnye osnovy psikhiki."] Moskva: IP RAN.

Sokolov E.N. (1996) The gestalt problem in neurobiology. [In Russian: "Problema gestal'ta v neryrobiologii."] Zhurnal Vysshey Nervnoy Deyatel'nosti imeni I.P. Pavlova, 46: 229–240.

Sokolov E.N. (2003) *Perception and the conditioned reflex. A new approach.* [In Russian: "Vospriyatie i uslovnyy refleks. Novyy vzglyad."] Moskva: UMK Psikhologiya.

Sokolov E.N. (2004) *Neurons of consciousness.* [In Russian: "Neyrony soznaniya."] Zhurnal Vysshei Shkoly Ekonomiki, 1: 3–15.

Sokolov E.N. and Nezlina N.I. (2003a) Long-term memory, neurogenesis and the novelty signal. [In Russian: "Dolgovremennaya pamyat', neyrogenez i signal novizny."] Zhurnal Vysshey Nervnoy Deyatel'nosti imeni I.P. Pavlova, 53: 451–463.

Sokolov E.N. and Nezlina N.I. (2003b) Long-term memory and neurogenesis. [In Russian: "Dolgovremennaya pamyat' i neyrogenez."] Zhurnal Vysshey Nervnoy Deyatel'nosti imeni I.P. Pavlova, 53: 623–642.

Sokolov E.N. and Nezlina N.I. (2007) The conditioned reflex: detector and command neurons. [In Russian: "Uslovnyy refleks: detector i kommandnyy neyron."] Zhurnal Vysshey Nervnoy Deyatel'nosti imeni I.P. Pavlova, 57: 5–22.

Sokolov E.N. and Palikhova T.N. (1999). Immediate plasticity of identifiable synapses in the land snail *Helix lucorum*. Acta Neurobiology Experimentalle, 59: 161–169.

Sokolov E.N, Satinskas R., Stabinyte D., Pleskacauskas A., Vaitkevicius H., Stanikunas R., and Shvegzda A. (2007) Encoding of stimulus movement parameters in the cat visual system. Neuroscience Behaviour Physiology, 37(4): 395–402.

Sokolov E.N. and Vaitkevicius G.G. (1989) *Neurointellect: From neuron to neurocomputer.* [In Russian: "Neyrointellekt: ot neyrona k neyrokomp'uteru."] Moskva: Nauka.

Spillmann L. (1999) From elements to perception: Local and global processing in visual neurons. Perception, 28: 1461–1492.

Spillmann L., Lascowski W., Lange K.W., et al. (2000). Stroke-blind for colors, faces and locations: Partial recovery after three years. Restorative Neurology and Neuroscience, 17: 89–103.

Spinks J.A., Naatanen A.R., and Lyytinen H. (2008) In memoriam: Evgenii Nikolaevich Sokolov (1920–2008). Psychophysiology, 45: 883–885.

Stabinyte D., Pleskaciauskas A., Satinskas R., and Vaitkevicius H. (1999a) Detection of movement direction by cells with directional receptive fields in the primary visual cortex of the cat. 1. Influence of the angular separation between stimuli. Biologija, 2: 61–65.

Stabinyte D., Pleskaciauskas A., Satinskas R., and Vaitkevicius H. (1999b) Detection of movement direction by cells with directional receptive fields in the primary visual cortex of the cat. 2. Influence of the relative luminance of two moving stimuli. Biologija, 2: 66–69.

Suga N. (1990) Biosonar and neural computation in bats. Scientific American, 262: 60–68.

Suga N. (2008) The neural circuit for tone-specific plasticity in the auditory system elicited by conditioning. Learning and Memory, 15 (4): 198–201.

Suga N., Jun Y., and Yunfeng Z. (1997) Cortical maps for hearing and egocentric selection for self-organization. Trends in Cognitive Sciences, 1997 (1): 13–20.

Svaetichin G. and MacNichol E.F. (1958) Retinal mechanisms for chromatic and achromatic vision. Annals of the New York Academy of Sciences, 74: 385–404.

Svarnik O.E., Anokhin K.V., and Alexandrov Yu.I. (2001). Distribution of neurons specialized for behavior and expression of transcriptional factor c-Fos in rat brain cortex during learning. [In Russian: "Raspredelenie povedencheski spetsializirovannykh neironov i ekspressiya transkriptsionnogo faktora c-Fos v kore golovnogo mozga krysy pri nauchenii."] Zhurnal Vysshey Nervnoy Deyatel'nosti imeni I.P. Pavlova, 1: 758–761.

Teplov B.M. (2006) *Psychological studies of camouflage (1923–1927).* [In Russian: "Psikhologicheskie issledovaniya v oblasti voenno-maskirovochnogo dela (1923–1927 gody)."] Moskva: BF Tverdislov.

Tiller W.A. (1997) *Science and human transformation: Subtle energies, intentionality and consciousness.* Walnut Creek, CA: Pavior.

Tootell R., Nelissen K., Vanduffel W., et al. (2004) Search for color "center(s)" in macaque visual cortex. Cerebral Cortex, 14: 353–363.

Tootell R., Tsao D., and Vanduffel W. (2003) Neuroimaging weighs in: humans meet macaques in "primate" visual cortex. Journal of Neuroscience, 23: 3981–3989.

Ukhtomskiy A.A. (1966) *The dominant.* [In Russian: "Dominanta."] Leningrad: Nauka.

Vinogradova O.S. (1975) *Hippocampus and memory.* [In Russian: "Gippokamp i pamyat."] Moskva: Nauka.

Walter W.G. (1963) *The living brain.* Oxford: W.W. Norton.

Walter W.G., Cooper R., Aldridge V.J., McCallum W.C., and Winter A.L. (1964) Contingent negative variation: an electric sign of sensorimotor association and expectancy in the human brain. Nature, 203: 380–384.

Weinberger N.M. (2004) Specific long-term memory traces in primary auditory cortex. Nature Reviews Neuroscience 5: 279–290.

Williams L.M. (2003) Nonconscious perception: the contribution of neuroimaging. In R. Meares and P. Nolan (Eds.), *The self in conversation.* Sydney: Watermark Press.

Yarbus A.L. (1965) *The role of eye movements in vision.* [In Russian: "Rol' dvizheniy glaz v protsesse zreniya."] Moskva: Nauka.

Zimachev M.M. and Chernorizov A.M. (2001) Structure of the frog's color space for different periods of behavioral activity [In Russian: "Struktura tsvetovogo prostranstva lyagushki v raznye periody povedencheskoy aktivnosti."] Vestnik MGU. Seriya 14. Psikhologiya, 4: 12–32.

INDEX